The Complete Idiot's Reference Card

Welcome to the Wonderful World of Ja...

By adding a JavaScript script to your HTML Web page, you can make your pag... you never dreamed of before. For example, you can:

- ➤ Animate text or graphics
- ➤ Create interactive loan applications
- ➤ Beat others at BlackJack
- ➤ Publish an online magazine with interactive links
- ➤ Calculate reams of sports stats
- ➤ Change background colors or spew random phrases when you click a button
- ➤ Show off your artwork in an interactive portfolio
- ➤ Give automated tours to users without any clicking

New Features in the Second Edition

- ➤ JavaScript 1.1 sports an additional set of new features, making JavaScript programming even more powerful.
- ➤ The Image object can replace Web graphics on-the-fly!
- ➤ The array object can organize, access, and sort sets of data.
- ➤ The Math.random( ) method generates random numbers with ease.
- ➤ You can automatically detect whether a user has certain plug-ins or mime types installed by using the navigator.plugins[ ] and navigator.mimeTypes[ ] objects.
- ➤ You can directly manipulate Java applets with JavaScript code, using LiveConnect. Call Java public methods from JavaScript!

The Bridge Between HTML and JavaScript: The <SCRIPT> Tag

```
<SCRIPT [LANGUAGE="JavaScript"] [SRC="scriptURL"]>
<!-- hide from non-JavaScript browsers -->
<!-- JavaScript statements and functions go here -->
//-->
</SCRIPT>
```

Que®

JavaScript Objects

Objects are the building blocks of your JavaScript scripts. Here's a handy reference to some of the things you can manipulate with JavaScript's built-in objects. Properties, methods, and events listed in bold are new to JavaScript 1.1.

The window Object

Properties	Methods	Events
frames[]	alert("*msg*")	onLoad
frames.length	confirm ("*msg*")	onUnload
Status	prompt ("*msg*")	**onBlur**
Self	open("*URL*", "name",	**onFocus**
	"characteristics")	
Parent	close()	onError
Top	**blur()**	
opener	**focus()**	
	scroll(x,y)	

The radio Object

Properties	Methods	Events
Name	click()	onClick
Length		
Value		
checked		
defaultChecked		
type		

The history Object

Properties	Methods	Events
length	go(delta)	
	go("string")	
	back()	
	forward()	

The document Object

Properties	Methods	Events
title	write("string")	onLoad
location	writeln("string")	onUnload
lastModified	clear()	
loadedDate	close()	
bgColor	open("*mimetype*")	
fgColor		
linkColor		
vlinkColor		
alinkColor		
forms[]		
forms.length		
links[]		
links.length		
anchors[]		
anchors.length		
applets[]		
embeds[]		
images[]		

The form Object

Properties	Methods	Events
name	submit()	onSubmit
method	**reset()**	**onReset**
action		
target		
elements[x]		

The text and textarea Objects

Properties	Methods	Events
name	focus()	onFocus
value	blur()	onBlur
defaultValue	select()	onSelect
type		onChange

The checkbox Object

Properties	Methods	Events
name	click()	onClick
value		
status		
defaultStatus		
checked		
type		

The select Object

Properties	Methods	Events
length		onFocus
name		onBlur
selectedIndex		onChange
type		
options[] *which*		
contain these		
subproperties:		
index		
length		
name		
selected		
text		
value		

The button Object

Properties	Methods	Events
value	click()	onClick
name		
type		

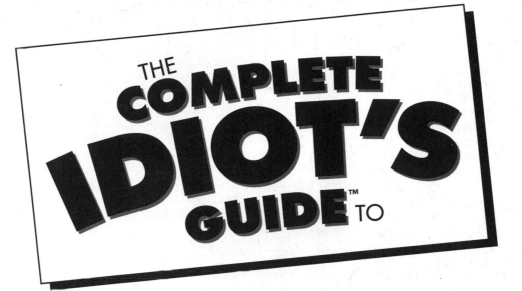

JavaScript

Second Edition

by Aaron Weiss

A Division of Prentice Hall Computer Publishing
201 West 103rd Street, Indianapolis, IN 46290 USA

"Homer, have you been up all night eating cheese?"

—Marge Simpson

©1997 Que® Corporation

Library of Congress Catalog Card Number: 96-72292

International Standard Book Number: 0-7897-1136-2

99 98 97   8 7 6 5 4 3 2 1

Interpretation of the printing code: the rightmost double-digit number is the year of the book's first printing; the rightmost single-digit number is the number of the book's printing. For example, a printing code of 97-1 shows that this copy of the book was printed during the first printing of the book in 1997.

Screen reproductions in this book were created by means of the program Collage Complete from Inner Media, Inc., Hollis, NH.

Printed in the United States of America

Publisher
Roland Elgey

Publishing Director
Lynn E. Zingraf

Editorial Services Director
Elizabeth Keaffaber

Managing Editor
Michael Cunningham

Director of Marketing
Lynn E. Zingraf

Acquisitions Editor
Martha O'Sullivan

Technical Specialist
Nadeem Muhammed

Product Development Specialist
John Gosney

Technical Editor
Kyle Bryant

Production Editor
Audra Gable

Cartoonist
Judd Winick

Book Designer
Barbara Kordesh

Cover Designer
Dan Armstrong

Indexer
Ginny Bess

Production Team
Angela Calvert
Cynthia Fields
Mary Hunt
Mindy Kuhn

We'd Like to Hear from You!

As part of our continuing effort to produce books of the highest possible quality, Que would like to hear your comments. To stay competitive, we *really* want you, as a computer book reader and user, to let us know what you like or dislike most about this book or other Que products.

You can mail comments, ideas, or suggestions for improving future editions to the address below, or send us a fax at 317-581-4663. For the online inclined, Macmillan Computer Publishing has a forum on CompuServe (type **GO QUEBOOKS** at any prompt) through which our staff and authors are available for questions and comments. The address of our Internet site is **http:// www.mcp.com/que** (World Wide Web).

Although we cannot provide general technical support, we're happy to help you resolve problems you encounter related to our books, disks, or other products. If you need such assistance, please contact our Tech Support department at 800-545-5914 ext. 3833.

To order other Que or Macmillan Computer Publishing books or products, please call our Customer Service department at 800-835-3202 ext. 666.

In addition to exploring our forum, please feel free to contact me personally to discuss your opinions of this book: I'm **104436,2300** on CompuServe, and I'm **jgosney@que.mcp.com** on the Internet.

Thanks in advance—your comments will help us to continue publishing the best books available on computer topics in today's market.

John Gosney
Product Development Specialist
Que Corporation
201 West 103rd Street
Indianapolis, Indiana 46290
USA

Contents at a Glance

Contents

Introduction

Welcome to The Complete Idiot's Guide to JavaScript, Second Edition!

The Complete Idiot's Guide to JavaScript, Second Edition introduces you, gentle reader, to the hottest property in cyberspace today: JavaScript. With JavaScript, a normal, everyday, Internet-familiar person can create Web pages with the finesse of an experienced guru. No mantras, no strange languages, and no expensive compilers are necessary—just a little common sense and an open mind.

This book explains what JavaScript is, how it works, what it's made of, and how you can use it. As a second edition, it also brings you up-to-date on the new features introduced in JavaScript 1.1. You'll discover the component parts that make up this language and come to understand all the esoteric pieces in a language that don't require a Ph.D. You'll even find several examples of JavaScript scripts in action that you can rip apart, change, and enhance.

What about the title of this book: The Complete Idiot's Guide? Well, it assumes that you're no idiot on your own turf. You know your job, you know what you want, you know how to get things done. But there's one thing you don't know: how to use JavaScript.

This book assumes that you've done a little Web surfing and have created some of your own Web pages. However, as you've surfed, you've come across things others have put together, and you want to learn how to do that, too. The underlying things (protocols, transmission layers, gateways, proxies) are of little concern to you; you just want to get the job done—quickly and easily—and at the same time, retain as much of your hair as possible.

Here are some more assumptions I've taken the liberty to make:

➤ You know what the World Wide Web is.

➤ You know what a browser is.

➤ You're familiar with HTML, the language of the Web.

➤ You've created some of your own Web pages.

➤ You like chocolate.

If, however, you feel you want more background on any of these assumptions, check out *The Complete Idiot's Guide to the Internet* (Peter Kent), *The Complete Idiot's Guide to the Internet with Windows 95* (Peter Kent), *The Complete Idiot's Guide to Creating an HTML Web Page* (Paul McFedries), or *The Complete Idiot's Guide to the World Wide Web* (Peter Kent).

How Do You Use This Book?

You don't have to read this book from cover to cover. If you want to find out what makes up JavaScript, go to the JavaScript internals chapters, Chapters 5 through 17; if you want to dive right in and start creating script pages, go to the examples chapters, Chapters 18 through 22. Each chapter is a self-contained unit with the information you need in order to use and understand one aspect of JavaScript. If you require information that's covered elsewhere in the book, you'll find plenty of cross-references.

There are a couple of conventions in this book to make it easier to use. For example, when you need to type something, it will appear like this:

Type **this**

Just type whatever is bold; it's as simple as that. If I don't know exactly what you'll have to type (because you have to supply some of the information), the unknown information appears in italics. For instance:

Type **this** *filename*

I don't know the file name, so you'll have to supply it.

Often it will be necessary to show longer examples of JavaScript. They will appear in a special typeface, arranged to mimic what appears on your screen:

```
Some of the lines will be in actual English.
Some of the lines will seem to be in a mutant dialect of English.
```

Again, don't panic.

If you want to understand more about the subject you are learning, you'll find some background information in boxes. Because this information is in boxes, you can quickly skip over the information if you want to avoid the gory details. Here are the special icons and boxes used in this book that help you learn just what you need:

Updates in Version 1.1

This icon marks information that is new to the second edition of this book, as a result of a feature introduced in JavaScript 1.1. If you're already familiar with JavaScript programming, look for this icon to quickly identify the newest JavaScript programming features.

Check This Out These boxes might contain helpful information or humorous anecdotes, neither of which is "need to know" information.

Techno Nerd Teaches Skip this background fodder (technical twaddle) unless you're truly interested.

Acknowledgments

The author (that's me) would like to thank a number of people for helping with this book. Not *just* helping either; these people have edited, tweaked, suggested, and most importantly *published* it. Martha O'Sullivan deftly commands the crew, which is helmed by John Gosney at the editor's chair and Audra Gable cementing the chapters in the production lair.

Lastly, of course, one mustn't overlook the ever-present contributions of MDEABSAHTF.

Trademarks

All terms mentioned in this book that are known to be trademarks have been appropriately capitalized. Que Corporation cannot attest to the accuracy of this information. Use of a term in this book should not be regarded as affecting the validity of any trademark or service mark. We simply don't have that sort of power.

Netscape Communications, the Netscape Communications logo, Netscape, and Netscape Navigator are trademarks of Netscape Communications Corporation.

JavaScript and Java are trademarks of Sun Microsystems, Inc.

Part 1
What's It All About?

You've heard the jargon everywhere: Java, JavaScript, live Web pages…. You've seen what the those things do: animation, buttons, custom content…. In a word, it's interactive multimedia for your Web page. You want it. But you hear that Java is a programming language, and your heart sinks. You're not a programmer.

Enter JavaScript, a way to get Java-powered pages with simple programming and without having a computer science degree! Step-by-steps included.

Before you dive head-first into the world of JavaScript, learn a little background info: what JavaScript is, what it does, and what it can do for you.

Coffee? In My Computer? I Prefer Decaf...

Extending the Web

In the "old days" of the World Wide Web (three whole years ago), there were two ways to get information (also called *content*) to the user. The primary way was through HTML (*HyperText Markup Language*), the language used to write Web pages. HTML enables you to present text and certain types of graphics (as well as *links* to connect one page to another page) either on the same computer or somewhere else in the world. As HTML has evolved (the current standard being worked on is version 3.2), other features have been added, such as forms, frames, tables, and so on. However, even with all the new features, HTML basically deals with Web content by:

➤ Formatting and displaying the content of a page.

➤ Waiting for the user to click something in the page.

➤ Depending on what the user clicks on, fetching something else (a new page, for example) and repeating the process.

Although this provides a wealth of possibilities for content manipulation (just spend a little time on the Web to see for yourself), it doesn't allow for more advanced things like accessing a database, ordering catalog items online, or making animated graphics within a Web page. For these capabilities, you need to understand the *Common Gateway Interface*, or *CGI*.

CGI provides a means of extending the capabilities of HTML by allowing the Web designer to write custom programs that interact with Web pages to do more complex things. A CGI program is a file that resides on the Web server and that the server runs in response to something inside the Web page. With CGI, you can:

➤ Create *image maps*, which are graphics that you can click on (see the following figure). Different areas of the graphic behave like unique HTML links, taking you to individual pages. (You used to have to know CGI programming to create one of these.)

Which part of an image you click determines what happens next.

An image on the image map

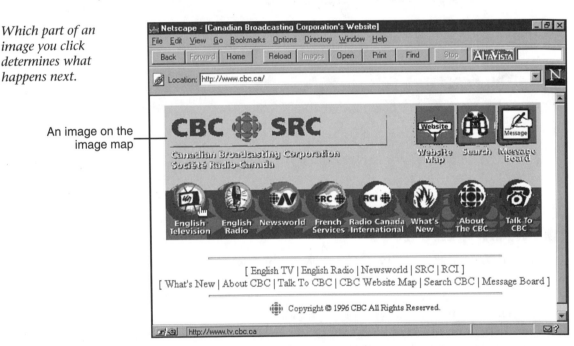

➤ Dynamically (on demand) create custom HTML pages and graphics. A common use is the "You are the 34,251th visitor" line you find on many pages.

➤ Create simple animations by having CGI send a sequence of graphics to the browser. This produces the Web equivalent of a "flip-book," where one graphic replaces the previous one.

➤ Interface with a database on the server to retrieve or add information. Online catalog ordering uses CGI, as well as the search engines (such as Yahoo, Lycos, and WebCrawler) that keep track of everything there is to find on the Web.

One disadvantage of CGI is that you *must* be a programmer to use it. Secondly, CGI requires that the user's actions be reported back to the server for interpretation and processing. The results of this processing then must be sent back to the user from the server. These extra transfers take time and reduce the "immediacy" of certain Web page interactions. Furthermore, you are limited to the CGI capabilities of your server; your provider might offer a Web server with incomplete CGI tools or with none at all. In addition, *multimedia* (sound, graphics, animation) has become all the rage, and everything in computers today has to support multimedia. CGI doesn't do this well.

Finally, to use CGI, you must have access to the CGI interface of the Web server that's serving up your pages. As I've mentioned, some providers might not support CGI access, or it might be offered for an extra (in many cases, costly) fee.

> **Techno Talk**
>
> **Pushy Servers**
> The technical term for CGI "flip-book" animation is *server push*. It's so named because the CGI program instructs the server to send (or "push") one graphic after another to the browser. Conversely, you could also use CGI to instruct the *browser* to "pull" one graphic after another from the server. This technique is (not surprisingly) called *client pull*.

In other words, CGI is more complex than most Web authors are interested in, and doesn't support all of the visually fancy things authors want to include in their pages. But something else is necessary, and that something is *Java*.

> **Techno Talk**
>
> **Most CGI Programs Are Written in Perl**
> Because the Internet originated within the UNIX world (before Windows computers or Macintoshes were hooked up to it), much of what drives the Internet (and the Web) is based in UNIX. CGI stems from this same root, and the *Perl* language is a UNIX-based language. However, a CGI program can be written in any language that the Web server supports.

Java: Web Programming for the Common Man

You can't surf the Web today without hearing about *Java*. Java, a programming language developed by Sun Microsystems, was designed to allow more power and flexibility for the presentation of material on the Web. With Java, you can...

➤ Create animations that sing and dance.

➤ Include prompts and dialog boxes that pop up while a user is filling out a form.

➤ Develop games and programs that actually run—right on the Web page.

➤ Calculate a loan in real-time based on user input.

➤ Display an accurate on-screen invoice reflecting a user's current purchases.

➤ Access databases and other information sources.

➤ Let your imagination wander.

Java works the floor in 3D rotating glory.

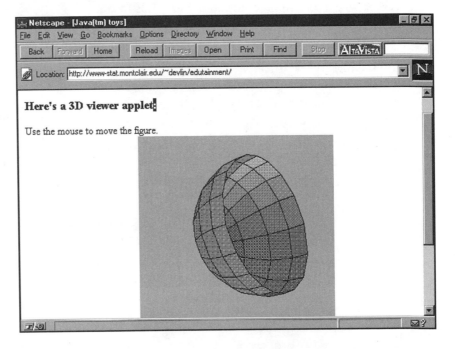

Before Java, if you wanted to view a graphic, play a movie, or listen to a sound file on the Web, you had to have a *helper application* (an independent program unrelated to the browser) installed on your computer and connected to your browser. Whenever a particular file (movie, sound, or whatever) was retrieved from the Web, the helper would be run to display or play back the file. If you didn't have the necessary helper, you had to find it, download it, and install it.

Java handles these things internally. No more helper applications, and no more CGI programming. All you need is a Java-enabled browser to view Java programs, and the Java Developers Kit to design them (it's available for free from Sun's Java Home Site, **http://java.sun.com/**). And, as an added bonus, the Java programs you create (called *applets* or *mini-applications*) will run on *any* Java-enabled browser on *any* platform: Macintosh, Windows, or UNIX. You don't need to create a program for each machine type. One size fits all.

However, Java is not without its problems. It also *is* a programming language, and as with all programming languages, you must learn it relatively well in order to use it. The applets you create must be *compiled* (by a compiler) before you can use them. A *compiler* is a special program that reads your own program and crunches it into machine-readable binary code. In spite of the existence of several nice development packages for building Java applets, compilers can be a hassle because you have to use them every time you make a change to your program, and it can take a long time to compile a program.

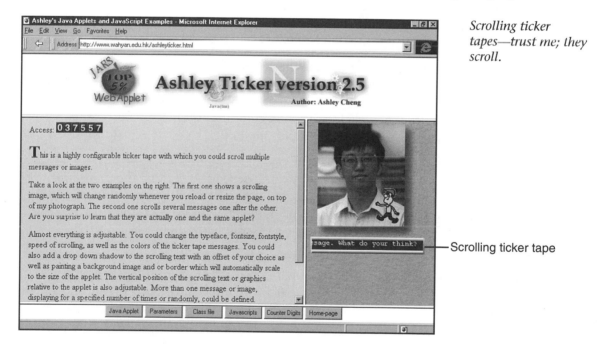

Scrolling ticker tapes—trust me; they scroll.

Scrolling ticker tape

So what you need is a way of getting the capability of Java without the added baggage of a full-blown programming language. Well, this time, Netscape comes to the rescue (with a little help from Sun) with JavaScript.

Enter JavaScript

JavaScript is a scripting language specifically designed to work with the World Wide Web. With JavaScript, you can take the power of HTML and the World Wide Web and extend it in a variety of ways.

Once upon a time (not too long ago), Sun Microsystems conjured up the complex and powerful programming language now known as Java. Although Java is highly capable, it's best suited for more complex tasks and experienced programmers. Netscape Communications saw the need for an in-between language—one that would allow individuals to design Web pages that could interact with the user or with Java applets, but that would require a minimum of programming experience. Always one to be first on the block, Netscape whipped up *LiveScript*.

LiveScript was more of a proposal than an actual language, but it convinced people that this "bridge-the-gap" idea was attractive. LiveScript was designed in the spirit of many simple scripting languages, but tailored with capabilities specifically designed for Web pages (HTML and form interaction, for example). To help the marketability of their new language, Netscape paired up with Sun, and *JavaScript* was born.

In theory, JavaScript is available for free to those who design Web browsers; this enables the designers to incorporate JavaScript compatibility into their browsers. In reality, Microsoft was the first to implement a version of JavaScript (which they named *JScript*), but they did not refer to the official JavaScript specifications. Thus, Microsoft Internet Explorer 3.0 is "mostly" JavaScript-compatible, but it's not 100%. (I explain this issue in more detail in Chapter 2.)

Recently, Netscape handed JavaScript over to an independent standards organization with the hope that all potential developers of Web browsers will have equal access to the official JavaScript implementation. As a result, hopefully, Internet Explorer 4.0 (due out sometime in the spring of 1997) will support JavaScript better than version 3.0 does.

Based on Java, JavaScript supports most of Java's expression constructs (another word for *statements*). However, JavaScript doesn't require a compiler or a knowledge of programming to get up and running. All you really need is an understanding of HTML and a little logic.

What's a "Scripting Language"?

It's impossible for a computer program to be all things to all people. Software publishers try their best to make sure their programs can handle most of what users want, but they can never anticipate everything. To make their programs more flexible, many provide the capability to extend or change how their program behaves through a *script*.

A *script* is nothing more than a sequence of program instructions (called *statements*). The program steps through the statements one at a time and performs whatever the script tells it. This is exactly the same as "programming," except that scripts tend to have simpler rules and require less learning time. Some examples of programs that provide scripting are dBASE, Paradox, and Microsoft Access (though there are many more). Some examples of stand-alone scripting languages are Perl and REXX.

Scripting languages make extending these packages easy. (And you don't have to be a programmer, purchase an expensive compiler, learn some strange pseudo-English language, or start wearing plaid shirts and pocket protectors.)

Thinking of Objects

Like Java, JavaScript is built on the concept of *objects*. Unlike Java, however, JavaScript provides a basic collection of objects for you to work with. While you can easily create new objects and object types, the ones provided give you a great deal of power.

As the word implies, an *object* is a thing—any thing. I don't mean to sound vague, but the term **object** is used to generically group a collection of different "blocks of stuff" together. In the world of computers, objects are different pieces (or building blocks) that make up a computer system or program. Objects shield a programmer (or a JavaScript writer) from having to understand how the operating system works.

You can think of objects as little black boxes. You poke things into it (which is called "setting an object's properties"), and the black box does something in response. Actually how it works isn't important, just that it does work. This is the basis for the concept of *object-oriented programming*, in which the programmer is more concerned with *what* an object is doing than *how* it gets the job done.

For example, if you had a "screen object," you could change the color of the computer screen by telling the screen object to set it's color property to, say, green. Whether the computer is a Macintosh or an IBM PC, the object would do the same thing.

In Chapter 5, you begin an up-close and personal look at objects in their natural habitat.

The Least You Need to Know

In this chapter, you took a quick look at the origin of JavaScript.

➤ The World Wide Web got its start through HTML, and HTML was extended and enhanced through CGI programming.

➤ Java came into being to satisfy the need to do more through the Web than either HTML or CGI could provide.

➤ JavaScript took Java one step further by making the power of Java available to Web authors who don't want to learn how to program.

Chapter 2

Navigator and Explorer: The World Wide Web on a Caffeine High

In This Chapter

➤ Browser wars: The JavaScript confusion

➤ Setups and configurations

➤ When browsers disagree

The JavaScript Confusion

Readers of the first edition of this book may recall simpler times—when JavaScript and Netscape Navigator 2.0 were the only team in town. For better *and* worse, the world of JavaScript has changed since those halcyon days of years past. Two major notes mark the evolution of JavaScript in the past year:

➤ Microsoft Internet Explorer 3.0 was released, with approximate support for JavaScript 1.0 (further explanation shortly).

➤ Netscape released JavaScript 1.1, which at the time of this writing, is supported only by Netscape Navigator 3.0.

The two points above have led to a fair amount of confusion among JavaScript authors and users. Talking about *2.0, 3.0. 1.1*—it's enough to drive someone into a dark corner with only a spoon and a brownie pie. Let me try to clarify the situation.

A Not-So-Zen Look at Browsers

Two versions of JavaScript are now on the market: 1.0 and 1.1. The previous edition of this book (*The Complete Idiot's Guide to JavaScript*) covered JavaScript 1.0. This edition covers JavaScript 1.1, which is largely similar to its predecessor but sports a few additional features.

At the time of this writing, *only* Netscape Navigator 3.0 supports JavaScript 1.1. For this reason, throughout this coverage, I'll denote any features of JavaScript that are new to version 1.1.

Both Netscape Navigator 2.0 and Microsoft Internet Explorer 3.0 support JavaScript 1.0. Therefore, any JavaScript programs that don't include the new 1.1 features should work with both of these browsers.

Jscript versus JavaScript

To add further confusion to the brew, although it is said that Microsoft Internet Explorer 3.0 supports JavaScript 1.0, that is not wholly, technically true. Microsoft did not design their JavaScript support based on the official reference documentation. Depending upon whom one believes, this was either because Netscape prevented Microsoft from accessing this reference material or because Microsoft did not want to "get into bed" with Netscape. In any case, Microsoft decided to "reverse engineer" JavaScript—to observe how JavaScript behaves and then create a programming language that behaves the same way. After doing so, Microsoft named their language "JScript" because it is a copy of JavaScript but not the "real thing." However, in their promotional press, Microsoft has vacillated, sometimes claiming that Internet Explorer supports "JScript" and other times saying that it supports "JavaScript."

Ultimately, JScript, or whatever one calls it, is mostly compatible with JavaScript 1.0. This means that most programs written in JavaScript 1.0 will work properly with both Netscape Navigator 2.0 and Microsoft Internet Explorer 3.0. However, in certain instances, JScript behaves differently from JavaScript. I'll cover a few of those instances later in this book.

A Brief Editorial

One hopes that in the near future the disparities between versions of JavaScript and browser support will fade away. Without some assurance of consistency between browsers' support for JavaScript, the language may face a dim future. Lack of standardization is one of the most fatal of flaws in technology. JavaScript's future health and well-being depends upon its reliability across platforms and across browsers.

By the time you read this book, the situation described may have changed—hopefully for the better. In a best-case scenario, Microsoft will include full official support for JavaScript 1.1 in their next release of Internet Explorer. If so, readers of this book, all JavaScript authors, and all users of the Web will be better off. A recent announcement that Netscape has handed JavaScript over to an independent standards body may prove to be the solution, allowing future browser revisions to support JavaScript equally.

Up and Running

Whether you currently use Netscape Navigator or Microsoft Internet Explorer, it's probably best to have both. If you need one or the other, you can get them from the Internet:

> Netscape Navigator 2.02, 3.0, and 4.0 (also known as "Communicator" when available) can be found at **http://www.netscape.com**.

> Microsoft Internet Explorer 3.0 and 4.0 (when available) can be found at **http://www.microsoft.com/ie/default.asp**.

If you choose to write JavaScript programs for Netscape 3.0 (JavaScript 1.1), remember that they will not work in Internet Explorer 3.0. Ideally, installing a copy of each browser (Netscape 2.0, 3.0, and Internet Explorer 3.0) provides the best environment for testing JavaScript programs. However, if you need to choose one, use Netscape Navigator 3.0 or 4.0, which support JavaScript 1.1. They lean more towards the future.

When it comes to configuring your browser to support JavaScript, there's little to do. By default, each browser above installs with JavaScript support enabled. To enable or disable JavaScript (obviously, one wants to enable JavaScript to make use of this book), follow these instructions:

> **Netscape Navigator 3.0:** Select **Options**, **Network Preferences**, **Languages**, **Enable JavaScript**.

> **Netscape Navigator 2.0:** The original release of 2.0 does not include an option for enabling or disabling JavaScript; it's always enabled. Install Navigator 2.02, which includes such a feature in **Options**, **Security Preferences**.

> **Microsoft Internet Explorer 3.0:** Select **View**, **Options**, **Security**, **Run ActiveX Scripts**. Despite its misleading label, enabling this option will enable JavaScript.

Browser Bias: Which JavaScript to Support?

Unfortunately, due to the currently inconsistent state of JavaScript support, you may need to decide which Web browser you "most" want to support. To get the most out of this book, you'd write JavaScript programs that conform to version 1.1 (the subject of this book). In doing so, you support only Netscape Navigator 3.0 users.

If you write JavaScript programs that do not use version 1.1's special features, Netscape Navigator 2.0 users will be able to view your program. Additionally, users of Microsoft Internet Explorer 3.0 may also be able to view these JavaScript programs. Then again, they may not; as I explained earlier, there are a few compatibility differences between Internet Explorer's and Netscape Navigator's JavaScript support!

Confusing as this is, here's what it boils down to:

➤ Write JavaScript 1.1 programs to exploit the full feature set of JavaScript and reach the most future users. Test these programs in Netscape Navigator 3.0.

➤ If you need to write JavaScript 1.0 programs, make sure they work best in Netscape Navigator 2.0. Certainly, you should still test them in Internet Explorer 3.0, but it is impossible to guarantee that *every* JavaScript program will functional equally in both browsers.

My Bias

Yes, I'm biased. This is not a form of corporate loyalty or blind nationalism. Rather, simplicity. I'm writing this book with Netscape Navigator 3.0 in mind. Therefore, I'll be covering JavaScript 1.1. Although I cannot comprehensively discuss every difference between JavaScript versions and browser support, I'll make these two efforts:

➤ When a feature is being discussed that is new to JavaScript 1.1 or has changed since 1.0, that will be noted.

➤ From time to time, I'll also point out differences in JavaScript support under Microsoft Internet Explorer 3.0. This is not meant to be a comprehensive survey of differences; no such list exists. However, certain variations have become well-known in the programming community.

The Least You Need to Know

➤ There are two versions of JavaScript. The original, covered in the previous edition of this book, was 1.0. A new version, 1.1, has been released; it sports some new features.

➤ As of the time of this writing, only Netscape Navigator 3.0 supports JavaScript 1.1.

➤ Both Netscape Navigator 2.0 and Microsoft Internet Explorer 3.0 support the older version of JavaScript (1.0).

➤ Microsoft Internet Explorer's support of JavaScript 1.0 is not perfect, but it is adequate in most cases.

➤ This book's bias is toward JavaScript 1.1 and Netscape Navigator 3.0.

Part 2
Let's Get Jivin'

Alright, now you're hooked. You've had a "taste of the bean," and you want to put a little sugar (the real stuff) on your Web site. You want to get rolling. To do that, you need a few things, not the least of which is a browser that can handle JavaScript.

At the present time, both Netscape Navigator 3.0 (and greater) and Microsoft Internet Explorer 3.0 (and greater) support JavaScript. (Other companies have licensed JavaScript technology for inclusion in future versions of their browsers, but they haven't released them yet.) So, set up your browser, kick the tires, and check out what's really brewing on the Web.

AL AND HIS TEAM WERE NOT THE BEST COMPUTER DEBUGGERS, BUT THEY SURE HAD STYLE.

Tag... You're It!

Giving HTML a Caffeine Boost

If you're interested in learning JavaScript programming (and I assume you are; this is the wrong book to be reading just for fun), you must be at least somewhat familiar with HTML by now. To quickly summarize, HTML is a markup language used to "describe" how a Web page should look. HTML is expressed through tags, which are written in the form:

```
<TAG>
```

Most tags surround the text on which they operate and, therefore, have to be paired in the manner:

```
<TAG> text to affect </TAG>
```

Web browsers such as Netscape and Internet Explorer interpret these markup tags and render the page to the screen according to the instructions built into the tags.

If this is material is new or surprising, I strongly recommend that you read a primer on HTML, such as Que's *The Complete Idiot's Guide to Creating an HTML Web Page*, by Paul McFedries.

Tag Attributes

Because this chapter refers to *attributes* of an HTML tag several times, you need to know what they are. As stated, a typical HTML tag looks like this: <TAG>. However, many tags accept further specifications that determine their final effect, such as:

`<TAG attribute1=x attribute2=y>`

That's all there is to it. When you use a tag that requires attributes or that can include attributes, it will be pointed out within the chapter.

The `<SCRIPT>` Tag

The tag to know for JavaScript programming is the <SCRIPT> tag. In short, it looks like this:

`<SCRIPT attributes> JavaScript program code </SCRIPT>`

The opening <SCRIPT> tag can include either of two attributes: the LANGUAGE attribute or the SRC attribute.

This is the standard opening <SCRIPT> tag, with the LANGUAGE attribute:

`<SCRIPT LANGUAGE="JavaScript">`

This tag simply defines the start of JavaScript program code and identifies the language the code is written in (which, obviously, is JavaScript). JavaScript's official documentation claims that the language attribute is mandatory; you cannot simply begin a section of code with <SCRIPT> alone because it helps the browser identify not only script code, but also the language the code is written in. (Currently, one other scripting language—*VBScript* from Microsoft—also uses the <SCRIPT> tag.) It should be noted, though, that in practice, omitting the LANGUAGE attribute from the <SCRIPT> tag doesn't cause any problems in most cases—especially when pages are viewed with a browser that supports only one scripting language (such as Navigator). For the future, however, it would be a good idea to stick to the rule and mark the end of a JavaScript code section with </SCRIPT>.

As an alternative to writing the JavaScript code within the Web page source itself, you can refer to JavaScript code that is saved in its own text file elsewhere on the server. This will behave just as if the code were typed directly into the Web page source (as it is in all of these examples). The following is the general format for such a code, which uses the SRC attribute:

```
<SCRIPT SRC="URL to your script file"> ...
</SCRIPT>
```

This would be an efficient way of reusing the same JavaScript code in several Web pages, without having to explicitly enter it into each one. You'd merely insert the call to the file. The text file of the JavaScript program must have a file name ending in .JS, as in the following example:

```
<SCRIPT SRC="http://www.epicmedia.com/funscript.js"> ... </SCRIPT>
```

Techno Talk

The URL (Earl) of Web?
URL stands for Uniform Resource Locator. It's a fancy way of identifying anything on the Internet anywhere in the world (a file, a document, a graphic, or a Web site, for example) with a unique *address*. Think of it as a global CyberZipCode: No two Web pages, FTP files, UseNet newsgroups, Gopher menus, or whatever can have the same URL.

Techno Talk

Beware of Outside Sources!

Currently, the SRC= attribute of the <SCRIPT> tag is only supported by Netscape Navigator 3.0 and greater. If you want your JavaScript pages to work with other browsers, such as Internet Explorer 3.0 and earlier versions of Netscape, you might want to avoid using the SRC= attribute and incorporating your JavaScript code within your pages. The possible exception to this might be Internet Explorer 4.0 (which might be released by the time you read this book). It might support the SRC attribute; however, at press time, this is not known for certain.

You place JavaScript code between <SCRIPT> tags wherever you want the code executed within a page. A tiny example of the HTML code of a Web page, with embedded JavaScript code, might look like this:

```
<HTML>
<HEAD>
   <TITLE>My Nifty Web Page</TITLE>
</HEAD>
<BODY>
<H1>
   Welcome to my Exciting Home Page,<BR>
```

```
    Where I talk about ME
</H1>
<HR>
<SCRIPT LANGUAGE="JavaScript">
JavaScript program code goes here
</SCRIPT>
</BODY>
</HTML>
```

Note that you needn't put all of the JavaScript code within one set of <SCRIPT> tags. You can use numerous <SCRIPT> </SCRIPT> pairs, inserting them wherever in the page you want to include JavaScript code. Having said that, there are three caveats to note:

➤ Place all JavaScript function definitions between the <HEAD> and </HEAD> tags at the top of the HTML page, as in this example:

```
<HTML>
<HEAD>
<TITLE>My Funky JavaScript Page</TITLE>
<SCRIPT LANGUAGE="JavaScript">
function func1(x, y, z) {
    statements
}

function func2(a, b, c) {
    statements
}
...
</SCRIPT>
</HEAD>
...
```

➤ Functions must be defined before they can be called. (You might not understand what that means just yet, but after you read Chapter 8, the skies will be clear.) To summarize, a *function* is a section of code that performs a specific task. It is like a self-contained miniprogram. For many reasons, in other areas of JavaScript code, you will find the need to *call* these functions—that is, refer to them by name and have them executed. You'll learn about functions in gruesome detail in Chapter 8. In the meantime, simply remember that following this rule will ensure that all functions have been defined before they are called in any JavaScript code further down the page.

Can You Keep a Secret?

With all the concern about security in CyberSpace these days, you're probably wondering about the "secrecy" of JavaScript. After all, if your prized script is written in the middle of an HTML file, all someone has to do is select the View Source option from the browser's menu, and your hard work is displayed plain as day...right?

Unfortunately, that is right. If you want to keep your script from being seen, place it in an external file and include it using the SRC= attribute of the <SCRIPT> tag. But, remember two important things when you do this:

➤ Make sure that the file ends in .JS.

➤ Understand that only users of Netscape Navigator 3.0 will be able to use your pages correctly (as neither Navigator 2.0 nor Internet Explorer 3.0 support the SRC= attribute).

➤ Any and all JavaScript code, including function definitions, applies only to the page it resides on. If you wanted to use the same JavaScript code in more than one page (and didn't want to type it over and over again), you could either save the JavaScript code as an external file and use the SRC= attribute of the <SCRIPT> tag to load it, or store the JavaScript code in one document of a *framed* collection of documents and reference the JavaScript functions from the other framed documents.

➤ Enclose *all* JavaScript code within HTML comment tags. An HTML comment tag looks like:

```
<!-- comments -->
```

➤ Anything within HTML comment tags is ignored by most browsers—except browsers that support JavaScript, which will recognize the presence of the JavaScript code and not ignore it. The rationale behind this is that those browsers that know nothing of JavaScript might display the code in the Web page itself, which would not be desirable at all. This also can be used to allow all browsers—whether or not they're JavaScript-capable—to view the contents of your page (if the contents itself can be viewed without the JavaScript support). Therefore, in the end, the recommended manner of including JavaScript code into a page is as follows:

```
<SCRIPT LANGUAGE="JavaScript">
<!--
    JavaScript program code goes here
// -->
</SCRIPT>
```

➤ Also, notice that the tail end of the comment statement includes two slash characters. The slashes tell JavaScript to ignore the rest of the line, so that JavaScript doesn't try to process the closing comment tag as a JavaScript statement.

It doesn't matter where your JavaScript statements go in your page; they are always evaluated (a fancy term for "made ready to run") *after* the page has finished loading into the browser (but *before* the browser actually displays the page to the user).

Rules of the Web

You need to keep some fundamental rules in mind when you're building your JavaScript pages:

➤ JavaScript scripts (enclosed within a <SCRIPT> tag) are not evaluated until *after* the page loads (but *before* the page is actually displayed).

➤ Scripts stored as separate files (read in with the SRC= attribute of the <SCRIPT> tag) are evaluated *before* any in-page script commands.

The Least You Need to Know

This chapter has introduced you to the new <SCRIPT> tag that extends HTML to allow you to plug JavaScript commands into your Web pages. You also learned the following rules about scripts:

➤ Scripts are evaluated *after* a page has finished loading but *before* the page is displayed.

➤ Any functions defined in scripts are not automatically executed when the page loads. They are stored until called by something else in the page.

➤ Scripts loaded through the SRC= attribute (in other words, scripts that are kept in separate files) are evaluated *before* inline (or "in-page") scripts.

➤ Netscape Navigator 3.0 and greater support the SRC= attribute (i.e., can load scripts from other files outside the page). Although Internet Explorer 3.0 does not support the SRC= attribute, it's possible that Internet Explorer 4.0 might.

➤ It's a good idea to place scripts inside comment tags to keep browsers that can't handle JavaScript from displaying them on the page.

Chapter 4

Off and Running... with Someone Else's Help

Starting the learning curve with anything can be a major task, and computer-related things always seem to be the worst. After gathering up your courage to actually begin, you have a pile of books, the computer screen blinking "unknown command" at you, and a growing frustration with the inhabitants of Silicon Valley. Computer languages can be very frustrating.

To try to take the edge off the process and "ease" your way into the world of JavaScript, take a page from some of the computer gurus that wander the Web:

➤ Observe what other people are doing with what you want to learn

➤ Analyze how they did it

➤ Adapt it to your own needs

Where Can I Find the Experts?

In other words, borrow from those who've already gotten the bugs out. No, this is not plagiarism; I'm not suggesting that you simply take someone else's hard work and put your name on it. (That would be ethically—and perhaps even legally—challengeable.) Instead, look at the script code that they wrote and use what they did to help you better understand how JavaScript interacts with the Web. If you want to try to play with the script (make your own changes), all you have to do is save the HTML document as a file on your computer.

With the explosion of JavaScript on the Web today, several sites have sprung up (literally overnight) that make excellent starting points for you to explore further. In this chapter, you'll take a quick tour through several of the newest, neatest, and best places to learn more about JavaScript.

Remember that Netscape Navigator 3.0 is our browser of choice. Depending on which version of JavaScript some of the sites below are programmed with, they may or may not function correctly using alternative browsers.

Netscape: Home of JavaScript

Point your browser at:

> http://home.netscape.com/comprod/products/navigator/version_3.0/
> index.html

You'll be whisked into the world of Netscape and Netscape Navigator 3.0, the company that developed JavaScript. Netscape Navigator has been the most popular browser on the Web to date, and although Microsoft Internet Explorer is catching up, as far as JavaScript goes, Netscape still holds the torch.

Netscape's pages change regularly, so you'll want to stop in from time to time to catch the latest information and updates to Navigator and the other products Netscape sells.

Finding your way from the Netscape Navigator 3.0 page to JavaScript information is as easy as one click. From the opening page, scroll down until you see the subsection titled **Building Blocks** (see the following figure). Then click the **JavaScript** link, and you're all set. From there, you will land smack-dab on the JavaScript page, wherein lie several examples of code (Java Resources and Examples) and a link leading to the "official" JavaScript documentation (JavaScript Authoring Guide).

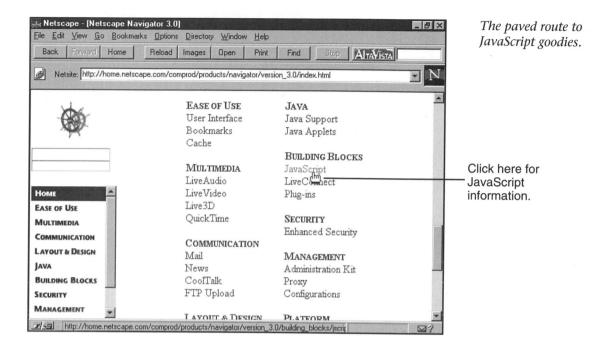

The paved route to JavaScript goodies.

Click here for JavaScript information.

Eyeing Some Code

Earlier I suggested that you take a long, hard look at other authors' JavaScript programs. Doing so requires that you first store a copy of the program itself, so let's see how you do that. It's relatively painless.

Several example JavaScript programs are on the Netscape JavaScript page. One of them is an "Interest Calculator," which calculates interest on a loan based on data the user inputs into the table. Click the link to the Interest Calculator to see it in action (as shown in the next figure).

Because JavaScript code is embedded within the HTML, merely save the HTML code for this page, and you will find the JavaScript program within it. You can easily see the HTML code by choosing the Navigator menu command **View**, **Document Source**. Alternatively, if the document in question resides within a frame (as is the case with the Interest Calculator mentioned above), click within the frame to bring it focus, and then select the **View**, **Frame Source** menu command. The second upcoming figure shows JavaScript source code.

That's gonna cost ya. Calculating loan payments—oh, the fun!

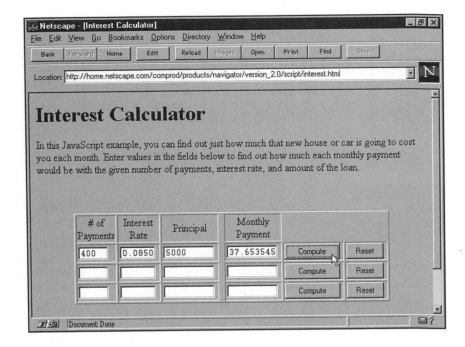

Viewing the HTML source for inspection and perusal.

Depending on what source viewer you've configured, you may or may not be able to save the file right from there. If you can't, you can simply select the Navigator command **File, Save As**. This displays a Save File dialog box, in which you can choose where to save the file. Be sure **HTML Files** is selected in the Save As Type list box, as shown here.

When you save the HTML source code, be sure to save it as an HTML file.

Select HTML Files as your file type.

The resulting file, with the name "somefile.htm" or "somefile.html" (depending on your system), can be viewed with any text editor. It is simply a plain text file, and within it you will find all the HTML tags that define the page, including any JavaScript programs.

Check This Out...

Caveat Capture

There is one exception to everything we've said about capturing the JavaScript code from a page. It all assumes that the code was embedded directly into the HTML. Some authors may keep the code in a separate file, using the SRC= attribute of the <SCRIPT> tag. In these cases, you can't retrieve the JavaScript program code.

Gamelan

Before Gamelan, there wasn't a central clearinghouse for Java and JavaScript material. Now, if you set your browser to **http://www.gamelan.com/**, you'll find an excellent collection of JavaScript pages, Java applets, and other Java-related nifties. The folks at EarthWeb (who maintain Gamelan) update the site daily, so there is always something new to check out. Gamelan breaks Java applets down into categories, and the areas covered are rather diverse: animation, communications, finance, games, special effects, networking, and so on. There's also an impressive list of links to other Java and JavaScript sites around the Net. At last glance, there were more than 180 sites in Gamelan's listing alone!

While you're poking around Gamelan, you might want to check out the Java Message Exchange (you'll find it listed in the sites category). The Message Exchange is a message board for the purpose of exchanging information on Java, JavaScript, and new JavaScript sites.

Gamelan: Learn to pronounce it right ("gamma-lahn"), and you're on your way to geekdom!

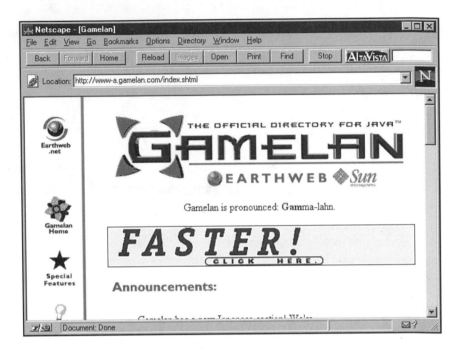

JavaScript Index

While Gamelan is Java-generic (it covers both Java and JavaScript), the JavaScript Index is devoted to JavaScript and its uses. Check out **http://www.c2.org/~andreww/javascript/**, and you'll find a comprehensive categorical breakdown of JavaScript pages and implementations. Some are pure JavaScript; others merge JavaScript with Java and other HTML techniques.

One nice section of the JavaScript Index is its Widgets section. A *widget* is simply a little bit of code which does something. From the standpoint of JavaScript, a widget is usually a little script that does something nifty: maybe a scroll bar, a background changer, or a pop-up help display. Widgets are great little scripts that you can borrow and combine with your own JavaScript code to create truly unique Web pages.

To borrow a widget, simply follow the same procedures outlined earlier with the Netscape example. Go to the page with the JavaScript program, and then save the HTML source (either by viewing the source and saving it from there or by using your browser's **File**, **Save As** menu command).

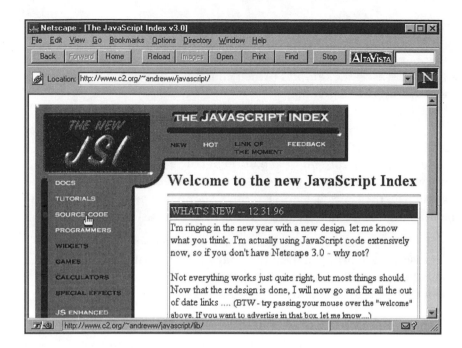

The JavaScript Index is just for us JavaScripters.

Conversations on JavaScript

Gamelan and the JavaScript Index are great for collecting JavaScript widgets and tutorial information. However, you're also likely to encounter a real stumper: the sort of problem that you simply can't solve. Perhaps your program doesn't work properly—or at all—and you cannot figure out why. Tutorials haven't helped, ice cream hasn't helped, and long bouts of sleep prove ineffective. In these cases, it's often best to chat with others on the subject. Often, someone else can offer advice for your specific problem.

Chat about JavaScript is available on the Internet via the same routes on which people chat about everything else.

UseNet

Your typical newsfeed, provided by your Internet service provider, should carry the newsgroup **comp.lang.javascript**. This is one great place to ask questions or answer questions!

Using Netscape Navigator, you can also connect to Netscape's private newsserver, **secnews.netscape.com**, and participate in the newsgroup **netscape.devs-javascript**. If you're not sure how to make this connection with Navigator, try the URL **snews://secnews.netscape.com/netscape.devs-javascript**.

Finally, Live Software, the creators of JavaScript (back when it was known as LiveScript, for the ancient history buffs out there), also offers two JavaScript-oriented chat groups on its newsserver. Point any news reader to **news.livesoftware.com** and check out the newsgroups **livesoftware.javascript.examples** (which contains examples of JavaScript code) and **livesoftware.javascript.developer**.

Mailing Lists

Another common, and often more content-driven, form of conversation occurs via mailing lists. When you join a mailing list, you receive messages that other users send to the list. You can merely read their messages, or you can respond by sending new messages back to the readers of the list. To participate in a mailing list, you must first "join" it.

To join the mailing list called **JavaScript Talk**, for example, send an e-mail message to the address **majordomo@listserv.bridge.net**. In the body of the message, type the line **subscribe javascript-talk**. Shortly thereafter, you'll receive a welcome message from the list, containing instructions for participation, and so forth.

Some additional mailing lists which discuss JavaScript include:

➤ **Obscure/Inquiry JavaScript List**   To join, send e-mail to **javascript-request@inquiry.com** with message body **subscribe**.

➤ **JavaScript Mailing List**   To join, send e-mail to **javascript-request@NETural.com** with message body **subscribe**.

Sample Platter of What You're Likely to Find

Now that you know where to look for lists of JavaScript-powered pages, here's a sampling of the many diverse things those pages can do.

JavaScript 1040EZ

Just in time for April 15, here's a site that uses JavaScript to fill out the 1040EZ form (known by some wags as "1040 STU-PID").

http://www.homepages.com/fun/1040EZ.html

You have a company known as Home Pages to thank for this little marvel.

Unit Conversion Calculator

These few nifties can convert from various units of measurement to others, all with the magic of JavaScript, authored by Jonathan Weesner.

> http://www.cyberstation.net/%7Ejweesner/conv.html

Mastermind

If you have any idea how to play the game Mastermind, JavaScripted by Ian Cameron, this page might appeal to you.

> http://dingo.uq.edu.au/~zzdcamer/master.htm

ColorCenter

This nifty JavaScript incarnation enables you to test various Web page color combinations; it's a quick way to decide what colors will work in your own design. ColorCenter was designed by Bill Dortch of hIdaho Design.

> http://www.hidaho.com/colorcenter/cc.html

Scrolling Text and Banners

Textual animation for those with a sweet tooth for eye candy, this script is the spawn of Craig Slagel (this site does not seem to work properly with Internet Explorer 3.0).

> http://www.boots.com/~craigel/java2.htm

These Are Nifty and New...

All of the above examples, while perfectly smart and snazzy, were also included in the first edition of this book. Below are some additional examples of JavaScript programs that take advantage of new features available in JavaScript 1.1/Netscape Navigator 3.0.

Follow the Bouncing Block

Using the image replacement capability of JavaScript 1.1, we see some nifty visual effects from the mind of Jason Bloomberg.

> http://www.lhouse.com/~jbloomberg/colors

Simple Animation

This is a basic but educational example of creating an animation with JavaScript 1.1, by Tim Wallace.

> http://www.essex1.com/people/timothy/30-anim.htm

Animated Menu

A useful example of using JavaScript 1.1 to highlight menu options as the mouse passes over, this is also by Tim Wallace.

> http://www.essex1.com/people/timothy/30-menu.htm

The Least You Need to Know

You've taken a whirlwind tour around the globe and through the Internet and have found that JavaScript is expanding at an explosive rate. You've seen that there are hundreds of sites (more and more springing up each day) with scripts and applets you can download and use or adapt to your own needs. You also learned that using someone else's scripting idea as a basis for your own is as simple as saving the script document and editing it.

Now that you have a few scripts from other JavaScripters, you're probably wondering what the devil those new lines in the script actually mean. That's what the next chapters cover: the inner workings of JavaScript.

Part 3
JavaScript: Espresso for the Masses

No matter how you cut it, JavaScript is a programming language—of sorts. It has rules, commands, special words that do special things, and a way of putting things together that you must be familiar with if you want to become a power JavaScripter.

The good news is that what makes up JavaScript is fairly close to English, and (with a little logic thrown in) it's very easy to use. Also, because it's a scripting language, you don't need a fancy compiler or another program to turn your script into something your browser can deal with. In fact, all you really need to create your own scripts is a browser, a simple word processor, and this book.

In this section, you step through the parts that make up the JavaScript language and see how the work together and what they do.

WHAT THE AMISH SAY ONLINE.

Objects, Names, and Literals

As you learned in Chapter 3, JavaScript programs reside within the HTML code of a page and enable you to perform a variety of tasks that interact with the user or the user's input. JavaScript is relatively easy to program—even for those who are unfamiliar with computer programming—and it is not generally intended for creating extremely large or complex programs. Readers who have had experience with other programming languages will find JavaScript extremely accessible. New users, however, might want to read the following chapters a few times, to make sure they grasp the concepts involved.

What's in a Name? (A Variable Name, That Is)

One of the basic fundamentals of a programming language is the variable. A *variable* is essentially a label to which you assign a "value" (what this value might be, you'll learn about shortly). Variables are also commonly used in mathematics. Anyone who recalls having stayed awake during those classes might still be scarred by such statements as "x=5." But that's good; the trauma will help you when it comes to JavaScript. (And students always want to know of what use algebra will be....)

JavaScript has variables (also known as *names* or *variable names*) all over the place, many of them created by you, the programmer. So, first spend some quality time understanding the ubiquitous variable:

➤ Because it is a label, the variable is used to refer to a given "value" in a program.

➤ The value that the label refers to may change, but the label will stay the same. For example, at one point in our program, the variable *x* might refer to the value 5, but at a later point in the program, x might refer to 10. This is not arbitrary; perhaps we have used x to track the number of items a user has chosen to purchase, and one user ordered 5 while another bought 10.

➤ The variable enables you to instruct the computer to perform a series of tasks or calculations, regardless of what the actual values might be. This, in a sense, is the heart (or one of the hearts, if that's possible) of a program—a JavaScript program in particular.

Tom, Dick42, and _Harry

Generally, it is up to you, the programmer, to decide on variable names. But as you might guess, JavaScript has a few rules that govern what names are allowable:

➤ The variable name must begin with a letter or an underscore character (_). The first character of a variable name cannot be a number or some other nonalphabetical character.

➤ You cannot use a space within a variable name.

➤ JavaScript is case-sensitive, so "a" is a completely different letter than "A." This has two important ramifications:

Watch your variable names. Although *cost*, *Cost*, and *COST* are all valid variable names, they are all different variable names.

Built-in JavaScript statements, which you'll learn about in subsequent chapters, are all lowercase. (You'll be reminded of this when the time comes.)

➤ You cannot use a "reserved word" as a variable name. A reserved word is a word that JavaScript already uses for some other purpose, such as a built-in command (an expression, object, or function, all of which are covered later). To give you an example, JavaScript reserves the word "if" for programming purposes. Therefore, you cannot create a variable named *if*. (For a complete list of JavaScript's reserved words, see Appendix A, "JavaScript: The Complete Overview," at the end of this book.)

As long as you abide by the preceding rules, JavaScript doesn't care what you choose to name a variable. As far as JavaScript is concerned, the same variable name will always refer to the same value placeholder, whether that name is x or inventory. However, you should care. As the programmer, you want to maximize your ability to understand and follow your own program. This is especially true when you inevitably must debug it (that is, find where problems are and attempt to fix them). So it is in your best interest to make up variable names that hold some human meaning in relation to the values they will represent.

For example, let's suppose that you have a Web page you're using to sell a product: You're hawking novelty mugs with pictures of your dog wearing a bikini. The prices of these may vary, depending on how many mugs the consumer chooses to purchase at one time. The first variable you'll need to name is the one that refers to the number of mugs ordered. Remember, you can name this variable anything (within the previous rules), such as x or bazoo. But, for the sake of programming clarity to the human mind, mugs is probably a good choice for a variable name. (Of course, orders would suffice, too, but you get the concept.)

There is a second variable in the preceding example, and that is the price of each mug. Let's say the single-mug purchase price is $9.95, but two mugs sell for $15.95, and three sell for $22.95. Because the price may vary and cannot be assumed to be constant, it will require a variable name, as well. Again, you could name the price variable mary or y, but something like price or cost seems to be a more reasonable choice.

Full of Value(s)

As you've read, variables are references to values. Now that you understand what a variable is, look at the values a variable might hold. In JavaScript, a variable might refer to any of three types of values, plus a special bonus value (I know this doesn't make sense yet, but bear with me).

➤ **Numeric value** This is what first comes to mind when people think of a variable. As in the previous examples, a variable name may refer to a numeric value; for example, price refers to the value 9.95, and mugs refers to the value 2.

➤ **String value** A string, in programming parlance, is a group of characters that is not a numeric value. For example, "bob" is a string. "]]]#!!!" is also a string. A string can be any length and can be made up of any characters, including numbers. Thus "a" is a string, and so is "400". Note, however, that the string "400" is not the numeric value 400. It is merely the characters "4," "0," and "0." It does not hold mathematical meaning to the computer. A variable may refer to a string. For example, you might create a variable called *surname*, and it might refer to the string "Carruthers". Or maybe you have a variable called *model*, which could refer to "C3PO".

Strings are always enclosed with quotation marks. Do the same in JavaScript code. JavaScript is only able to distinguish between a variable name cost and a string value "cost" if you enclose string values within quotation marks. You can use either double or single quotation marks to enclose a string ("cost" or 'cost'). In the case of nested strings—where you have to insert one string value within a phrase that is already within quotation marks—use double quotation marks to set off the whole phrase, and use single quotation marks to set off each value within it (for example, "callmyfunction ('bob','jane','white')"). You will see another example of this when we discuss event handlers in Chapter 9.

➤ **Boolean value** "Boolean" is a humorous-sounding word that simply means "true or false." It comes from the lingo of logic studies. A variable may refer to a Boolean value, which means it can be true or false. In this sense, the variable is referring to a condition, and not to substantive content as in the two previous examples.

And the special bonus value is this:

➤ **null** A variable may refer simply to the word and concept "null." In JavaScript, null means "nothing." No value, nada. Note that this is not zero because zero is a numeric value. Null is simply nothing. A little weird, I admit, but it has its uses on certain occasions. And it's good talk at parties. (Joe: "So, can there ever really be total 'nothingness?'" Bill: "Yes, in JavaScript there can be.")

Handing Out Assignments

When you create a variable name and refer it to a value, you are making an assignment. For example, in our earlier example, we "assigned the numeric value 5 to the variable mugs." Although you'll discover more complex assignments in Chapter 7, the following basics serve as a useful grounding (you'll learn exactly how and where to place these commands as part of a JavaScript program in Chapter 7).

Your Basic Assignment

A basic assignment in JavaScript is made with this construction:

```
var variablename = value;
```

where var is the keyword that precedes all assignments, variablename stands for the name of the variable, and value stands for the value you are assigning to the variable. For example:

```
var mugs = 2;
var price = 9.95;
```

Assigning a String to a Variable

When making an assignment to a string value, it is vital to place the string within quotation marks (either the double or single kind). Here are two examples:

```
var surname = "Carruthers";
var model = 'C3PO';
```

Note that if you do not include the quotation marks, JavaScript will think you are assigning the value of one variable to another variable; for example:

```
var surname = carruthers;
```

JavaScript will think you want to assign the value of the variable `carruthers` to the variable `surname`. Because `carruthers` is a nonexistent variable, JavaScript will display an error message to alert you. This is not what you want in this case (although at other times, you might want to assign one variable's value to another).

Boolean Assignments

Boolean values usually represent conditions such as matters in which there can be only a true or false status. A Boolean value assigned to a variable simply looks like this:

```
var married = true;
var dead = false;
```

...And Don't Forget Null

And, for the sake of closure, an assignment of the special bonus value, null:

```
var variablename = null;
```

You may or may not encounter actual applications of the null value assignment in later chapters. It's not crucial, and it may not come up very often. A common technique among programmers who want a variable to contain "nothing" is to assign numeric variables the value 0 (for example, `total = 0`) and to assign string variables the value "" (for example, `surname = ""`). This is because, in many instances, we want numerical variables to begin with a value of zero (as in variables which keep count of something, for example), and we often want string variables to begin as a string with no characters.

The Plain (Literal) Truth

A value that is not married (assigned) to a variable is known as a literal. This is such a simple concept that it might actually be a tad confusing at first.

➤ The numeric value 5 is a literal.

➤ The string "mary worth" is a literal.

What is the point of any of this? Recall that variables are most often used to track potentially changing values. In some instances, you will want to refer to a value, but it may be one constant amount. For example, perhaps the price of your product is $9.95, and it is always $9.95 in all cases.

In these instances, you still have the option to assign a variable name to a constant value, which often makes reading the JavaScript program easier for human debugging purposes. However, you do not need to use a variable at all in these cases. You may simply want to write out 9.95 whenever it is needed in a calculation within the JavaScript program. This is a reasonable practice in some cases, but in others it would be more comprehensible to use a meaningful variable name.

Check This Out...

Stay Still
A *constant* is a label whose value never changes. A typical example from "the real world" is PI. We use the label PI or that funny symbol Π, yet it always represents the same actual number. We may choose to use a similar technique in JavaScript programming for ease of reading and for ease of future program modifications.

The following examples use a variable assignment and the * sign, which is a multiplication symbol (we'll learn more about that in the next chapter). To illustrate a literal versus a variable name, consider the following:

Using variables:

```
var price = 9.95;
var total = mugs * price;
```

Using literals:

```
var total = mugs * 9.95;
```

Although both sets of commands yield the same results, there are different reasons to select one approach or the other. In the first case (using variables), the calculation for the variable total is very easy for a human reading the program code to understand (for debugging purposes). In the second case, it might not be so obvious to a human reader just what the 9.95 represents. If there is a problem with the program, analyzing it may be more difficult because of this.

Second, imagine that there might be many instances of calculations within the program that utilize the 9.95 price. If the price were to change, it would take some time to manually edit the JavaScript program to reflect the price change. On the other hand, in the first example, you would only need to change the value assigned to price one time, and because price is used to represent the value throughout the remainder of the program, all other calculations would remain accurate without your having to find them and change them.

Treating Values Like Objects

So far, you've learned about two important topics (variable names and their assigned values) and one minor topic (literals). Now, it is time to move up one rung on the ladder of abstraction to a very relevant concept in JavaScript programming: the object.

In JavaScript, an *object* is an umbrella concept under which a set of variables resides. This may be a tough concept at first, so let me explain it several different ways. Consider a sweater. A sweater, by the JavaScript definition, is an "object" that possesses several noteworthy qualities or *properties*. For example, a sweater may possess properties of material, size, color, and price.

Note that each property sounds like the variables discussed earlier. That is exactly what they are. Thus, an object is a sort of "supervariable" that contains a set of subvariables. Another example of an object would be an individual person. A person, as an object, contains a set of properties, some of which are useful for our particular application—such as first name, surname, age, gender, and marital status.

Also take note of how objects can fit inside other larger objects. For example, a person object could be part of a family object. A family object might have properties such as size, ethnicity, combined income, and persons (each of which, in turn, possesses its own individual person object properties previously described). Therefore, an object can also be a property of another object. Confusing? Somewhat, but useful as well, as you shall see.

In JavaScript lingo, you denote an object and its properties in the form *object.property*. For example, recall the sweater object. Imagine that in JavaScript, you create an object called *sweater* (for now, don't worry about how you create an object). You then create several properties for the sweater object: material, size, color, and price. In JavaScript syntax, you would refer to those properties in program code like this:

```
sweater.material
sweater.size
sweater.color
sweater.price
```

Each of the preceding is a variable of the same sort discussed at the opening of this chapter. Therefore, you can assign appropriate values to each of them. Examples include the following:

```
sweater.material = "argyle";
sweater.size = "M";
sweater.color = "violet";
sweater.price = 29.95;
```

Objects are common in JavaScript programs, so this is an important concept to nail down. Object properties exist in the order in which they were originally defined. You won't learn how to define objects until Chapter 8, but you should remember this point.

A la Carte Versus Prepackaged Objects

Keep in mind that you don't have to create objects. They're necessary only if they are useful to the tasks of your JavaScript program. A simple program that merely performs calculations using two variables may not need any objects. However, in addition to objects that you may choose to create, JavaScript also includes a number of pre-made objects. These exist to help you achieve certain ends in your program. But before you take a closer look at some built-in objects, you need to learn about functions, and all of that fun takes place in Chapter 8.

So far, you've looked at variables, the values that may be assigned to them, literals, and objects, which are superset groups of variables (known as properties). Here, break for tea and crackers, which are provided in the rec room down the hall. See you in a bit.

The Least You Need to Know

➤ A variable name is a label that you use to refer to some sort of value. You should choose meaningful variable names so that you can tell what they stand for when you have to debug (look for problems in) your program.

➤ A value is the contents assigned to a variable. Values may take the form of numeric data, character strings, Boolean values, or the special null symbol (written as the word null).

➤ A literal is simply a value used in code without being assigned to a variable. (That is, it is written out explicitly.) Literals have specific uses in particular circumstances, but they generally make code more difficult for human readers to understand.

➤ An object in JavaScript is a superset variable, under which a set of subvariables (or properties) relate. It is easiest to understand by example: a sweater is an object that possesses the properties of material, size, color, and price. Objects can also serve as properties for other objects.

Operators and Expressions

If this chapter were a sequel to the previous one—and it is—it would pick up where we left off—and it will. Variables, values, and objects are merely part of the JavaScript story. They all deal with ways to contain data. In this chapter, you're going to look at methods of manipulating data in order to generate new and improved (or at least useful) data. I guarantee this will be fun. If it's not, you get a free video rental from your local video store down the street. Tell them I sent you; they'll take care of you.

Let's Play Operation!

An operator is a command that interprets given values or variables and produces a result. Does that make any sense? Perhaps not, but that's a textbook definition. As usual, examples are the best explanation.

A common and easy-to-understand form of operators are arithmetic operators. They are used to perform calculations on given data. Here is an arithmetic operator:

```
+
```

Neat, huh? That's not nearly so confusing as the definition made it seem. Of course, + can't perform anything on its own—it needs data to work with. Here's where values come in, either in the form of variables or literals. In techno-talk, the values used with an operator are called operands. Thus, consider the following:

```
3 + 8
```

In the above, 3 and 8 are operands, and the + is the operator. That example used literals for values; more commonly in JavaScript programs, you would see operands that are variables:

```
total = mugs * price
```

The asterisk (*) is the operator for "multiply." JavaScript offers a wide array of arithmetic operators, which you can use with your values, whether they are literals or variables (or variables in the form of properties of objects). The following table attractively highlights some of the common arithmetic operators available in JavaScript.

Common Arithmetic Operators for Fun and Profit

Operator	What It Does
+	addition
−	subtraction
*	multiplication
/	division
%	modulus (returns the remainder of a division)

One Lump or Two? Binary and Unary Operators

The preceding arithmetic operators are known as *binary* operators. This is because they work their magic given two values (binary meaning "two"). That is why the binary syntax, as illustrated in the examples, can generally be described as `operand1 operator operand2`.

A couple of notable unary operators exist. These only call for one operand, which will be a variable. There are three unary operators in JavaScript to know: increment, decrement, and negation. Here's an example of each.

Unary Increment ++

This operator will increase by one the value of the operand (variable) supplied to it. Thus, mugs++ will increase the value of the current value of mugs by 1. You might (as further detailed later in this chapter) use this in an assignment:

```
sales = mugs++;
```

ie sales = 2 mugs, 3 mugs etc

Note the position of the ++ relative to mugs. In the preceding example, sales will be assigned the current value of mugs, and then the value of mugs will be increased by 1. Because the value of mugs was increased *after* mugs' value was assigned to sales, sales does not gain the benefit of the increment. This is as opposed to

```
sales = ++mugs;
```

where mugs will first be increased by 1, and that result will be assigned to sales. This is an important distinction because if you use one when you mean the other, your later calculations may be off by 1.

Unary Decrement --

This operator works just like the unary increment, but in the opposite direction. It decreases the value of the specific variable operand by one. Therefore, the operator mugs– will decrease the value of mugs by 1.

You can use the unary decrement operator in assignments just as you use the unary increment. Again, keep in mind the difference between –mugs and mugs– when used in an assignment (as explained in the previous unary increment section).

Unary Negation –

Finally, there is the unary negation operator. Simply, it negates the value of the operand. Thus, if the variable mugs currently holds the value 5, –mugs would return the value –5. Of course, if mugs was already –5, the unary negation operator would return the value 5 (because the negation of –5 is 5).

No More Math, But More Operators

There are several other varieties of operators besides arithmetic. Each one works by relating two or more variables in some way. Operators are of central importance in JavaScript programming because they are the main way to evaluate current conditions and change future conditions. Let's take a spin through the nonarithmetic operators: assignments, comparisons, and logicals.

Assignment Operators

You've already encountered one form of assignment operator: the equal sign (=). This is the most basic and common assignment operator and, as you've learned, it is used to assign one value—either a literal or a variable—to a variable.

```
price = 9.95;
price = cost;
```

In the first case, a literal is assigned to the variable price. In the second case, the current value of the variable cost (whatever that may be) is assigned to the variable price. Simple enough.

The other assignment operators are shortcuts to arithmetic operators, which combine assignments and arithmetic in one fell swoop. Witness this:

```
total += price;
```
ie. total plus price = total

In longhand, using the aforementioned arithmetic operators, the above could also be written like this:

```
total = total + price;
```

One common application of this technique is updating a running total. Perhaps you're keeping track of cumulative gross profit and want to keep adding new purchase orders to that gross. If the current value of total was 10, and price was 5, the above would sum those two values and assign the new result (15) back to the variable total. Note that both of the above methods produce exactly the same result. The += method is simply shorter to write.

Similarly, you can also use the following hybrid assignment operators:

```
total -= price; SAME AS total = total - price;
total *= price; SAME AS total = total * price;
total /= price; SAME AS total = total / price;
total %= price; SAME AS total = total % price; (see arithmetic operator table)
```

Comparison Operators

Often, you have to compare two values to make some sort of determination of what to do next. These comparisons can grow to be quite complex, but you will, of course, start with the basics. The rationale behind these operators should be fairly understandable if you can avoid getting bogged down in the symbols.

The most basic and obvious comparison operator is the equals operator (==). This operator can compare two values and determine if they are equal. The result of any comparison, including this one, is true or false.

Here is a very simple equality comparison:

```
mugs == 10
```

If the value of the variable mugs is 10, and thus equal to the literal value 10, the above comparison will yield a true result. If mugs refers to any value other than 10, the result will be false. This result is most commonly used to direct the flow of the program or to generate a condition-specific action (which you'll learn more about later).

Similarly, you could use the not equals (!=) comparison operator, as in this example:

```
mugs != 10
```

Now this is where you might get confused. The above will again compare the value of mugs with the literal value 10. However, this time we asked if they were "not equal." Therefore, if mugs is 5, the above comparison will yield a true result. If mugs is 10, the above will be false.

Two other common comparison operators are greater than (>) and less than (<). They are used in the following manner:

```
mugs > 10
mugs < 10
```

If mugs is a value greater than (but not including) 10, the first statement above yields true; otherwise it yields false. Similarly, if mugs is a value less than (but not including) 10, the second statement above yields true; otherwise it yields false.

Finally, a pair of comparison operators is inclusive of the tested value: greater than or equal to (>=) and less than or equal to (<=). Here are examples of their use:

```
mugs >= 10
mugs <= 10
```

These work the same as the > and < operators, except that they do include the tested value (10, in our example). Note, therefore, that if the value of mugs is 10, both comparisons above would yield true.

Not Just for Vulcans Anymore: Logical Operators

Some of the previously mentioned folks who stayed awake in algebra class may recall that horrific week spent learning "logic." The magic words of a logician are AND, OR, and NOT. Although this makes for less-than-stimulating dinner date conversation, it has many uses in JavaScript programs.

Logical operators are quite similar in usage to comparison operators. They also sort of "compare" two values and provide a true or false result. The major difference in practice is that the logical operators usually "compare" comparison operators. What?? Once again, some examples are in order.

&& (a.k.a the AND Operator)

The && operator looks at two comparisons, and if each is true in and of itself, the && operator returns a true. Try it this way:

```
( mugs > 5 ) && ( price < 10 )
```

The above statement first evaluates the comparison mugs > 5. That will be either true or false. Then it evaluates price < 10. That will also be either true or false. Finally, if the first comparison is true AND the second comparison is true, the logical operation will yield true. If either or both comparisons are false, the whole result is false.

It helps a lot to think of these logical comparisons in the context of an English sentence. We use them exactly the same way in verbal language: "If your father comes home early AND my paycheck cleared, we will go out for dinner." The example sentence contains both a logical comparison and a resulting action. But for now, as far as JavaScript goes, just consider the logical comparison. The resulting actions will come later.

|| (a.k.a the OR Operator)

The OR operator is less finicky than the AND operator. It requires that only one of the two comparisons be true in order for it to return a true for the whole logical comparison. For example:

```
( mugs > 5 ) || ( price < 10 )
```

Just as with the && operator, both comparisons above are evaluated. If either is true, the OR operator returns a true. Of course, if both are true, it still returns a true. Only if both comparisons yield false results will the || operator yield a false result.

Take this English sentence for example: "If your father comes home early OR my paycheck cleared, we'll go out for dinner." Only one condition needs to be satisfied for the family to chow down, in this case.

[handwritten: Basically you get out the opposite of what you put in!]

! (a.k.a the NOT Operator)

This one is twisted. The NOT operator is a unary operator and, therefore, takes only one operand. That operand is often a comparison operator, in which case the negation of the comparison is returned. Try selling that on a T-shirt! To explain from another angle, if the operand is true, a ! operation on it will result in false. And vice versa.

In the following example, let's assume that mugs holds the value 5.

```
!(mugs == 5)
```

[handwritten: if they do = 5 ∴ false]

[handwritten: they = 5 ∴ false]

Above, mugs == 5 results in true because it is true. However, because it's included in a NOT operation, the result of the whole phrase above is false. Of course, if you're clever, you might realize that the comparison (mugs != 5) would return the same result as !(mugs == 5); that result would be false. This is correct, and therefore, in many cases, the NOT operator is unnecessary because the same evaluation can be made with a comparison operator. However, programmers tend to like NOT operators because they often result in more compact code (although not in the previous example, where the comparison operator is, in fact, shorter).

String Operators: The Loom of JavaScript

You've reached the last of the operators. Whew. String operators are intended to work with string values, which you should recall are not numerals or arithmetic expressions. In addition, the comparison operators can be used with strings. Because strings are not numerals, how string operators work requires a little explanation.

Checking for equality between two strings is fairly straightforward. Suppose you supply the following test (use literals for clarity, although in many cases you'd be using variable names):

```
"dogs" == "cats"
```

Clearly, the two strings are not equal (the same), so the comparison has a false result. For two strings to pass an equality test, they have to be exactly the same, character for character.

However, because "dogs" cannot be greater than "cats" (depending who you ask!), the statement "dogs" > "cats" is simply nonsensical to JavaScript. The same applies to the <, >=, and <= operators. Of course, the "not equal" != operator could apply to two strings.

The exception to the above rule that strings cannot be compared with greater than and less than is if the strings represent possible numerals. Let's suppose the string in question is "54". In this case, JavaScript will attempt to convert the string to a numeral for comparison purposes (remember: strings cannot actually be compared to numbers, but

JavaScript automatically tries to convert the string to a number). Therefore, "54" > "12" does make sense to JavaScript and is exactly the same as 54 > 12. But JavaScript can perform this conversion only if the string contains only numerals; "dog54" would not be converted to a numeral, and the above comparison would again be nonsensical and generate an error or unpredictable results.

Finally, strings can be concatenated with the + operator, or the += assignment operator. Concatenation is the process of combining multiple strings to yield one new, bigger string. You may want to construct a message for the user, tailored to be appropriate for varying conditions. For example, the line

```
"dogs " + "are cute"
```

would yield the string "dogs are cute" (note the space in the above, which prevents the words "dogs" and "are" from being directly smooshed together). Also, if you had previously assigned "dogs " to the variable named phrase, this line

```
phrase += "are cute"
```

would assign the entire string "dogs are cute" to the variable named phrase.

Full of Expressions

Programming types like to throw around the term "expressions." In a sense, by now, you're already familiar with what an expression is, even though I haven't explicitly defined it yet. I wanted to keep some suspense in this tale, after all.

An expression, in programming circles, is any phrase of program code that represents one evaluation, result, or assignment. You've already used a variety of expressions so far, such as:

```
mugs = 5;
```

and

```
(price > 10)
```

There is no critical need for a specific definition of an expression; it's just a term that programmers use to refer to these little portions of code. Every little segment covered in examples thus far is an expression.

There is one sort of JavaScript that's worth special note, though. A conditional expression is basically a shorthand way to assign a value to a variable based on the results of a certain condition. A conditional expression looks like this:

```
(condition) ? valueiftrue : valueiffalse
```

If the condition is true, the resulting value is whatever is specified in the position where valueiftrue is above; if the condition is false, the value returned is whatever is positioned where valueiffalse is above. A common use for this sort of conditional expression is in an assignment operation, in which a variable is assigned the result of the above expression. For a clearer example, imagine that you include a bonus gift—a pencil—with all mug orders fewer than 10, and you include a teddy bear with all orders of 10 mugs or more. You can use the following conditional expression to make this determination:

```
bonus = (mugs >= 10) ? "teddy" : "pencil";
```

The variable bonus will be assigned a string value of "teddy" for orders of 10 or more mugs, or it will be assigned "pencil" on orders for fewer than 10 mugs.

The Least You Need to Know

➤ Operators serve to bring values and/or variables together and yield new results.

➤ Arithmetic operators are used for basic math calculations, as well as for incrementing and decrementing numeric variables.

➤ Comparison operators are used to evaluate specified cases, such as whether one variable has a greater value than another, whether they are equal, and so forth.

➤ Logical operators evaluate comparisons against AND, OR, and NOT conditions to determine whether a series of conditions is true or false.

➤ String operators compare and/or concatenate strings of characters.

➤ Expressions are JavaScript "phrases" that yield assignments, evaluations, or results.

Chapter 7

Making a Statement

In This Chapter

➤ A statement about statements

➤ Conditional: if...else

➤ Loop de loops: while and for

➤ Dealing with objects

➤ Leftovers: the remaining statements

➤ The philosophy of the statement

By now, you've explored most of the building blocks of a mature JavaScript program. Variables are assigned values, and objects are made up of subvariables known as properties. Variables can be operated on for mathematical purposes, or they can be compared or in some other way evaluated, thereby making expressions. An expression is any one "phrase" of JavaScript code, such as an assignment operator or a comparison operator. Finally, you have the statement, which just happens to be the subject of this chapter.

The Anatomy of a Statement

A *statement* brings expressions together with certain keywords to make the JavaScript equivalent of an English sentence. That is, using any or all of the building blocks discussed thus far to create program logic is the whole purpose of a JavaScript. Statements define and control the flow of the program.

Think of statements as the bones of a JavaScript program. All of the statements in your code comprise the skeleton, which determines the overall shape of the program. The JavaScript language provides a small but useful set of statements that you can use to direct program flow.

Check This Out...

Execute and Flow

Two common terms in programming jargon are necessary in this chapter. When JavaScript reads and performs the actions specified in each statement of code, it is *executing* the program. Normally, JavaScript executes each statement in sequence, in the order in which the statements are written. This is called the *flow*. By default, execution flow follows in sequence. Many of the statements described in this chapter are used to alter program flow—that is, to move execution to a specified region of code. In this way, you build the overall logic of the program. Doing this correctly is one of the challenges of programming, and it often takes some debugging to correct errors in your original logic.

The If...else Statement

It's no coincidence, then, that statements are bookended by keywords that strongly resemble English language statements. One very common JavaScript statement is the If...else statement, which functions just as it sounds in English. The following would be an English usage version of an If...else statement:

> "If I earn at least $500 this week, I can pay the electric bill; I must pay the bill, or else my lights will be shut off."

You can generate the exact same sentiment in JavaScript using only two variables: income and lights. Presume that the variable income has been previously assigned some numeric value representing this week's earnings. The variable lights will be assigned on the condition of the income and will receive a Boolean value (true or false) because there are only two possible outcomes for the lights: remain on or shut off. Given all this, the

JavaScript version of the preceding statement, using the JavaScript If...else construction, would look like this:

```
if (income >= 500) {
   lights = true;
} else {
   lights = false;
}
```

Given this statement, JavaScript would first evaluate the expression (income >= 500). If this returns a true result, JavaScript executes the statements within the first set of brackets {}. If the expression is false, JavaScript skips ahead to the else clause and executes the statements within the set of brackets immediately below the else keyword. You can include as many statements as you want within the brackets of a clause, but you must remember to end each statement with a semicolon (;) as in this example:

```
if (income >= 500) {
   lights = true;
   savings = income - bills;
}
```

To JavaScript, the semicolon is the signal that one statement has finished and another is about to begin.

The formatting in both of the previous examples is purely a matter of taste. JavaScript doesn't care where you put breaks in the lines, as long as you include all of the correct syntax (the brackets, the semicolons, and so on). However, for the human reader, using a consistent and somewhat logical format throughout the code will make debugging in the future much easier and much less insanity-inducing.

Now you see how a statement in JavaScript serves as the outline in which most assignments, expressions, and function calls (we haven't covered those just yet) occur. The If...else statement is merely one way to control the logic flow of a JavaScript program.

> **Check This Out...**
>
> **Partnering Parentheses**
> One very simple way to keep track of parentheses is to indent all the code within a pair of parentheses to the same level (as the examples demonstrate). If you have another pair of parentheses within a pair, indent again. That way, all the statements that are part of one "block" of code will be visually lined up, and mismatched parentheses will be much easier to spot.

The while Statement

The while statement is another way to control program flow and execution. It functions in the following way:

```
while (condition) {
    statements
}
```

In this example, the series of statements within the brackets are executed for as long as the specified condition holds true. The simplest example of a while statement is a simple loop. A *loop* results when a statement or series of statements are repeated some number of times until some condition changes. Therefore, the while statement is a classic loop. In this simple example, you will keep appending the string "repeat" to a variable named phrase until the loop has executed 10 times:

```
count = 1;
phrase= "";
while ( count <= 10 ) {
    phrase += "repeat ";
    count++;
}
```

Let's consider a line-by-line analysis of the above code, which pulls together several concepts from previous chapters.

In line one, you assign the value 1 to the variable count. Because you will be using this as a counter, you must assign it an initial value. In this case, you would like count to begin with the value 1, so that is your initial assignment.

In line two, you want to be sure that the string variable phrase starts out empty. To do this, you can assign an "empty string" to it, as you can see in this syntax:

```
phrase="";
```

This will prepare the string for usage in the loop that follows.

In line three, you construct a while statement. The while loop is defined to proceed as long as the value of count is less than or equal to 10.

In line four, you begin the statements that comprise the body of the while loop; therefore, an opening bracket precedes the first statement. In this line, you use an assignment operator to concatenate (combine) the string value "string" to the existing value of the variable phrase.

In line five, you increment the counter variable count by 1, using the unary increment operator.

The final result of the example will be that count will hold the value 11, and phrase will hold the string "repeat repeat repeat repeat repeat repeat repeat repeat repeat repeat". Notice that when count has reached 10, it will move through the loop one last time, adding the final "repeat" to phrase and incrementing count to 11. Then, when the while condition is tested again, it will be false, and the loop will cease. JavaScript would then drop down to the next statement following the while condition's bracketed statements.

The for Statement

The for statement is another statement that creates a loop circumstance. It is much like the while statement and, in fact, in many programming situations, either statement could serve the same role even though their particular syntaxes differ. The real difference is that for statements are more specifically tailored to handle numerical loops. The while statement, although capable of the same (as illustrated in the previous example), is somewhat more flexible in its capability to function on conditions other than numerical loops.

Check This Out...

Update That Loop

In any loop, it is presumed that the variable in the test condition is going to change. If the test condition does not change, the loop will never execute if the condition is false, or it will never stop executing if the condition is true (this is called an "endless loop"). In a counting loop, you change the counter variable with the "loop update expression." This expression is part of the statement definition, as in the for statement. In this example, you use the unary increment operator as your loop update expression; it increases the value of the loop counter count by 1 at each pass through the loop.

The for statement is followed by an initial expression (which is often a variable assignment, but may be another statement), a test condition, a loop update expression, and finally, a block of statements to execute. An example would look frighteningly similar to this:

```
phrase = "";
for (count = 1; count <= 10; count++) {
    phrase += "repeat ";
}
```

Watch Your Syntax

In programming, *syntax* refers to the "rules of grammar" (in other words, what words or symbols go where). For example, most statements begin with a keyword (such as for) that identifies the statement. They are followed by a set of parentheses in which special conditions are specified. All of this is syntax: The order of what goes where. If you accidentally violate a syntax rule, such as leaving out a parenthesis or semicolon, you will experience a syntax error. JavaScript will alert you of this when you try to execute the program (load the Web page), and then you'll have to fix it.

Again, let's analyze the example line by line:

In line one, you assign an empty string to the variable phrase as preparation.

In line two, you define the for statement. The counter variable count is set to 1 to start with, and your test condition for the loop determines whether count is less than or equal to 10. The loop update expression uses the unary increment operator to bump the value of count up by 1.

In line three, you use the statement that makes up the loop itself. It will be executed as long as the test condition remains true. In this case, you use an assignment operator to concatenate the value "repeat" to the string variable phrase.

This example would produce the same results as the while loop: The variable count would hold the value 11, and the variable phrase would hold the string "repeat" in ten consecutive repetitions.

As stated, this is quite similar in logic to the previously described while statement. The major differences are that the initial variable assignment for the loop counter and the expression that increments the loop counter are both included in the for statement definition heading (they are the expressions within parentheses following the keyword for). This is why the for statement is more suited for these sorts of arithmetic loops, whereas the while statement is flexible enough for other sorts of loops; the while statement has fewer restrictions on the expressions that can affect the test condition.

The break and continue Statements Bring It All Together

Sometimes you will want to jump out of the execution of a loop (as in the while and for statements) in mid-loop. Here is a classic scenario that might demand this sort of "eject from loop" capability. Suppose that you want a facility in your Web page that will total the gross profit of all the purchases made from your site that day. However, you are running a promotion, and every 10th person to make a purchase receives the order for free! Therefore, when you're calculating the total gross for the day, you must make exceptions for every 10th order.

This is how the loop will work: Look at each purchase made, and then add its price to a running total until you've reached the end of the purchases. Simple loop. Now for the exception: Check each purchase to see if it is a whole integer multiple of 10 (which would mean it was a 10th purchase). If it is, do not add its price to the grand running total. This example will use the continue statement, which is used to drop out of a series of statements within a loop and return to the top of the loop.

The example code contains three simple variables:

➤ orders, which holds the current number of orders for the day.

➤ count, which is the loop counter (this begins at 0).

➤ total, which contains the gross running total (this begins at 0).

In addition, you have one object, named price. Price has the properties 1, 2, 3, and so on, where each property represents one item purchased and holds the value of its price. For example, price.1 might equal 9.95, price.2 might equal 14.95, and so on.

Also, recall that you can refer to objects and properties in the format *object*[*property*], as in price[1], which is how you will describe them within the loop code itself.

Here is the code you will use:

```
total = 0;
for (count = 1; count <= orders; count++) {
   if (( count % 10 ) == 0 )
     {continue;}

   total += price[count];
}
```

Notice: Count Those Parentheses

In the continue statement example, take note of the line containing the if keyword. It is followed by double parentheses because you have two sets of "nested" parenthetical expressions. Nesting occurs when you have one parenthetical expression within another parenthetical expression. For example: the if comparison must be in one set of parentheses, as in if (comparison). However, the comparison itself is also enclosed in parentheses, as in (count % 10), to prevent any possible misinterpretation by JavaScript. As you can see, it's very important that you keep track of your opening and closing parentheses, and that every pair matches up; otherwise, you're likely to get syntax errors. And going back through your program to look for missing parentheses is less than fun. Therefore, refer to the "Partnering Parentheses" sidebar (earlier in this chapter) for tips on visually aligning them in your code to make counting the pairs easier.

Now let's consider what took place in the previous example. Several concepts are going on in the previous example, all of which are covered at some point in this book.

In the first line (total = 0), you initialize the summation variable total to zero.

In the second line, you declare the parameters of the for loop. You begin count at 0 on the presumption that the properties of the object price also began numbering from 0. (Be sure to keep an eye out for such things in your own program.) You set the for loop condition to remain true while count is less than or equal to the total number of orders. Finally, you set the loop updater to increment count by one. Note that count is not incremented on the first pass through the loop, and thus remains at 0 until the second pass.

On the third line, below the for declaration, you have the set of brackets within which the loop statements are enclosed. In this case, your loop statement is an if statement. (Recall that the if statement is followed by its own bracketed statements, which is why there are two sets of brackets in the example. If you follow them closely, you will see that they make sense.) The if statement checks to see whether the current order in question was a 10th purchase. It does this by using the "modulo" arithmetic operator. Consider: you could divide the current value of count by 10. If the current order were a 10th purchase (an even multiple of 10), this division would yield a remainder of 0. The modulo operator can be used to return the remainder of a division. Therefore, the expression count%10 will return the value 0 on every 10th purchase.

On the fourth line, you've got the bracketed expression immediately below the if clause, which determines what to do if the condition is true (that is, if this is a 10th purchase). Note that your if-true statement is continue. This will cause JavaScript to ignore the remainder of the statements in the brackets of the for statement and return to the top of the for loop. This will not re-initialize count to zero; it will just continue with the loop as normal.

On the fifth line, you do not need an else statement because the previous if statement will ignore the remainder of the loop statement on this pass when the condition is true. If the condition is false (that is, if count represents any purchase other than a 10th one), execution will necessarily drop to the final statement in the for loop.

On the last line, the final statement adds the value of the current property of the object price to the running total.

The break statement is similar to the continue statement in usage, but it behaves in one notably different way. Instead of causing the loop to skip ahead to its next trip through, the break statement immediately drops out of the loop entirely. That is, it aborts the loop on the spot and moves on to the next statement following the loop in the JavaScript program. If you were to replace continue in the previous example with break, when you reached the first 10th purchase in the loop—which would be purchase number 10—the whole loop would end. Clearly, that's not what you want in this example, but in other cases, it might be.

Object-Related Statements

Two statements are designed specifically for the purpose of dealing with objects. Recall once again that an object is a variable that contains a set of subvariables known as properties. Your prototypical object example was the sweater object, which contained the properties material, color, size, and price. The following statements work with a given object to help you navigate and/or manipulate its properties. As always, this will make more sense after you look at examples.

The for...in Statement

The for...in statement is a specialized loop that's similar to the for statement, but with the purpose of looping through the properties of a particular object. Imagine again your sweater object. Perhaps a customer has chosen to order a sweater, and in other portions of your Web page, he has selected each property that interests him—maybe cotton, black, and XL. Of course, the price property is determined by you, the retailer, based on the sort of sweater he chose.

Now the sweater object's four properties have each been assigned a value. Imagine then that you are outputting an invoice to the screen for the customer to verify. You need to state the values of each of the sweater's properties, which requires moving through each property in sweater and printing its value. Sound like a loop? It is a loop! And, because it is a loop within an object, you need a for...in statement. Quel coincidence!

61

The loop parameters in the for...in statement are much simpler than the for statement. There is no need to initialize a counter, to test for a condition, or to update the counter (such as by incrementing it). The for...in loop works only one way: From the first property to the last in the given object. Therefore, the for...in statement looks like this:

```
for ( counter in objectname ) {
   statements
}
```

The counter is any variable name you want to supply as a counter. *Objectname* is the name of the object whose properties you are interested in. Let's take an easy example. Loop through the properties of the sweater object and add the value of each to a string. Later, that string may be used for some other purpose, such as to output to the screen. Your counter will be named count, your object is sweater, and your string will be named descrip (as in "purchase description").

```
descrip = "";
for ( count in sweater ) {
   descrip += sweater[count] + " ";
}
```

Voilà! In this example, you first assign the variable descrip to an empty string. Then you define the for...in statement. One statement follows within the loop. It simply concatenates the value of each property of sweater to the current contents of the variable descrip. Note that you are, in fact, adding the expression sweater[count] + " " to the variable descrip. This inserts blank spaces between the values so the string value will be more readable if and when it is output later.

At the conclusion of this JavaScript program, the variable descrip might contain a string value such as "cotton black XL 24.95". The exact order of the values in the string depends on the order in which the properties in the object sweater were originally created.

The with Statement

Yet again, you are concerned with only one object. The purpose of the with statement is to tell JavaScript which object you are currently concerned with. After you identify the object, any references to variables in the bracketed statements that follow are assumed to be properties of that object.

In practice, the with statement looks like this:

```
with ( objectname ) {
  statements
}
```

Imagine that you are going to assign values to the sweater object's properties. You don't need to use the with statement; after all, you could assign values in the format sweater.color = black. However, you can also use the with statement in the following way:

```
with ( sweater ) {
    material = cotton;
    color = black;
    size = XL;
}
```

Granted, the with statement doesn't exactly rival sliced bread or those nifty sandwich makers as far as inventions of the century go, but it does save on keystrokes, and it also helps improve the formatting and readability of the JavaScript program. Those are always positive qualities when it comes time to debug.

The comment Statement

If you found the with statement to be short on excitement, this one is even duller. The comment statement is simply a way by which you can insert your own comments into the JavaScript program for future reference. JavaScript itself completely ignores them. This isn't to denigrate the utility of comments. Including comments in your program is an extremely useful way of reminding yourself what the heck is going on in case you must return to the code at a later date. Programming is one of those things where, when you are steeped in the development of a program, everything you do makes sense to you; however, if you return to the program two months later to make some changes or corrections, you'll have absolutely no idea what your code means anymore. This, then, requires you to carefully reread the code to understand it again. Therefore, including English commentary in code is a good thing; it's just not an exciting thing.

Comments Comments Everywhere

This is the second appearance of comments in this book. Previously, you saw how comments work in relation to HTML code. If you recall, the big pep talk was about including the entire JavaScript program within HTML comment tags in order to prevent non-JavaScript browsers from displaying the code on-screen.

The comments you are learning about now are meant to prevent the JavaScript browser from attempting to execute in-code reminders for humans. Comments are used to explain to you, the human, what is going on in the code. Therefore, you don't want JavaScript to attempt to execute the comments because it will only wind up producing errors.

There are two ways to denote comments in your JavaScript program, depending on whether they fit on one line or span multiple lines. For one-liners, simply precede the commentary with double slash marks (//). For multiline comments, place the symbols /* at the beginning of the text and place the symbols */ at the end.

Here are two examples of well-commented code:

```
// this counter will be used to track the number of sweaters ordered
count = 0;


/* the following loop will go through each order and process it accordingly.
First, we'll check to see if the size is in stock. Then we'll see if the color is
in stock.
Lastly, we'll see if the purchaser's name is on our blacklist, in which case we
will secretly jack up the price by adding unreasonable shipping and handling costs
*/
for ( count=1; count <= orders ; count++ ) {
    ...
```

The var Statement

The var statement is included more often as a matter of style than for necessity. In theory, you should precede variable assignments with the word var. For example, the following statement:

```
counter = 0;
```

should theoretically be written like this:

```
var counter = 0;
```

As you may have noticed, you have not been doing this throughout your examples, and I keep using the words "in theory." That's because you don't actually have to use it. JavaScript knows when you are assigning a variable, but some purists consider it good form to include the var word for program readability.

Having said that, I need to tell you that it *is* necessary in one case to write out var; however, you haven't encountered that scenario yet. But you will encounter it when you learn about functions, which just happens to be in the next chapter.

The Least You Need to Know

➤ Statements serve as the connective tissue of a JavaScript program. They control a program's flow.

➤ Statements have this syntax: statement definition, followed by statements to execute if definition is true—which are enclosed in curly brackets { }.

➤ The if...else statement tests a condition, and then it executes the stuff within the first set of brackets if true, or it executes whatever is within the second set of brackets if false:

```
if (condition) {
    statements if true
} else {
    statements if false
}
```

➤ The while statement sets up a loop if the given condition is true:

```
while (condition) {
    statements
}
```

➤ The for statement sets up a loop that performs the bracketed statements until a specified counter meets a condition:

```
for (initialize counter; condition; update counter) {
statements
}
```

➤ You can deal solely with an object using the for...in statement:

```
for (counter in object) {
    statements
}
```

and the with statement:

```
with (object) {
    statements
}
```

➤ Commenting your code is unexciting, but it is strongly recommended. Use // before single-line comments, and surround multiline comments with /* and */:

```
//This is a single-line comment
```

and

```
/*Here we have a multiple line comment
that goes into some detail about the code which follows*/
```

Chapter 8

Conjunction Junction, What's a Function?

In This Chapter

➤ The function of a function

➤ Parameters and results

➤ Defining a function

➤ Calling a function

➤ The power of object creation

➤ Making a method

If statements are the connective tissue of a JavaScript program, functions are the blood. (See, that high school anatomy course really *has* paid off.) Any JavaScript program beyond the most basic will include functions. Some are built into JavaScript (those are listed in Appendix A at the end of this book); however, you will create other functions.

That's great, and very nice to know, but what is a function? A very apropos question. Could you ask it again, and this time a little louder?

What Is a Function?

Much better. A function is like a miniprogram unto itself. It can be "called" from the rest of the JavaScript program. A function is composed of JavaScript code, which, if executed, accomplishes some task. The set of code composing the function is given a name or label of some sort. That name then comes to represent a particular function, or set of code. Creating a function is not the same as calling a function. In this chapter, you will see how a function is "defined" (that is, how you write out the code that belongs to the labeled function). When it is executed, a function is called from some other section of JavaScript code. You will see how this is done, as well.

Check This Out...

Calling All Functions!
When you "call" a function, you are instructing JavaScript to execute that function. Remember that a function is a miniprogram of JavaScript code. So "calling" it means to execute the code that comprises a particular function.

You often use a function to define a procedure that will be called upon regularly. By doing so, you program and name a set routine so you can call it repeatedly without having to redefine it over and over. To make an analogy to real life, throughout the day you have many functions in your daily activities. You might consider sleep a function. Likewise, eating lunch is a function. Between these predefined activities, you act out other tasks, which are sometimes similar to loops and conditional statements.

For example, perhaps you are watching television. While doing so, certain conditions may occur: if hungry; if sleepy; if bladder full. These are like conditional statements in a JavaScript program. Upon evaluation of these conditions, you may choose to call upon a predefined function. For example, if hungry, eat lunch; if bladder full, run to bathroom. In each case, eat lunch and run to bathroom are functions because they refer to a defined series of actions. That series, however, must have been defined only once sometime in the past. For instance, the function "run to bathroom" may have been "defined" when you were toilet-trained. Since then, you have simply called that function to execute it when necessary. A vivid image, no doubt.

So far in the statements you have used in this book, you have called upon only very simple actions. Soon you will learn how to create and define functions—whole sets of actions that can vary in size from one statement to a whole other program in and of itself—which can then be called from statements.

The Role of Parameters

Functions frequently, although not necessarily, accept parameters when they are called. A parameter is a specified value that somehow plays a role in the doings of the function's actions. Let's recall the lunch function from real life. Although the procedure for eating lunch is predefined, there are a few variables you do need to take note of. The most obvious is, "what food will you be eating for lunch?" "What beverage will accompany this food?"

Function Notation

You specify the variables included in a function by listing them within parentheses beside the function name. An example might be lunch (food,beverage). It is common practice, in a book such as this, to write a function name in the format lunch(). This simply means that you're speaking of the function named lunch, although you're not considering its particular variables at this time.

In this sense, you can say that the function lunch() takes two parameters: foodstuff and beverage. When you feel peckish just around noon, you call your lunch function with these two parameters, which you could note in the following way:

```
lunch("pizza", "Coke");
```

In this example, you invoke your lunch() function with the specifics of a pizza and a Coke. Similarly, functions in JavaScript can also take parameters. When you define the function (which you will do shortly), you must decide which parameters the function will require. When you define a function, you don't know what the specific parameter values will be. That is determined when you call the function, somewhere else in the JavaScript program. When you define the function lunch(), you might name the parameters food-stuff and beverage, for instance. Only when you later call the function lunch() will you use actual values for these parameters.

Returned Results

At the conclusion of a function, you will often (but not always) want to return some sort of result to the program. Again, with the lunch example, you might say that the function lunch() accepts two parameters, foodstuff and beverage, and returns one result: a variable called satisfaction, which will contain a logical value true or false.

By this logic, the lunch() function processes the foodstuff and beverage specified to it ("pizza" and "Coke" in this case) and then returns a true or a false value for the variable satisfaction. The calling program (in this example, that would be you, the person) then examines this result and decides what to do from there. It may choose to call the function again with new parameters (for example, if satisfaction was returned as false, you might want to run for more food), or it may choose to move on with the remainder of the program (if satisfaction is returned as true, for example).

69

Now I'm Hungry: Defining and Calling a Function

The formal template for a function definition looks like this:

```
function functionname(parameter1, parameter2, ...) {
    statements
}
```

Therefore, the formal JavaScript definition for the lunch() function would have looked like this:

```
function lunch(foodstuff, beverage) {
  eat foodstuff;
  drink beverage;
  satisfaction = (evaluation of satisfaction);
  return satisfaction;
}
```

Of course, the statements within brackets in this example are all fake, because there are no real JavaScript statements that define eating food. Remember that the above function is not executed unless it is called from somewhere else in the JavaScript program. Merely defining it does not execute it.

In addition, let me pass along an important word about parameters that I briefly touched upon earlier. When you name parameters in the function definition, you are essentially creating variables. Whatever values are passed to the function in the function call will be assigned to the variables you have named in the function definition (in the order that they are listed in the function call). So if you called the previous function with the following call,

```
lunch("pizza", "Coke");
```

within the statements of the function lunch(), the variable foodstuff will contain the string value "pizza," and the variable beverage will contain the string value "Coke". In this function call, you have passed literals as the parameter values. Alternatively, if you call the function with this statement,

```
lunch(choice1, choice2);
```

the variable foodstuff will contain the value of the variable choice1; likewise, beverage will contain the value of the variable choice2. In this function call, you have passed the contents of variables as parameter values.

Would You Like Parameters with That Function?

A function does not have to accept any parameters. The one you are writing may not need any. In these cases, you simply continue to use the () where they are required (in the function definition and function calls), but you put nothing in between, as in these examples:

```
function noparams() {
    statements
}

or

noparams();
```

More About Function Calls

You'll see several function calls in action in later examples. For now, however, you should get a grasp on the two forms of function calls. You have just seen one common form: the plain function call. It exists, as written, in the following form:

```
functionname(parameter1, ...);
```

However, recall the role of the "return" value. In the lunch() example, after the function completes (the meal has been consumed), the function returns the value of the variable satisfaction, which is a logical value of true or false. Where is this value returned to? Mid-air? In the plain function calls above, the value is not returned anywhere. It has nowhere to go. To make a function call that can accept a returned value, you make the call within an assignment. For example:

```
morefood = lunch("pizza", "Coke");
```

In this case, the function lunch() will be called, and the food will be processed just as in the plain function call. In addition, though, the logical value that is returned from the function will be assigned to the variable morefood. From there, you might use morefood in future conditional evaluations later in the program.

Therefore, for the calling program to accept a return value from a function, the call is made in this form:

```
variableforreturn = functionname(parameter1, ...);
```

Let's Make a Function!

Now you're ready to define a real JavaScript function. No more talk about lunch. You will build on an example that was already coded in the previous chapter. In Chapter 7, you wrote a small segment of JavaScript code that calculated the daily gross profit on product purchases via a Web page. The special exception was that every 10th purchase was free, so for every 10th purchase, a zero was added to your cumulative total.

Now let's turn that segment into an official function. The task: Calculate daily gross profit, leaving every 10th purchase out of the total. Return total gross.

To do that, you first define the function, which will be called promotion():

```
function promotion(orders, price) {
```

As you can see, you are sending two parameters to the function: orders, which represents the total number of orders for the day, and price, which is an object for which each property is a price of sale for a given order.

Note that price is an object, which must have been created prior to calling the function; however, you have not yet learned how to create an object because doing so is a variation on creating functions. For now, assume the object price was created elsewhere in the JavaScript program. By the end of this chapter, you'll know how to create objects for real.

Finally, write the { statements } section of the function.

```
        var total = 0;

    for (var count = 1; count <= orders; count++) {
        if (( count % 10 ) == 0 ) {
            continue;
        }

        total += price[count];
    }

        return total
    }
```

For the most part, the example above is the same as the example code for the continue statement that was used in Chapter 7. There are a couple of differences to note:

➤ **The semicolons** Remember that each statement should end with a semicolon. In this case, the variable assignment to total is one statement; the entire for statement is one statement; and so is the if clause within the for statement. The final statement—return—does not need a semicolon because it is the final statement before the closing bracket. If you refer to the code above, you'll find that this paragraph does make sense.

I should add that JavaScript is flexible about the semicolon rule. Code without semicolons works fine as well, as long as two statements aren't on the same line. However, if you type two statements on the same line (such as "sales=0;price=9.95"), the semicolon is mandatory.

➤ **The var statement, which is used twice**   In the previous chapter, you learned that the var statement is superfluous except in one special case. Welcome to the special case. The "special case" is when you're making new variables within a function. Any variables you create solely for use within the function (such as a loop counter), should be made with a var statement. If you do it this way, the variable holds its value only within the function statements. One advantage to this is that it might prevent you from overwriting the value of a variable with the same name that exists elsewhere in the JavaScript program.

Motherly Advice

It's because of this "special case" var situation that you're encouraged to always use a var statement when assigning values to variables. Doing so would prevent any possible mistakes that might occur if you forgot to use a var statement when it really was necessary. Ultimately, the choice is yours. If you trust yourself to remember to use var statements within functions, you may opt to forego them elsewhere. On the other hand, if you tend to forget where you put your pen down five seconds ago, perhaps the recommended var usage is the way to go.

The Whole Burrito: A Finished Function

For the purposes of science and education, in the previous example, you sort of decapitated the function definition from the entire function body. Now you'll rejoin the two parts and wind up with one fully mature, living, working function.

```
function promotion(orders, price) {
    var total = 0;

    for (var count = 1; count <= orders; count++) {
        if (( count % 10 ) == 0 ) {
```

```
        continue;
    }

    total += price[count];
}

return total;
}
```

Because this function's entire purpose in life is to calculate and return a value, you want to call it in an assignment. So, wherever it is in your JavaScript program that you want to execute this function and use its result, you would call it with an expression such as:

```
total = promotion(orders, price);
```

Although you needn't call the function with variable names that match the parameter names, in this case, you have done so simply because the variable names are equally sensible labels in both portions of the program.

Making the Call

You can make a function call in any valid location for a statement. For example, you might include a function call in an if...else statement, as in

```
if (hunger == true) {
    morefood = lunch("pizza", "Coke");
} else {
    watchtv("NBC");
}
```

Here, the fictitious function lunch() is called if the hunger condition is true, and the equally fictitious function watchtv is called if the hunger condition is false.

Also note that a function can call another function in the course of its { statements }. However, there is an important rule (which you'll see again in a later chapter) that a function must have been defined before any calls are made to it. Therefore, if you are calling one function from another, the function being called has to have been defined previously in the JavaScript program (before the definition of the function making the call).

Even more interesting, a function can be passed as a parameter to another function. This makes sense if you think about it. Consider the promotion() function defined earlier. It returns a result of the gross profit for the day. Suppose you have another function, weekly, which performs a weekly gross summary and takes two parameters: total sales for the week (wkorders) and gross daily profit for the current day (the promotion() function). It returns the value for current gross weekly sales. One might then call weekly with this statement:

```
weektotal = weekly(wkorders , promotion(orders,
price));
```

Method Programming

Supposedly, Marlon Brando was a classic method actor. Of course, he was largely before my time (and I stress "largely"), but there are methods in JavaScript programming as well. Follow this closely: In JavaScript, a *method* is a function that is a property of an object.

Thus far, you have seen one type of object property: the common garden-variety variable. An example was

```
sweater.color
```

Top Loading
Because functions must be defined before they can be called, the best way to avoid potential problems is to simply place all function definitions at the top of your JavaScript program, above any other programming. Some people recommend placing all of the function definitions at the very top of the Web page between the <HEAD> and </HEAD> tags so they will always be loaded before anything else. (You'll see an example of that in a later chapter.)

However, it is possible for the property—and not the variable—to be a function. Thus, imagine you have a function that calculates the price of a sweater based on other characteristics, such as its material. The function itself doesn't matter now. You'll just assume that the function fprice() has been defined and takes the parameter material. It is assigned to the object property price. Now your whole sweater object looks like this:

```
sweater.material
sweater.color
sweater.size
sweater.price()
```

The first three properties are variables and may be assigned values (as in the first example below) or may be assigned to other variables (as in the second example):

```
sweater.material = "argyle";
```

or

```
buystock = sweater.material;
```

However, the fourth property is a method—a function within the object. Therefore, assigning a value to it is nonsensical. Instead, it is something that you call. For instance, you might call the method sweater.price() and assign the returned result to some other variable, as in this example:

```
total += sweater.price();
```

That's really all there is to a method. It is a function just like those discussed throughout this chapter; the only difference is that it exists as a property of an object instead of "on its own."

Methods are created when an object is created. You haven't yet learned how to create an object, and doing so is the only remaining building block you need to know for writing full-fledged JavaScript programs. Therefore, Que proudly presents...the creation process.

Object Creationism

An object is, truth be told, a function. To use an object such as sweater in your program, you first need to define its function. That provides the structure for the object.

The function, in this case, takes parameters that represent each property. But, as you'll repeat, the function merely defines the structure of the object; it does not create the object itself. Thus, although you are ultimately interested in creating a sweater object, its definition needn't be called sweater. Imagine, for example, that you sell several sorts of topwear, such as sweaters, T-shirts, and tank tops. All of these may be defined by the same object definition. Later, however, you'll create separate objects to represent each. Let's do this by example.

For your first example, define a topwear object that does not contain a method. Instead, it contains three regular variable properties: material, color, and size. Succeeding the function definition, watch the { statements } section.

```
function topwear(material, color, size) {
    this.material = material;
    this.color = color;
    this.size = size;
}
```

Again, this example merely defines the structure of the object; it does not actually create an instance of the object. You'll do that in a minute. Note, in the example, the use of the term "this." In a sense, think of it as JavaScript shorthand for "this object that you're considering." (There is another situation in which you will use the this keyword; you'll find out about it in a later chapter. For now, just note its use in defining an object.)

At this stage of the play, you have created the skeleton for any object that will be based on topwear. By skeleton, I mean that you have defined what sort of properties and methods this object would contain. But you haven't yet created an actual instance of an object, such as a sweater object with properties containing actual values. You do that by assigning the above function to a variable, using a special function call known as the new function call. Here's an example:

```
sweater = new topwear("cotton" , "black" , "XL");
```

This example accomplished two feats. First, it created an actual object sweater—just like the one you've been referring to throughout these chapters (except this one doesn't have a price property). Second, it assigned some values to each of sweater's properties. Therefore, after executing the above expression, the following now exists in the mind of your JavaScript program:

sweater.material   which is currently the value "cotton"

sweater.color   which is currently the value "black"

sweater.size   which is currently the value "XL"

Now this object and its properties may be used in the program in any of the circumstances in which you've used objects. So you can create any number of new objects based on the topwear object definition. Simply use the new function call, as shown here:

```
tanktop = new topwear("nylon" , "white" , "M");
tshirt = new topwear("twill" , "pink" , "XXL");
```

Now you have tanktop.material, tanktop.color, tanktop.size, and so on and so on for as many new objects as you choose to create. Go wild.

Method Making

Defining an object that contains method properties is basically the same procedure as above. Recall that a method is a property that is, itself, a type of function. So, re-create the topwear definition to include a price calculating function—the one based on material, which you used in an earlier method example and called fprice.

First, you have to create the fprice() method definition (here, you'll use some silly formula to determine the garment price):

```
function fprice() {
    // Base price is $10, add various amounts based on material
    var startprice = 10.00;
    var addcost = 0;
```

```
        if (this.material == "cotton") {
           addcost = 5.50;
        }

        if (this.material == "nylon") {
           addcost = 2.50;
        }

        if (this.material == "silk") {
           addcost = 20.00;
        }

        return startprice + addcost;
     }
```

Notice, above, the use of this.material. This is a useful form of JavaScript shorthand. Because fprice() is not an independent function but a method of an object, this.property refers to properties in the parent object (topwear). Now that this method definition is created, you will include a call to it in your topwear object definition.

```
function topwear(material , color , size) {
   this.material = material;
   this.color = color;
   this.size = size;
   this.price = fprice;
}
```

Above, when you create the "hook" between the price method of the topwear object and the fprice() function, you simply type the name of the function (with no parentheses or parameters). At this time, you don't want to call the fprice() function, so you merely attach it to the topwear object type.

Finally, create the new object sweater once again.

```
sweater = new topwear("cotton" , "black" , "XL");
```

This time, the object sweater contains these properties:

```
sweater.material
sweater.color
sweater.size
sweater.price()
```

78

To access the price of a particular sweater, you would call the method sweater.price() with an expression such as

```
price = sweater.price();
```

So, quick quiz: Given all of the above, what would the value of price be?

Answer: Price is assigned the value of sweater.price. sweater.price, in turn, refers to the method fprice(), which is part of the object sweater. sweater is an object with properties defined by the definition topwear. sweater.material holds the value "cotton". fprice calculates a total cost based on this material property, which works out to 15.50. Therefore, sweater.price holds the value 15.50, and finally then, price is assigned the value 15.50.

As is good practice when reading programming books, read the previous passage a few more times and follow its logic through the code segments illustrated in the example.

Congratulations are in order. This completes the last of the building blocks of JavaScript programming. Everything you do from now on in JavaScript is based on the concepts covered in Chapters 5 through 8: variables, objects, literals, operators, statements, functions, and methods. The next few chapters will explore how these apply to specific JavaScript and Web-related applications. But first, it's time for an intermission for rest and recovery (for me, that is; you can continue reading whenever you want).

The Least You Need to Know

This chapter strongly demands a close reading. Nonetheless, contractual obligations being what they are, here's the obligatory summary:

➤ A function is a self-contained program code element that is defined one time. It may be called upon by the remainder of the JavaScript program at any time to perform its actions.

➤ Functions may accept parameters—values given to them upon calling—and may return results to the calling program.

➤ Functions are defined with this statement:

```
function funcname(parameter1, parameter2, ...) {
    statements
}
```

➤ Functions can be called with a plain call:

```
funcname(parameter1, ...);
```

or in an assignment operator expression if returned results are desired:

```
variable = funcname(parameter1, ...);
```

➤ Object definitions are created by defining a function that describes the properties of the object (really, it's a good idea to read the chapter to grasp this).

➤ Methods are functions that are properties of objects. First their functions are defined, and then they are assigned to a property in the object definition.

➤ An actual instance of an object is created by making an assignment operator call to an object-defining function using the keyword new. Huh? It's like this:

```
objectname = new objfunction(property1, property2, ...);
```

➤ All functions should be defined in the JavaScript program prior to any other code.

An Eye on Events

Welcome back from intermission. (I had cookies.) Thus far, we've looked at several building blocks for writing JavaScript programs: operators, names, statements, and functions. The natural question, then, begs: "How do I make something useful out of all this?"

In answer to this question, I'll first show you several interactive and reactive facilities of JavaScript (in this case, event handling). In short, that is what enables your JavaScript program to recognize and react to user actions within a Web page. First, however, allow me to finish my cookie...crunch crunch—mmm—okay. Thanks.

The Main Event

By and large, the execution of your JavaScript programs needs to be "triggered" by something. Although you may, in some cases, want code to execute immediately when the page loads, much of JavaScript's usefulness comes in its capability to be triggered.

Consider the mugs and sweaters you've been selling in program examples in the previous chapters. Most of those examples revolve around calculations you would perform upon receipt of a new purchase order from a Web user. Thus, receiving a new order triggers those JavaScript programs. Anything that might trigger execution of JavaScript code is known as an *event*.

Events are most often triggered by the user of your Web page. Common events include clicking on page elements (radio buttons, form submit buttons, URL links, and so on), entering values, and positioning the mouse pointer over certain elements. Your JavaScript programs that reside in the HTML source of the page will usually be triggered by these various events. Therefore, you need to learn what these events are, how to watch for them, and how to trigger JavaScript code in response.

Who They Are

Each event has a name by which you'll refer to it, so the logical place to begin is with a name and description of each event JavaScript is capable of recognizing. The eight events are covered in the following subsections.

Click

The Click event occurs when a user clicks the mouse button on either a link or a form element. Form elements include buttons, checkboxes, and "reset" or "submit" buttons (see the following figure).

New to JavaScript 1.1 is the ability for the Click event to cancel an action. For instance, imagine that a user clicks a hyperlink. The new Click event can be called to display a confirmation box; from there, if the user chooses "Cancel," his browser will not follow the hyperlink.

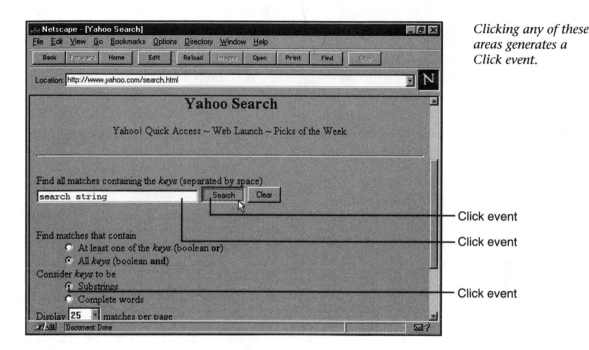

Clicking any of these areas generates a Click event.

Focus

The Focus event occurs when a user clicks or uses the Tab key to bring attention to a given form element. That is, when a user clicks a form element to activate it and prepare it to accept an entry, a Focus event occurs. For certain form elements, such as a button, clicking on it triggers both a Click and Focus event. Form elements such as text boxes, though, don't possess Click events, although they do trigger a Focus event when clicked on. Note that the Focus event occurs before the user enters data into the element; focus merely occurs when the element is activated for use. (Because some people use the Tab key to move between form elements, that also triggers a Focus event as each element becomes active.)

Blur

The Blur event is the opposite of the Focus event: it occurs when a user removes the focus from a currently in-focus form element, either by clicking or tabbing to another form element (thus moving the focus to a new element) or by clicking on some inactive region of the page (thus removing focus from all elements).

Both the Focus event and the Blur event are enhanced in JavaScript 1.1. Bringing focus into a window (such as the browser window) or a frame can now trigger the Focus event. You can use this feature, for example, to change the background color of a frame when the user brings focus to it. Likewise, the Blur event can be trigged by removing the focus from a window or a frame. For example, imagine a scenario in which a user clicks within a frame to bring it focus, and the Focus event changes the background frame color. You might choose a certain color, such as medium blue, to represent that this frame is "active." When the user clicks outside the frame, the Blur event is triggered, which might change the background frame color to some other shade, such as light blue, to represent that its "inactive."

Change

The Change event occurs after a user modifies the input into a form element such as a text input area. It also occurs if a selection is made from a selection box (the form element that allows a user to make a selection from a scrolling list of choices). Note that the Change event occurs only after a modified entry loses focus. That is, the moment a user begins entering data into a form element, the Change event is not triggered. It is triggered when the user finishes entering data (i.e., when he removes focus from the element by clicking elsewhere).

Modifying the text input area or choosing an entry from the selection box generates a Change event (when focus leaves the element).

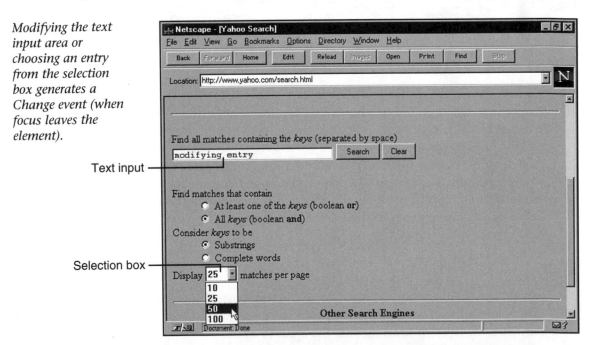

MouseOver

The MouseOver event occurs when the mouse pointer is over a link. While using the Web, you may have noticed that when you move the pointer over a link within a page, the URL address of that link appears in the status bar. That is an example of a MouseOver event.

 New to JavaScript 1.1, the MouseOver event can also be triggered when the pointer passes over a defined area within a client-side image map.

MouseOut (New to JavaScript 1.1)

 Somewhat the reverse of the MouseOver event is the MouseOut event, which occurs when the mouse leaves the region over a hyperlink or an area within a client-side image map. If areas or hyperlinks are adjacent to one another on a Web page, a MouseOut event might also lead to a MouseOver event as the user moves the pointer away from one link and over another. You can use this combination, for instance, to highlight an option as the user passes his mouse pointer over it.

Select

A Select event occurs when a user selects text within a form's text entry element (highlights the area of text by dragging the mouse across it while holding down the left button). A user might do this just before modifying the text in the entry. The following figure shows selected text in a form entry element.

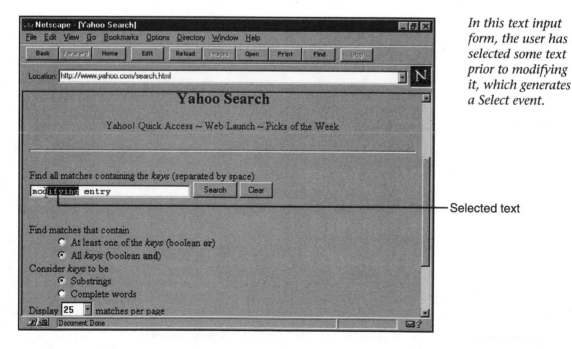

In this text input form, the user has selected some text prior to modifying it, which generates a Select event.

Selected text

Submit and Reset

A Submit event occurs when a user clicks the "Submit" button of a form element (see the following figure). Note that this event occurs before the form is actually submitted (as defined in the <FORM> tag). This enables you to trigger JavaScript code that might perform some analysis or evaluation, and as a result, it allows or prevents the form from actually being submitted.

A Submit event is generated when the user clicks the Submit button. In JavaScript 1.1, clicking the Reset button triggers a Reset event.

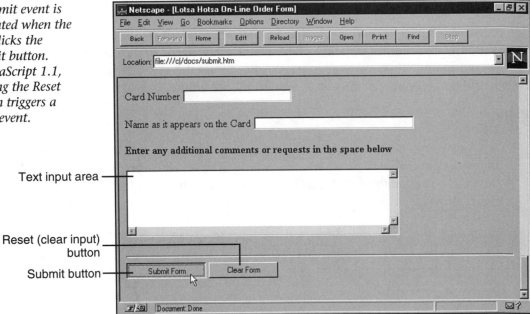

New to JavaScript 1.1 is Reset, a sibling to the Submit event. The Reset event occurs when the user clicks the "Reset" button in a form. Any JavaScript code triggered by this event is executed before the form data is reset.

The eight events you just read about are the basic events that may occur in a Web page as a result of user interaction. From these events, you will choose which are relevant to watch for within your particular page, and what JavaScript code to trigger as a result.

One Eye Open: Watching for Events

For each particular page element (link, form, and so on), you specify events to watch for in the form of an attribute of the tag that defines that element. Event attributes take this form:

```
onEvent="JavaScript code"
```

First, consider a simple example; after all, specifics make more sense than general definitions.

Recall the link tag in HTML. In typical HTML, you would define a link in the following way:

```
<A HREF="url to link to">Text to appear highlighted in page</A>
```

The user browsing your Web page sees "Text to appear highlighted in page" as a colored link. If he clicks that link, he is taken to the new page defined by the URL specified in the HREF attribute.

This is typical HTML. Now, let's add event watching to it. Suppose you want to launch a certain JavaScript program if the user moves the mouse over the link. That would require a MouseOver event trigger. Recall that you watch for an event with the attribute—in this case, you watch for `onMouseOver="JavaScript code"`. To do so, you add the attribute into the tag that defines the link, modifying the example in this way:

```
<A HREF="url to link to" onMouseOver="JavaScript code">Text to
appear highlighted in page</A>
```

For example, you can change the message in the browser's status bar to display the resulting action of clicking a button:

```
<form>
<input type=button value="Roll Dice" onMouseOver="window.status='Click this button
to roll the dice and begin a new round'">
</form>
```

Techno Talk

Keystone Caps

Remember that JavaScript is case-sensitive. Within JavaScript code, it matters whether you refer to a variable with upper- or lowercase letters. Referring to JavaScript statements with uppercase letters will result in errors. However, HTML code is not case-sensitive. Tags and their attributes (which includes onEvent attributes) can be in either upper- or lowercase. For the purposes of writing this book, though, I use "onEvent" because it is easier to read than "onevent." Do remember that any JavaScript code included between the quotation marks in the onEvent attribute is subject to JavaScript's case-sensitivity.

Between the Lines: Calling an Event Handler

Let's consider the portion of the preceding link that you've been labeling "JavaScript code" (which follows the onEvent= portion of the attribute). What should go in there?

The first rule is that you must include the surrounding double quotation marks. So no matter what, the event watcher must say onEvent="somethingsomething". The actions specified between the double quotation marks are known as the event handler. This makes sense because they describe how to handle the event when it's triggered. The event handler is your JavaScript program code.

Basically, you would call two types of JavaScript event handlers between those double quotation marks: the function call and explicit code. In JavaScript 1.1, you have a third option: resetting an event handler in JavaScript. The following sections cover the three types of event handlers in greater detail.

Function Call

The function call is the most common and desirable event handler. This is why functions are so useful. In a nicely constructed Web page, you define each function intended to handle a particular event at the top of the page in the <HEAD> section. Then, in the course of the page, you call each function as required by your event watchers (the onEvent attributes).

In the case of a function call event handler, the previous link example might resemble this:

```
<A HREF="http://www.yahoo.com" onMouseOver="myfunction(parameter)">Text to appear
highlighted in page</A>
```

In this example, when a user positions the mouse pointer over the link (which would take him to **http://www.yahoo.com** if he actually clicked it), the JavaScript function myfunction(parameter) is called.

Important Parameter Bulletin

Note that the onEvent attribute requires double quotation marks around its definition. This means that if you want to send a string literal as a parameter in the function call, you cannot use double quotation marks to specify the literal. For example, suppose you want to call printfancy ("Nice work!") as the event handler. To do so, you have to use single quotation marks for the string literal so it won't be misinterpreted as the close of the onEvent attribute. Thus, you have to write onEvent="printfancy ('Nice work!')".

Explicit Code

Besides the elegant solution of a function call, you can write out explicit JavaScript statements within the double quotation marks. You can write an entire JavaScript program of any length, but anything more than a statement or two is probably a good candidate for a function. You should remember two notable rules if you write out JavaScript code as an event handler:

➤ You cannot use any double quotation marks. You're limited to using single quotation marks (') anywhere a quotation mark is needed, because a double quotation mark (") would be interpreted as closing the onEvent attribute.

➤ You should separate the JavaScript statements with semicolons.

> **Event Handler Rules** You cannot specify an external file as the JavaScript event handler within the onEvent attribute. However, as previously discussed, you can include external JavaScript functions at the HEAD of the Web page with the `<SCRIPT src="URL of myfuncs.js">` and `</SCRIPT>` tags, and those functions may then be called normally as event handlers in the onEvent attribute.

Here is an example of the same link definition, but with explicit JavaScript code as the event handler:

```
<A HREF="http://www.yahoo.com" onMouseOver="total=0 ;
for (count=0;count<=10;count++) {total += 5} ;
half=total/2">Text to appear highlighted in page</A>
```

Now, I didn't say this example did anything useful; in this case, when the user moves the pointer over the link, the event handler is executed. It adds the value 5 to the variable total ten times in a loop, and then assigns half of total to the variable half. Perhaps at some later stage in the Web page, these variables will be used for some further calculations. In any case, the above is an example of explicit JavaScript code as an event handler.

Resetting an Event Handler in JavaScript 1.1

 Both event handlers above (function calls and explicit code) were specified within HTML tags. In JavaScript 1.1, it's also possible to set an event handler within JavaScript code.

For instance, suppose your Web page has a form button named ClickMe. You can define an event handler for ClickMe within JavaScript code as follows:

```
document.formname.ClickMe.onclick = function1
```

In this example, ClickMe is a button within the form *formname*. We've assigned function1 to be the event handler for a Click event of ClickMe. Note that the function above is not followed by the traditional parentheses, as in function1(). When setting an event handler in JavaScript code, you leave out the parentheses; including them would cause the function to execute immediately.

Using code like that you just saw, you can change the event handler assigned to an event, even if that event handler was previously defined in HTML tags. You'll see a simple example of this later in the chapter.

Examples, Exemplars, and Instantiations

At this point, you know the events, you know how to watch for them in HTML tags, and you know how to call the JavaScript event handlers. In fact, that's all you need to know. However, for the sake of clarity, let's run through examples of event triggers for some more types of events. Although they all follow the same rules (outlined earlier), it's nice to see how a specific event is handled so you can refer to it later on.

onClick

Imagine a form in which the user will click a checkbox to indicate his marital status. Upon clicking—whether they check it on or off—you might want to trigger a JavaScript function that uses the marital status in some other calculation. (Keep in mind that forms are defined with <FORM> tags in HTML; however, the specifics of that are not the subject of this book.) Assuming you know how to define a form element, the following is the line that defines the checkbox and onClick event trigger:

```
<INPUT name=married TYPE="checkbox" onClick="marstat(this.checked)">Married?
```

The preceding line first defines a checkbox according to conventional HTML standards. Then you include the onClick attribute discussed in this chapter. Note that you make a function call as the event handler. And presumably, you defined the JavaScript function "marstat()" earlier in the page. So far, this is just like previous examples of event triggers.

However, what might strike you as different, upon first glance, is the fact that you pass the parameter this.checked to the function marstat(). What is this.checked? It's composed of two parts—this and checked. Let's consider each, as this concept will reappear in subsequent examples.

The above is a form, and after all, it is the data entered into this form that you want to pass to the event-handling function. A form is considered an object in JavaScript, and as you may recall, an object possesses a set of properties. Because the form above happens to be a checkbox form, as far as JavaScript is concerned, it's a checkbox object. The checkbox object is a built-in JavaScript object that contains four properties, one of which is named checked. The checked property is a Boolean value indicating whether the checkbox is checked on (true) or off (false).

Therefore, this.checked refers to the property checked, which is part of the object "this form," which happens to be a checkbox object. So in the previous function call, this.checked represents a Boolean value reflecting the state of the checkbox, and that is the parameter that the JavaScript function marstat desires.

onClick and Canceling an Event

As I mentioned earlier in the chapter, JavaScript 1.1 adds the capability to cancel an onClick event. Let's look at a typical use of this. Suppose you have a form with a Submit button. When the user clicks the Submit button, you want him to confirm that he truly wants to submit the form data. Below is the HTML code for the Submit button:

```
<INPUT NAME=submit TYPE="submit" VALUE="Submit Data" onClick="return
confirm('Submit Data?')">
```

Notice the event handler you've assigned to the onClick event above: "return confirm('Submit Data?')". This calls the JavaScript confirm() function, which displays an "OK or Cancel" window for the user. If the user selects Cancel, it is returned to the onClick event, which cancels the process of submitting the form. Obviously, then, if the user selects OK, the onClick event proceeds with the form submission.

onFocus

In this case, you will create an event trigger that will occur if the user moves the page focus to this form. The form will be a simple one-line entry blank, but that doesn't matter; this action is triggered by the activation of the form element, not by the data that is placed into it. When focus is placed on this element, an explicit JavaScript statement is executed.

```
<INPUT NAME=age TYPE="" ROWS=1 SIZE="3" onFocus="window.status='Nice _focus'">
Your age?
```

Again, you watch for and trigger this event just as in all previous examples. Instead of calling a JavaScript function upon triggering, you execute a JavaScript statement. In this case, you assign a string value (note the single quotation marks) to an object property. You won't learn about the window object until the next chapter; for now, just note that this particular JavaScript statement will cause the specific string value to appear in the Web browser's status line.

When the user brings focus to the form element, the onFocus event changes the message in the window's status line.

Clicking here brings focus.

Clicking anywhere here removes focus.

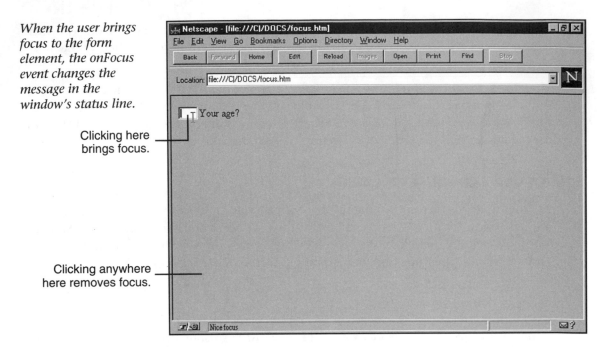

onSubmit

In this example, you'll watch for the user attempting to submit a form. Perhaps you've provided a text box in which the user is to enter an e-mail address. After entering the address, the user must click the Submit button (typical HTML form design). Suppose you also wrote a JavaScript function that can look at the information the user entered and determine whether it is a plausible e-mail address (i.e., that it has the proper format for an e-mail address). The following code will trigger this hypothetical function, evalform (address), when the user attempts to submit the form.

```
<FORM onSubmit="evalform(this.email.value)">
<INPUT NAME=email TYPE="text" ROWS=1 SIZE="20">Enter your e-mail address
<INPUT NAME=submit TYPE="submit">
<INPUT NAME=reset TYPE="reset">
</FORM>
```

Alrighty then. As this is the final onEvent example, it's the most complicated. Let's tear this beast apart and see what's going on up there.

For now, completely ignore the onSubmit attribute; we'll look at it last. Everything else should look like a typical HTML form. After the <FORM> tag, you define a text entry blank that is one row high and 20 spaces wide. You name this element email, using the NAME=

attribute. (This name does not appear on the screen; it is for program reference only.) The text following the <INPUT> tag will appear on the screen beside the element. Again, this is standard HTML form syntax.

Below that line, you create another element, a Submit button, and below that, you create a Reset button (in case the user wants to clear the text-entry element). Now look at the event handling in this form, which is defined in the opening <FORM> tag. Because you want to call your function when the user submits the form via the Submit button, you use an onSubmit event watcher. Then, as in the previous examples, you define the event handler as a function call to the function evalform(). This should be familiar territory by now. What's worth special note, however, is the syntax of the parameter you are sending to the evalform() function. The evalform() function (if it existed) would accept the user's input into the text-entry element of the form and determine whether it were a plausible e-mail address. You refer to this data with the name this.email.value. Why?

As usual, "this" refers to the main object in question: this form. The text-entry element is a property of the form, and it is named whatever you named it with the NAME= attribute. (Psst! You named it email.) Finally, email itself (the text-entry element) is also an object—another built-in JavaScript object (the text-entry form element is a built-in object, which you named email within this particular page). One of the properties of the text element object is value, which contains the actual data entered into the element. So there it is: this.email.value refers to the data entered into the text element named email, which is a property of "this" form in question.

The preceding code will pass the correct user input to the function evalform(parameter). This function should then return a true or false value upon making its evaluation—because the JavaScript statement return true or return false is the last statement in the function definition. If it returns a value of true, the submission will proceed in whatever manner you intend to handle it (usually this is done with the METHOD= attribute of the <FORM> tag, but you didn't include it here because it is the stuff of HTML coding, not JavaScript). If it returns a false value, the submission will not proceed.

Resetting Event Handlers in JavaScript 1.1

Earlier in this chapter, you learned that in JavaScript 1.1, you can set or assign event handlers within JavaScript code. You saw that in the following example:

```
document.formname.ClickMe.onclick = function1
```

Now let's elaborate on the above code to see how you can better take advantage of this new feature of JavaScript 1.1. Imagine, for instance, that your page contains two form elements: a button and a checkbox. When the user clicks the button, the onClick event calls an event handler; however, *which* event handler it calls depends upon whether the checkbox is checked or unchecked.

Consider the JavaScript 1.1 code below:

```
<SCRIPT>
function event1()
 {window.alert("Checkbox enabled")}
function event2()
 {window.alert("Checkbox disabled")}
function check()
{
if (document.Formica.checkbox.status == true)
 {document.Formica.ClickMe.onclick = event1}
 else {document.Formica.ClickMe.onclick = event2}
}
</SCRIPT>
<FORM NAME="Formica">
<INPUT TYPE="checkbox" NAME=checkbox STATUS=true onClick="check()">Checkbox
Enabled<HR>
<INPUT TYPE="button" NAME=ClickMe VALUE="Click Me!">
</FORM>
<SCRIPT>check()</SCRIPT>
```

In the above code, you first defined three functions: event1(), event2(), and check(). Both event1() and event2() are event handlers for an onClick event of the ClickMe button. The function check() is our focal point: it determines the status of the checkbox and sets the appropriate event handler (either event1 or event2) to the onClick event for the ClickMe button.

In action, if the user enables the checkbox and then clicks the ClickMe button, a JavaScript alert window appears, stating that the checkbox is enabled. Conversely, if the user disables the checkbox and then clicks the ClickMe button, an alert window appears, stating that the checkbox is disabled.

Notice that you define an onClick event in the HTML tag for the checkbox, thus calling the check() function and properly assigning the event handler for the ClickMe button.

Finally, notice the final line of code in the above example:

```
<SCRIPT>check()</SCRIPT>
```

This explicitly calls the check() function one time so that the ClickMe event handler is properly set before the user first clicks the checkbox.

The Least You Need to Know

Once again, reading the full chapter is an excellent idea. The following list is a fair summary, but it's far from detailed instruction.

➤ An event is any user action such as a click, mouse movement, text selection, or form entry.

➤ Event handlers are the JavaScript programs that execute when triggered by a specified event.

➤ Event handlers can be triggered using the onEvent="JavaScript code" attribute within the tag defining the element being watched.

➤ Events that can be triggered include onClick, onFocus, onBlur, onChange, onMouseOver, onSelect, and onSubmit.

➤ In JavaScript 1.1, the onBlur and onFocus events now also apply to windows and frames.

➤ JavaScript 1.1 now includes the events onReset and onMouseOut.

➤ Event handlers can be set or reset in JavaScript 1.1 within JavaScript code, as in:

```
document.formname.button.onclick = functionname
```

How Much Is That Object in the Window?

In This Chapter

➤ What's behind your window

➤ Setting the status bar

➤ Referring to frames

➤ User interactions

➤ Building new windows and razing them

➤ Geraldo Rivera finds Twix bars buried in the Andes

As you've seen, the purpose of JavaScript is to play a role in the workings of a Web page. In Chapters 5–8, you first learned the programming foundations of the JavaScript language itself. Then I ate cookies. In Chapter 9, you saw one way to integrate JavaScript programs in the functionality of a Web page—via event triggers.

Welcome, then, on to Chapter 10. You now begin a journey into using JavaScript to interact with and/or control various characteristics of the Web page itself. You'll start at the top with what is known to programming cognoscenti and exterior decorators alike as "the window."

The Looking Glass

Imagine launching your Web browser. After some hard drive activity, the browser pops onto the screen, and you are presented with an initial Web page. It is that space on your screen where the Web page appears that is the "window." In fact, your Web browser is mostly one huge window, although it has some navigational controls above the window and perhaps some status information below the window.

Your "window into the Web" is, in fact, "the window."

The window ⎯

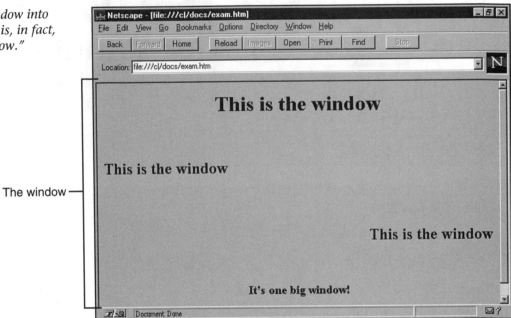

Everything that appears within a Web page, therefore, must appear within the window. For this reason, the window is called the "top-level" object. Recall the JavaScript definition of an object (such as the sweater object). Everything about the sweater—material, color, size, and price—is a property of the sweater. In this case, everything about the Web page—its colors, background image, form elements, and so on—is a property of the window. In terms of JavaScript, then, the window is considered an object.

That is the thrust of this chapter: looking at the window instead of merely looking through it.

Properties

The window object contains several properties that you might need to reference, along with some nifty examples as your bonus gift. Keep reading.

The status Property

Look at the bottom of the window in the previous picture. The small area in the bottom frame of the window currently reads "Document: Done."

That area is the status line, and the Web browser uses it to report...well...status messages to the person using the browser. In this case, the status message tells you the document has finished loading. You, as a proprietor of JavaScript and controller of the window object, can conjure up your own messages to display on the status line.

The basic template for setting the status message text is this:

```
window.status = "messagetext"
```

The most likely places you would use the status property are in an onEvent trigger or the function that acts as an event handler. To create an example of the latter, you can create a Web page with two buttons on it. Label one "Try me!" and the other "Over here!" When the user clicks either, the status line will display an appropriate message. You'll define a function msg(msgtext) to act as the event handler.

```
<html><body><head>
<script language="JavaScript">
function msg(msgtext)
{window.status=msgtext}
</script></head>
<form><input type=button value="Try me!" onClick="msg('That was nice')"></form>
<form><input type=button value="Over here!" onClick="msg('Hey there')"></form>
</body></html>
```

The function accepts a parameter from the onEvent call and assigns that value to window.status. That's the relevant heart of this example. Down below, where you define the form element buttons, you use the traditional onEvent call as discussed in Chapter 9. Note that you pass string literals to the function; you enclose them in single quotation marks.

If you load the above file into your Web browser, you'll see a window with two buttons. Clicking either of them brings up its associated status line message, as shown here.

Have fun clicking buttons and setting the window's status message.

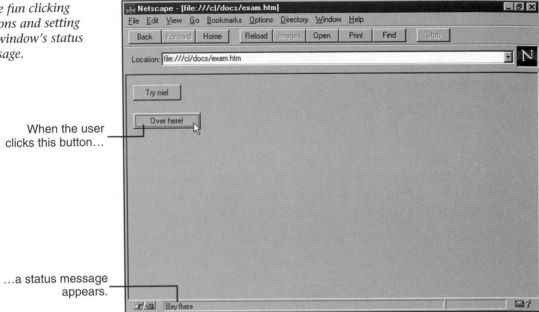

When the user clicks this button...

...a status message appears.

The opener Property

1.1 As you'll see later in this chapter, you can cause a window to open a new window by using the open() method. A new feature of JavaScript 1.1 is the opener property, which refers to the window that opened the current window. For example, suppose you have these two windows: Window1 (which caused Window2 to open) and Window2 (assuming you're currently within Window2). In this case, the following code

```
window.opener
```

would refer to Window1.

Using the opener property, you can cause changes to the opening window using code within the current window. For instance, suppose again that Window1 has opened Window2. In JavaScript code that has been loaded into Window2, you could make the statement

```
window.opener.close()
```

which would close the window that opened the current window (Window1, in this example).

In a similar vein, you could change the background color of the opening window with this statement:

```
window.opener.document.bgColor="yellow"
```

The self Object

Some claim it pretentious to refer to yourself, but in JavaScript you won't be ostracized for doing so. In fact, sometimes, you have good reason to. Technically, self is a synonym for window. Therefore

```
self.status = "Wake up!"
```

is the same as

```
window.status = "Wake up!"
```

However, the JavaScript creators realized the potential conflict. Let's say you created a form element in your page that has the internal name "status" (as defined by the NAME= attribute of the form element tag). In this case, if you ever referred to it in a window property construction, it would be unclear whether you meant the window status line property or the form named status.

Therefore, you have the option of using self.property in cases where there may be ambiguity. Of course, you might not create any ambiguity in the first place when naming your form elements—but just in case, self is there for you.

Frames

Frames aren't discussed much in this book because they are a Netscape HTML invention. And, in general, I've avoided overly complex HTML codes because this is a book about JavaScript and not HTML. Nonetheless, the two are bedfellows: They both contribute to a Web page's design and functionality.

If you don't already know how to code frames into HTML, this book isn't the place to learn. But as a reminder, frames are subwindows within the main window of a Web page. Thus, the top-level window of the Web page pictured here contains three frames.

It's quite logical, then, that each frame is a property of the window object. In turn, each frame has its own properties because each is its own minidocument and thus possesses the properties that any document would have (Chapter 12 covers all this).

This window object contains three frames.

One frame —

A second frame —

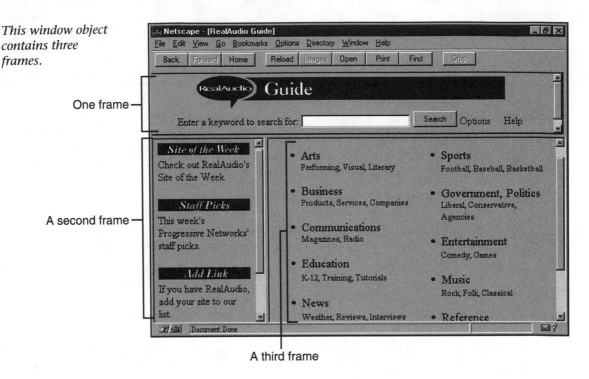

A third frame

Each frame is referred to as window.frame[0], window.frame[1], and so on. Therefore, as you'll see when we talk about document properties in Chapter 12, the properties within a frame can be described as window.frame[0].property. For now, this is all you need to know: Each frame is a property of the window object.

Methods

In the spirit of "many different names for the same thing," you might remember that a method is a function that is part of an object. (You coded a method called sweater.price() back in Chapter 8.) Thus, the object window also has a set of methods associated with it. You can (and will) use these for a variety of useful purposes; therefore, you will now embark on a guided tour of window object methods.

alert()

What better way to let the user know something than by shoving it in his face? Enter the alert. An alert, in general-speak, is one of those message windows that appears on-screen to tell you something. Usually, it has an "OK" button you click to signal that you've read this urgent message and would like to continue. The following figure shows a typical alert.

Code red! Alert! Abandon ship! This is a common alert window.

Consider the hypothetical example where you requested that the user enter his e-mail address into a form text-entry element. You saw previously (in Chapter 9) that you can use an onSubmit event trigger to check the user's entry for validity before allowing the submission to proceed. Let's build on that example. Suppose the submitted address is deemed nonplausible, and you want to display an alert telling the user that he is an abject liar.

The format for the alert method is: window.alert ("message").

After the user acknowledges the alert by clicking the "OK" button, JavaScript will move on to the next statement in your code or function. To reprise, your function evalform() was triggered by the following:

```
<FORM onSubmit="evalform(this.email.value)">
<INPUT NAME=email TYPE="text" ROWS=1 SIZE="20">Enter your e-mail address
<INPUT NAME=submit TYPE="submit">
<INPUT NAME=reset TYPE="reset">
</FORM>
```

Presumably, then, you have defined the function evalform() earlier in your document. It might go a little something like this:

```
function evalform (address)
{ crucial = address.indexOf ("@") ;
//the above uses a method of the string object to locate an at-sign in
//the submitted form
if (crucial != —1)
 { return true } ;
else
 { window.alert ("Your e-mail address is invalid! You are an abject liar!") ;
   return false }

}
```

The preceding function accepts a parameter, which is the submitted e-mail address to validate. The address.indexOf property is a method of the string object (covered in Appendix A at the end of this book), which returns the position of the specified character

103

within the string. In this case, you're searching for an @ symbol because all valid e-mail addresses have this symbol. The position of that symbol is assigned to the variable crucial and will be a value of –1 if the symbol is not found in the string. This will be your only test because this is simply an example.

Following that, you use a standard if...else clause: if the @ symbol is not located, the window.alert method is called to give an appropriate scolding to the user. Also note that the Boolean false is returned to prevent submission of the form. Lastly, the else clause takes care of the condition where the @ was located and simply returns a logical true, which allows the submission to proceed.

confirm()

The confirm() method is another type of message box. If you've ever used a computer— and at this stage of the book, I deeply hope you have—you've seen confirmation messages. They typically pose a question or proposition, and you are asked to choose between OK and Cancel.

This is how you use the confirm() method of the window object:

```
window.confirm ("message")
```

This method returns a true value if the user opts for the OK option or a false if he selects Cancel. In some cases, because a result is returned, you might want to call this method as somevariable = window.confirm ("message").

Next, you add a confirm() method to the e-mail validation function. In this case, if you determine that the address is valid, you repeat it to the user in a confirmation message so he can verify its accuracy. To do so, simply add the following highlighted code to your evalform() function:

```
function evalform (address)
{ crucial = address.indexOf ("@") ;
if (crucial != —1)
 { message = "You entered " + address + " —— is this correct?";
   return window.confirm (message) } ;
else
 { window.alert ("Your e-mail address is invalid! You are an abject liar!") ;
   return false }
}
```

You've added only two lines to the previous version of this function, and both occur in the true (address is valid) condition. First, you created the message to use in the confirm()

method by making a variable message to which you assigned three concatenated strings using the string concatenate operator (+). Below that, you called the window.confirm() method with the previously made message, which is what the user will see. Note that you make the method call as part of a return statement; the confirm() method will return a true or false, and you want to pass that result back to the calling form, which will then proceed with or cease the submission.

Now let's assume you executed this little e-mail entry JavaScript program and entered an e-mail address that passed validation. The previous code would generate something that looked like the following figure.

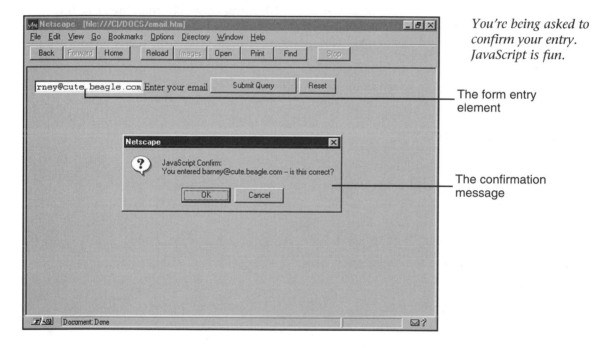

You're being asked to confirm your entry. JavaScript is fun.

The form entry element

The confirmation message

prompt()

The prompt() method displays a nifty message box, into which you may ask the user to enter some sort of information. That information is then assigned to the variable to which this method is assigned, to be used as you may want for any other purpose. For this example, consider a new scenario: You present a series of form buttons, each one of which represents an astrological sign. Somewhere in the Web page, the user is told to click whichever sign belongs to him. Upon doing so, you then prompt the user to enter his age.

The prompt() method works as follows:

```
somevariable = window.prompt ("prompt message" , defaultvalue)
```

You Make the Call Note that although you don't do anything else with his age in this particular example, you may choose to use it for any other programming purpose you like.

The prompt message represents the proposition you want to put to the user. The defaultvalue represents some data that you'd like to appear in the prompt by default. If you have no preferred default value, just enter two double quotation marks in that spot like this: "".

In this example, you'll validate the age the user enters to be somewhere within the known human lifespan. If it fails this test, a scolding alert will appear, and then he will be asked to enter his age again. If the age he enters this time passes, the user will be thanked.

Here is the full code of your little programming feat:

```
<script language="JavaScript">
function getage ()
{ age=window.prompt ("How old are you?","") ;
if ((age<1) ¦¦ (age>120))
{ window.alert ("Why must you turn this page into a house of lies?") ;
getage () }
else
{ window.alert ("Thank you.") }
}
</script>
<FORM>
<INPUT NAME=gemini TYPE=button value="Gemini" onClick="getage()">Click your sign
</FORM>
```

Several examples are worth noting in this program. Jump to the final line first—the <FORM> definition. Here, as usual, you define a form element (a button) and include the onClick event trigger. To handle the event, you call the function getage(), which takes no parameters. Standard stuff.

Now up to the function definition itself (at the top of the program). The first statement in the function definition is your prompt() method. It asks the user "How old are you?" and presents her with an entry blank with no default value. Whatever the user enters is assigned to the variable age. You then test age for validity, using an if...else statement. Note the nifty conditional in the if clause, which uses a logical operator (OR) on two comparison operators.

Should the age be deemed invalid (outside the range 1–120), an alert appears, accusing the user of duplicity. Note that after the accusatory alert, the function getage() is then called again. (Yes, it calls itself.) That essentially restarts the function, thus letting the user start all over with the age prompt.

On the other hand, if the age falls within the acceptable range, an alert appears, merely thanking the user for his input and ending the function. The following figure shows the prompt method in action.

Not poking or prodding, just prompting.

focus() and blur()

Newcomers to JavaScript 1.1, these two methods simply enable you to bring focus to or remove focus from a specific window object. For instance, recall the new opener property (covered earlier in the chapter):

```
window.opener.focus()
```

This would return focus to the window that opened the current window. Similarly, you could remove focus from the current window using this code:

```
window.blur()
```

scroll()

Another neat addition to JavaScript 1.1 is the scroll() method. This allows you to scroll a specified window to an x,y pixel coordinate point. For reference, the coordinate 0,0 always refers to the upper-left corner of a window. Thus,

```
window.scroll(0,0)
```

would scroll the current window to its upper-left corner. Increasing the y value scrolls the window further down the document, while increasing the x value scrolls the window further toward the right of the document. You can even scroll a window other than the current one by using this statement:

```
window.opener.scroll(0,200)
```

107

open() and close()

Finally, at the sunset of your journey into the window object, consider methods that give rise and fall to windows themselves.

You can use the open() method to create an entirely new browser window. When you do, the current window remains in place, but a new window is opened on the desktop. The new window is essentially another Web browser, and you define its characteristics—including size, title, document to open, navigation buttons to make available, and so forth—with the open() method.

Why would you use this method? Perhaps, in your Web page, you want to show the user an example of something on another Web page. Instead of loading that example page within your current window and eliminating your explanation from the screen, you might open a new adjacent window that contains the example. At the end of the example, the user could either manually close the new window himself or choose some "I'm done" button, which would trigger the close() method to close the new window.

The formats for these methods are:

```
window.open ("UrlToOpen","windowname","feature1,feature2,feature3,etc.")
window.close ()
```

The window.close() method must be contained in JavaScript code within the window to be closed. One window can't close another window; a window can only close itself (window suicide). Therefore, using the window.close() method is simple; just include a call to it as the event handler for some element, such as a form button, that indicates to the user he is done with the window.

The window.open() method has a few more parameters, as you can see. However, the first two parameters are straightforward:

➤ UrlToOpen is the address of the document you want to be opened in that window (for example, **http://mydoc.html**).

➤ windowname gives the window an internal name, which may be used for other references. (Note, this name doesn't seem to appear anywhere on the visible window itself.)

Finally, you may provide any, all, or none of the list of possible feature characteristics of the new window. Separate each feature by a comma but not a space, just as presented in the template example for the previous method. The possible features include:

toolbar=yes or no   Determines whether to include the standard Back, Forward, Home toolbar.

location= yes or no	Determines whether to show the current URL location.
directories=yes or no	Determines whether to show "What's New," "What's Cool," or other buttons.
status=yes or no	Determines whether a status bar is displayed at the bottom of the window.
menubar=yes or no	Determines whether to include a menu bar at the top of the window.
scrollbars=yes or no	Determines whether to create scroll bars if the document exceeds the window size.
resizable=yes or no	Determines whether the user may resize the window.
copyhistory=yes or no	Determines whether this new window should inherit the current window's session history.
width=# pixels	Defines how wide the window should be, measured in pixels.
height=# pixels	Defines how tall the window should be, measured in pixels.

How Many Pixels in an Inch?

Noncomputer nerds might not be used to measuring sizes in pixels. But that is the standard measurement tool for the images on a computer screen. For the purposes of creating your window sizes, use the following guidelines: A standard VGA screen on a 13–14 inch monitor (which is the most common screen size in use) is 640 pixels wide by 480 pixels high. Therefore, determine what percentage of the screen you want your new window to eat up, and use the 640×480 scale accordingly. Furthermore, many users use screen sizes of 800×600 on 14–15 inch monitors, while those with 17-inch monitors more commonly use 1,024×768 pixels. At this point, 640×480 is still considered the most common standard size against which to measure your windows.

Given all of the features previously described, let's create an onEvent trigger that will create a new window using some of the above features.

```
<INPUT NAME=newwin TYPE=button value="Click me for a new window"
_onClick="window.open ('http://
mydoc.html','newwin','toolbar=no,status=yes,scrollbars=no,
_resizable=no,width=320,height=240')">
```

109

Check This Out...

Assume True If you don't specify a window feature in the open() method call, it will default to yes. Therefore, if you want a feature false, be sure to list it and assign it "no" in the open() method call.

I know that looks messy, but it's really just a long list of parameters. Note the use of single quotation marks within the open method call, which are used because of the double quotation marks that must surround the onClick definition.

As a certain animated pig who shall remain nameless used to say, "As far as window objects go, th-th-th-that's all folks!" (Well, he said something like that. It was a long time ago.)

The Least You Need to Know

➤ The entire window through which a Web page is viewed is a JavaScript object known as window.property.

➤ All elements and characteristics of a Web page are properties of the window object.

➤ window.status="message" defines the status bar message.

➤ window.opener refers to the window that opened the current window.

➤ window.frame[*x*].property refers to property of frame number *x*.

➤ window.alert ("message") is a method that displays an alert box.

➤ window.confirm ("message") is a method that displays a confirmation box; it returns true if the user selects OK and false if the user clicks CANCEL.

➤ somevariable=window.prompt ("message","defaultvalue") is a method that displays a prompt box and assigns the user's input to somevariable.

➤ window.focus() and window.blur() can bring focus to or remove focus from a specified window.

➤ window.scroll(x,y) scrolls the specified window to the pixel coordinates x,y. (0,0 always refers to the upper-left corner of the document.)

➤ window.open ("UrlToOpen","windowname","feature1,feature2,etc") launches a new window with feature characteristics.

➤ window.close() kills the window that uses this method call (window suicide).

Chapter 11

Mapping and Tracking: Locations and Histories

In This Chapter

➤ Picking apart a meaty URL

➤ URLs back in time

➤ Guiding visitors by the wallet

The location object refers to the current URL—that is, the address of the page currently loaded. This object provides several properties with which you can play with various characteristics of the URL. The history object contains the current list of other URLs that have been visited in the present session. It, too, can be sliced, diced, and analyzed.

Wherefore Art Thou, URL?

The location object contains the current URL. Therefore, imagine that the address of your Web page is this:

> http://my.isp.com/~me/mypage.html

In this case, the location object refers to that address. The object's properties will seek out various portions of the URL. The location object is rather straightforward and nonconfusing, which is a good thing. The location object contains eight properties, and they behave in the following manners.

href

location.href contains the string value of the entire URL. Thus, given the previous sample URL, the value of location.href would be "http://my.isp.com/~me/mypage.html".

One possible use of this property is to pass it as a parameter to the window.open call. Perhaps you want to open a new window, which connects to the same URL as the current window (so you can look at another portion of the same page at the same time you're looking at the current portion of the page). Simply use this call:

```
window.open(location.href, "windowname", "feature1, feature2, ...");
```

You can also launch a new page without opening a new window. If you simply assign a new URL to location.href, the browser will attempt to connect to a new page. For example:

```
location.href = " http://my.isp.com/~me/mypage.html ";
```

Of course, if you do this, you'll effectively be leaving your current page, including any other JavaScript programs that are in it.

host

The location.host property holds only the hostname and port of the current page's URL. Take a look at the previous example URL

http://my.isp.com/~me/mypage.html

where the "hostname" would be my.isp.com. That's the Internet name of the computer on which the page resides. In the previous example, no port is specified in the URL and, therefore, location.host will only contain the value "my.isp.com". If a port were specified in the URL, it might look like this:

http://my.isp.com:80/~me/mypage.html

"80" is the port in this example. If this were your URL, location.host would contain the string value "my.isp.com:80". (Because the default port for a Web page is 80, it is usually not specified; but some URLs use a different port, in which case it will be specified.) One possible use for this property is to construct a string for a user message or HTML link. That is, suppose you want to write a JavaScript function that you might use in numerous Web pages. The purpose of the function is to provide an HTML link on-screen that the user can click to jump to another document in a set of pages. Because your function doesn't know which machine it will be on, it could use the location.host property to concatenate an appropriate string for later output in the window as a link.

Home Port

A computer is more like an apartment block than a single family home: It has a street address (its IP address, such as my.isp.com), but it also has a series of "apartments" within that address. In net-speak, these apartments are called ports. A computer "listens" on different ports for different types of connections. Generally speaking, Web servers listen for requests on port 80. However, some servers are configured differently and listen on another port. In such cases, when addressing this machine with a URL, you must specify the alternate port to send the request to. Therefore, if my.isp.com listens for Web requests on port 8080, you could send an URL such as **http://my.isp.com:8080/~me/mypage.html**.

Assigning a value to location.host will generate an error because it is nonsensical. However, you can assign an entire URL to location.href, which would then connect to that URL. You cannot connect to just a host. Thus, assigning a value to location.host is of no use.

hostname

At the risk of sounding redundant, let me say that the property location.hostname will return just the host-name portion of the URL. Recall in the case above that host refers to hostname:port. Likewise, hostname refers only to the name. Yes, it is true: If there is a URL with no port specified, location.host and location.hostname contain the same value.

port

The property location.port simply contains the value of the port number in the URL, if specified, as explained previously. Note that if a port was not specified in the URL, location.port contains no value. It does not contain the default 80 port unless the 80 was specified in the URL.

pathname

Once again, let's look at your example URL:

> **http://my.isp.com/~me/mypage.html**

The pathname is the portion of the URL that describes the location of the Web document on the host computer. The pathname begins with and includes the slash (/) immediately succeeding the hostname (or the port, if it were specified). In the above,

> **/~me/mypage.html**

is the pathname. Therefore, this is the value that location.pathname would contain.

Assigning a value to this property, as in

```
location.pathname = "~me/otherdocs/newdoc.html";
```

will cause the Web browser to load that document into the current window. This is similar to when you assigned a value to location.href, except that the new document will come from the same host as the current document.

protocol

The protocol property contains the leftmost portion of the URL, which contains the name of the protocol to use in retrieving the specified file (Web document). The example URL used the HTTP protocol, as is most common on the Web. However, some URLs may contain different protocols, such as

> **file://hostname/pathname**
> **gopher://hostname/pathname**

FTP, for instance, is the File Transfer Protocol and is another common way in which files can be delivered across the Internet. Gopher is yet another information-retrieval protocol, which had its heydey before the explosion of the Web (and HHTP—the HyperText Transport Protocol). Many sites still offer information via the Gopher protocol.

In your http://my.isp.com/~me/mypage.html example, location.protocol would contain the value "http:". In the previous examples, location.protocol would contain "file:" and "gopher:", respectively.

By checking the location.protocol property, the JavaScript program can determine if the page it currently resides in was delivered by HTTP, FTP, or Gopher. Conceivably (although not commonly), this could later be used in the JavaScript program to direct the user elsewhere, or to inform the user of restrictions (for example, "Sorry, but to hear the streaming audio on this page you must retrieve the page using HTTP").

hash

Some URLs contain special hash mark values following the pathname. For example:

> **http://my.isp.com/~me/mypage.html#tuesday**

The hash mark (#) specifies the name of an anchor to jump to in the Web page. An anchor is a place on a page that has been marked (via the HTML tags that make up the page) as a jump-to point. This allows users to be directed to specific spots within a page, instead of always at the very top. The above URL attempts to bring the user to the anchor known as "tuesday" in the page mypage.html.

Bookmanchor

Readers who are familiar with the popular application FrontPage should note that the folks at Microsoft have broken from tradition a bit—possibly causing some confusion with their terminology. Commonly, marked locations within a page are called *anchors*, as we've described them in this section. However, Microsoft has apparently decided to call these locations "bookmarks" instead of "anchors." What's more, Netscape Navigator uses the term bookmarks to refer to URLs that have been saved by the user for future use (a "hot list"). Microsoft uses the term "Favorites" to refer to the same item as Netscape's "Bookmarks." Confused yet? The point is, sometimes you might see these hash marked locations referred to as anchors, and sometimes as bookmarks.

Thus, the location.hash property would contain the value following the hash mark (in the preceding case, it would be tuesday).

Assigning a value to location.hash will cause the Web page to jump to that anchor. Note that of the properties you've seen so far, this may be one of the most useful.

search

Yet another variation on the URL is a search parameter following the pathname, denoted with a question mark (?). A form entry is probably the most common use for a search parameter. When a user enters form data into a form element and then clicks the "submit" button, the following URL is called:

http://my.isp.com/~me/myprogram?formdata

The property location.search would contain the value following the question mark. The most sensible use of this parameter would be in the page that receives the submitted form data.

Jump Around

Because it jumps to new locations within the same page, location.hash is more desirable than throwing out your current page, such as when you assign new values to location.href or location.pathname. You can use the location.hash property in event handlers, for example, to bring the user to specific locations within the current page.

For example, suppose you have two pages. One of them accepts user input in a form entry. It then sends that input to another page. This other page contains a JavaScript function that evaluates the submitted form data. Therefore, you can make a call to this function with evalform(location.search), which would pass the submitted form as a parameter.

Re-Form School

As per my usual disclaimer, this book isn't an HTML guide. However, just to refresh your memory, I'll briefly mention how a form is submitted. You define a form element with the <FORM> tag. This tag may take several attributes, one of which is the METHOD= attribute. METHOD= may be assigned either GET or POST. This defines how the form data will be submitted to the server. The details are technical, but GET is the most popular method. It is also the method that generates the ?formdata syntax in a URL.

The ACTION= attribute specifies which URL to send the submitted data to. This URL will presumably be designed to process the form data in some way.

Thus, a <FORM> definition might look like this:

```
<FORM METHOD=GET ACTION="http://some.isp.com/~someone/someprogram">
```

The preceding set of properties for the location object gives you all you need to pluck the current URL for any relevant information. Next, you look at the history object, which keeps track of previously visited URLs.

Let's Do the Time Warp Again: The history Object

The history object is an interesting beast. You're probably familiar with the standard browser history list, which is usually available via a menu (in Netscape Navigator, it's on the Go menu). Upon accessing the history list, you're presented with a list of the pages you accessed in this browsing session. You may then choose to quickly jump to one of those previously visited URLs.

The history object lets you send the user to somewhere in the history list from within a JavaScript program. The object contains two properties and three methods. So let's take a drive past each, shall we?

Historic Properties

First, here's a look at the properties: current and length.

current

The history.current property contains the value of the current URL. Yes, that would make it equivalent to location.href. Note that, as you'll see in a moment, the history list is referenced in a relative manner. That is, however, that many items are in the list, position 0 is the current item. (This will become relevant in a few short paragraphs.)

length

Depending on how many pages the user has visited during this session, the history list can be of any length. The property history.length contains the current length of the history list.

It's worth noting that the history object does not contain any values that reflect the actual URLs in the history list. Therefore, you cannot, for example, perform some action that reads the value of "URL number 3 in the history list." The history object is designed for navigating the history list. That's where its methods come into the picture.

Ways of Old: Historic Methods

Now here is a discussion of the history object's three methods: back(), forward(), and go().

back()

This method has a very logical behavior: history.back() simply moves the user to the URL one place previous in the history list (previous to the current position). It is the same as if the user clicked the "back" or left-pointing arrow in the Web browser's navigation toolbar.

Just as with any instance where you bring the user to a new page, you give up control from your JavaScript program. The user may never return—or he may go anywhere else that the new page links to. Therefore, it usually makes the most sense to utilize these JavaScript methods (which call up new pages) between sets of pages you have designed. In this way, your pages can all contain appropriate JavaScript programs to move the user along to where you want him to go.

forward()

Can you guess what this method does? I bet you can. history.forward() moves the user one URL forward, relative to the current position in the history list.

go(offset) or go(substring)

Finally, you can use the go() method to jump to a particular position in the history list, instead of merely making one hop backward or forward. You can use this method to refer to the desired position in the history list in two different ways.

go(offset) accepts an integer parameter, positive or negative, as offset. If the parameter is a positive integer, the program will move the user that many places forward in the history list. If the parameter is negative, it'll move the user that many places backward (previous to the current position) in the history list. Your current position is always place zero.

Note, however, that this applies only to Netscape Navigator, and *not* to Internet Explorer 3.0. Internet Explorer's handling of the go() method is very unreliable. For example, this line

```
history.go(2);
```

will send the user two locations forward in the history if he is using Netscape. On the other hand, if he's using Internet Explorer 3.0, the line will send the user forward in the history, but not necessarily the number of locations specified! Likewise, this line

```
history.go(-3);
```

will send the user three locations backward in the history list if he's using Netscape. Similarly, this negative number will also send the user backward in Internet Explorer's history list, but not necessarily the specified number of locations. This is a real quirk in Internet Explorer 3.0, one that many hope to find rectified in version 4.0. For now, I would advise coding for Netscape Navigator, because it follows the "official" JavaScript rules for behavior.

Alternatively, you can send go() a string instead of an integer value. For example:

```
history.go("mugs.html");
```

In this case, JavaScript will search for the newest history list URL that contains the specified string somewhere within its URL string. Again, this only works properly in Netscape Navigator, not Internet Explorer 3.0. Therefore, if the history list contains the URL **http://some.isp.com/~someone/mugs.html**, that's where the user will be sent by the above example (unless, of course, there is another URL that also contains "mugs.html" and has been added to the list more recently).

Remember that URLs are added to the history list when the user visits a page. Therefore, the URLs closest to the end of the history list are the newest; those closest to the beginning are the oldest.

In Closing...

You now have an eyeful of the JavaScript objects that allow you to play around with URL references. Their most applicable use is probably in guiding users around your pages, within functions that determine where to guide them based on certain conditions. For example, let's say you make a special offer to customers who order 10 or more mugs from your page. You might want to take them to another page from which they can select a gift of their choice. Thus, you can create a JavaScript function based on an if...else statement, which sends them to the gift-choosing page on the true condition (perhaps by assigning the gift page's URL to location.href), or which doesn't send them on to the gift page in the false condition. (Or perhaps you might send them to some other page that advertises the "buy 10, get a free gift" deal.)

Briefly, that example would look like this:

```
function giftdeal(mugs) {
   if (mugs>=10) {
      location.href = "http://mysite.com/~me/giftpage.html";
   } else {
      location.href="http://mysite.com/~me/giftad.html";
   }
}
```

The Least You Need to Know

➤ The location object possesses several properties that relate to portions of the current URL.

➤ location.href contains the value of the entire URL.

➤ Properties host, hostname, port, pathname, and protocol each contain the value of their respective portions of the URL.

➤ location.hash and location.search contain the values of the strings following an anchor specification and form data, respectively.

➤ The history object allows for navigation through the current session's URL history list.

➤ history.back() and history.forward() move the user back or forward one URL in the history list.

➤ history.go(integer) moves to the URL that is integer places away from the current URL; negative integers move backward (earlier) in the list from the current URL, and positive integers move forward (later in the list).

➤ history.go("substring") moves to the newest URL in the history list that contains "substring" somewhere within it.

➤ The history.go() method does not work reliably in Internet Explorer 3.0, but it might be corrected in version 4.0.

Chapter 12

The Document Shuffle

In This Chapter

➤ This is a document

➤ Colorful changes

➤ Objects of objects—links and anchors

➤ Output is good

➤ Hello, good-bye: interactive events

At various times throughout these chapters, the terms "Web page" and "document" are used somewhat interchangeably. At least, I've never made clear if there is any distinction between the two. In this spin 'round the chapter-o-wheel, you're going to look at documents. More specifically, you're going to learn how you can fiddle with documents using JavaScript.

This, then, is the second chapter in which you examine JavaScript practices that interact with the Web page. Previously, you saw how to affect window elements (by opening new windows and creating message boxes, for example). Now you'll define what a document is and learn how to manipulate it. And if there's time, I'll also explain how to make no-fail chicken soup from scratch.

Document Defined

In Web parlance, a *document* is the file of HTML codes that describe a given page. A *page* is what appears within the browser window.

A typical HTML document contains a variety of characteristics other than the content of the page itself. These include a background image (often called a background "texture"), background color, foreground color, and the colors of hypertext links. In traditional HTML, these traits are all defined as attributes of the <BODY> tag.

Like the Web browser's window, the document object is also a built-in object of JavaScript. It has its own set of properties and methods with which you can influence various aspects of the current document. Like your previous tours of duty, this chapter takes you through the properties and methods of the document object and shows you how to use them in everyday life.

Welcome to the Property

The document object has a whole gaggle of properties associated with it. Most of these properties mimic characteristics that may have been defined in HTML tags. But it's far from redundant mimicry; allowing you to access the properties via JavaScript opens up the possibility of changing a document's original characteristics, if you want.

The first property examples that follow illustrate this concept.

bgColor and fgColor

Two of the most basic characteristics of a document are its colors. A document has two main colors: a background color and a foreground color. The background color defines the color of the "page" itself, while the foreground color defines the color of the text that appears on the page.

In documents, colors are specified in what is known as a hexadecimal triplet. Each color specification actually contains three specifications: red, blue, and green. Thus, you define the background color, for instance, by specifying how much red, blue, and green to mix together to yield the final color. Each color will have a value from 0 to 255, 0 being a complete lack of the color, and 255 being 100 percent of the color.

Okay, that explains the "triplet" part of "hexadecimal triplet." Now let's explain the "hexademical" part. You see, JavaScript doesn't like "normal" numbers, such as 255. It prefers a different numbering system known as hexadecimal. The system we humans commonly use is known as decimal. Many computer programs can convert decimal numbers to hexadecimal for you, but for a brief tutorial on how to do that, see the "I'm a Human Calculator" sidebar on the next page.

The value of document.bgColor is the hexadecimal triplet that defines the current page's background color. A possible value would be "000000," or pure black. Note that the long hexadecimal number is, in fact, three 2-digit hexadecimal numbers in a row. The leftmost two digits represent the Red value, the second two represent Green, and the rightmost two represent Blue. Another possible value would be "FFFFFF," which is pure white. Likewise, "FF0000" would be pure red. You can, in turn, alter the current background color by assigning a new hexadecimal triplet to document.bgColor. For example, regardless of what the current page's background color is, this JavaScript assignment

```
document.bgColor = "#00FF00"
```

changes the background to pure green. Note the hash mark (#) in the above assignment. It is traditional to place the hash mark in front of a hexadecimal number. If you leave it out of the assignment, it will still work. But note that if you retrieve the value of document.bgColor, it will contain a hash mark preceding the hexadecimal triplet regardless of whether you included it or not.

Along these same lines, document.fgColor will contain the hexadecimal triplet that represents the text color. And, similarly, assigning a new value to this property will change the text color.

Manipulating all of these possible combinations is a pain. Although this is the only way to fine-tune the exact color you will use, JavaScript does provide a shortcut. Instead of the hexadecimal triplet, you can assign a string literal specifying one of JavaScript's built-in color names. JavaScript has a long list of predefined colors, such as "aliceblue" and "crimson" and "palegreen." (See Appendix A at the end of this book for the full list.) Therefore, instead of using an assignment such as this:

```
document.bgColor="#000000"
```

you can write this:

```
document.bgColor="black"
```

I'm a Human Calculator

Hexadecimal is a base-16 numbering system, which contains the base values 0–F. That is, beyond 9 comes A, B, C, D, E, and F. Your common decimal system uses base-10 numbering, which only has the base values 0–9. Converting a decimal number, which you're used to, to a hexadecimal number, requires some addition and multiplication.

In this chapter, you're only considering 2-digit hexadecimal numbers that represent red, green, or blue values (although in decimal, these same values would be 3 digits long because decimal has fewer possible values for one digit to hold). To convert a hexadecimal number to decimal, then, use the following formula:

```
(lefthand hexadecimal digit * 16) + (righthand hexadecimal digit)
Note that a hex. digit of A = 10, B = 11, etc., to F = 15
```

What?? To put it to work, consider the hexadecimal value 05:

```
(0 * 16) + (5) = decimal value of 5
```

Okay, that one was easy. So now consider the hexadecimal value 1A:

```
(1 * 16) + (10) = decimal value of 26
```

For another example, use hexadecimal value C5:

```
(12 * 16) + (5) = 197
```

Finally, here's the maximum 2-digit hex value of FF:

```
(15 * 16) + (15) = 255
```

This should give you enough knowledge to guess-timate hex values for the color specification; from there, you can fiddle with the exact values to create the exact color you're looking for.

More Colors: alinkColor, vlinkColor, and linkColor

You can specify three other colors in a document. Each of these properties functions the same way as the previous two—they simply affect the color of different characteristics of the page.

alinkColor	Defines the color of an "activated" link. An activated link is a link that has been clicked, but for which the mouse button has yet to be released.

vlinkColor	Defines the color of a link that has already been visited.
linkColor	Defines the color of a link that has not yet been visited and is not currently being clicked.

You can use each of the above in the standard ways for object properties: you can either retrieve the value from or assign a new value to document.alinkColor, document.vlinkColor, and document.linkColor. If you've coded HTML before, you might have noticed that you can set these same colors in standard HTML tags. So why bother with JavaScript? Because by using JavaScript, you can change the colors in a given page at any time you want—on the fly—perhaps as a result of certain user events. In HTML, you can define the colors only once for the life of the page.

The title Property

The property document.title holds the value of the title of the document as defined in the HTML tags <TITLE> and </TITLE>. The title is what appears in the browser window's upper border and in the bookmark list if the page is bookmarked by a user. The title does not actually appear within the content of the page itself.

As usual, you can retrieve the document's title from this property, or you can assign a new title to the document via this property.

The anchors Property

An anchor is a spot in a page that has been marked with a "name" within the HTML code. Links can then point to anchors to send a user to specific locations within a single page. Anchors are defined in HTML with the <A NAME=> tag.

The document.anchors property is an array (that is, an object in and of itself) that contains the value of each anchor on the page, in the order in which they were defined in the HTML code. Suppose your page has five anchors defined within it. In that case, there are five properties in the object document.anchors:

```
document.anchors[0]
document.anchors[1]
...etc...
document.anchors[5]
```

Each of the above contains the name of the anchor corresponding to the order in which it was defined. So if you named and defined your anchors in the order Monday, Tuesday, Wednesday, Thursday, Friday, those would be the values contained in document.anchors[0] to document.anchors[5], respectively.

125

You may use the property length, as in document.anchors.length to retrieve the total number of anchors defined.

Note that you would not use an assignment to document.anchors to bring the user to an anchor within the document. That could be done several ways in JavaScript. Remember that an anchor is specified in an URL with a hash mark following the pathname. Thus, you could assign the entire URL with a hash mark and desired anchor name to document.URL.

The links Property

In the same spirit as the anchors property, you have the links property. Most pages contain several link definitions throughout the HTML code, as created by the <A HREF=> tag.

document.links is another object array that contains each of the links specified in the current page. As with document.anchors, there are as many properties of document.links as there are links in the page, as indicated here:

```
document.links[0]
document.links[1]
...etc...
```

You can retrieve the total number of links in the document using the property document.links.length. As usual, you can change the value of a particular link by assigning a new string to one of the above properties, as in

```
document.links[2] = "http://www.yahoo.com"
```

Imagine a scenario where this reassignment may be useful. Say you have a link in the page that (on-screen) reads "Click here to continue." Perhaps, though, you would like that link to take some users to one URL and take other users to a different URL, depending on some other condition, such as whether they've purchased more than a certain quantity of mugs.

Image Maps and Hyperlinks

More advanced readers may be wondering how image maps fold into the mix. An image map is an image with subregions defined as hyperlinks. The answer is quite easy: each area within the image map is simply a hyperlink and thus part of the document.links[] array. So if the third hyperlink on a page is an area region of an image map, it can be referred to as document.links[2] (remember that the first hyperlink is element 0 of the array).

To do so, you can use an if...else statement to evaluate the user's mug purchase, and on each condition, you can assign a different URL specification to the above link. This would be transparent to the user. He would simply click the link labeled "Click here to continue," and he'd be taken to an appropriate page as determined by your JavaScript program.

Some Miscellaneous Properties

A few properties aren't of vital consequence and don't require a particularly detailed explanation. Each is relatively straightforward and may not find tremendous usage in your JavaScript programs. However, they're nice to know, especially when you get into those typical JavaScript arguments with friends and colleagues.

The lastModified Property

This property simply contains a string value reflecting the date that the document was last modified. A function might use this property, for instance, to communicate to the user how "fresh" the current page is, in case some of its information may potentially become outdated.

The referrer Property

This property contains the URL of the page that led to the current page. That is, if the user reached the current page via a link from another page, this property contains the URL of the page that linked him here. You might consider using this property to track statistics about which sites users are jumping to yours from.

The URL Property

This last property allows you to change which document is displayed in the current browser window. Executing a statement such as this

```
document.URL="nextpage.html"
```

will immediately load *nextpage.html* into the current window.

Forms

As with anchors and links, the document object contains an array of properties for each form defined in the document. However, there's more to forms than simply a value (as was the case for anchors and links). Therefore, you will learn about forms in depth in their own chapter, Chapter 13.

Images

New to JavaScript 1.1, the document object now contains an array property that refers to each image in the current page. This array and its related Image object allow for a variety of new possibilities; that is the detailed subject of Chapter 16.

Applets

Also newly added to JavaScript 1.1 is the applets array and Applet object of the document object. With the ability to reference Java applets in the current page, you can communicate between JavaScript and Java applets. In unifying this partnership between siblings, I point you toward Chapter 25 for a full discussion on using the applets array and the Applet object.

Methods to This Madness

In fact, there are five methods to this madness called the document object. The methods of the document object are, fortunately, relatively straightforward and useful.

The clear() Method

It shouldn't take the Amazing Kreskin to deduce the function of the document.clear() method. Once called, it clears the contents of the current window. Note that this doesn't affect the actual contents of the document as defined in the HTML tags. Nor does the clear() method clear any variable values or anything else. It is purely cosmetic: It merely clears the display window. Of course, you may not want to clear the window unless you plan to display further text in it. Fortunately, there are two methods for doing just that.

write() and writeln()

You can use both of these methods to output HTML to the current window. As the parameter to either method, you pass on a string that contains the HTML code that contains what you want sent to the window.

For example, suppose you want the string "Thank you for ordering" written in the window in large type. The HTML <H1> and </H1> tags are one way to generate text in a large font size. Therefore, you could simply use this method call:

```
document.write ("<H1>Thank you for ordering!</H1>")
```

Alternatively, you might have constructed a string somewhere else in your JavaScript code and assigned that to a variable, such as phrase. In this case, you can simply pass the variable phrase as the parameter to the method call, like this:

```
document.write (phrase)
```

The difference between write() and writeln() is that the writeln() appends a newline character to the end of the output. A newline character is basically like a carriage return. However, keep in mind that these methods output their parameters as HTML. And remember that HTML ignores newline characters when it comes to outputting to the screen.

What does the above mean? It means that HTML does not insert line breaks in screen output unless you specify a line break using either <BR> or <P> tags. Any "natural" line breaks in your HTML code, such as those created when you hit return, are ignored. The only time this is not true (when carriage returns are honored) is for text that resides between <PRE> and </PRE> tags. Those tags define a section of text that is "preformatted," and it appears on-screen in the browser's defined monospace font—a font in which all characters are of equal width (it's often Courier).

Thus, in most cases, there will be no effective difference between the write() and writeln() methods unless your string parameter contains HTML code that places the output within <PRE> and </PRE> tags.

Bonus Events

It so happens that the document object also has two relevant event triggers worth mentioning: onLoad and onUnload.

The onLoad Event

You can use this event trigger to launch a particular JavaScript program or function upon the completion of initially loading the document. Perhaps you coded a JavaScript function that displays an alert message to the user before he even begins reading the page. The onLoad event would be useful for this purpose.

You include the event as an attribute of the document's <BODY> tag, as in:

```
<BODY onLoad="welcome()">
```

Check This Out...

Watch Your HEAD The <BODY> tag occurs very early on in the HTML document. This highlights the need to define your functions as early in the document as possible—specifically, within the <HEAD> </HEAD> section, which is one of the only places prior to the <BODY> tag that you have an opportunity to do so.

129

In this example, the onLoad event handler is set to call the function welcome( ), which performs some feat of programming, such as displaying an alert window that requires the user to read an important disclaimer before he begins looking at the page. (Users will likely find this very annoying, but you could program it.)

The onUnload Event

This event is triggered when the user "unloads" or exits the document. It would also be defined as an attribute of the <BODY> tag. You might, for example, use this to show a message to the user after he chooses to leave your page, such as by calling a function that writes the text "You come back now, you hear?" into the document window.

```
<BODY onLoad="welcome()" onUnload="bye()">
```

As it stands, the only major aspect of JavaScript remaining to be covered is the forms objects (although there are a few more advanced topics lying in wait beyond the forms chapter). And wouldn't you know, I have it covered—in the next chapter in fact. So don't stop reading here. This is like the last 50 steps in an 8K run. Just a few more properties...maybe a method or two...you're almost there!

The Least You Need to Know

➤ The document is the HTML file that loads as a Web page in the browser window.

➤ JavaScript contains a document object, which possesses a number of properties through which you can read or modify characteristics of the current document.

➤ You can use document.bgColor and document.fgColor to alter the colors of the background or foreground text, respectively. Colors are defined in hexadecimal RGB values.

➤ document.anchors and document.links are arrays that contain the values of a document's defined anchors or links, respectively. For example, document.link[2] refers to the third link defined in the document (remember, the first link is link[0]).

➤ You can use the method document.write("string") to output HTML tagged text to the current window.

➤ Use the event triggers onLoad and onUnload to watch for users opening or exiting your page. Both are defined as attributes in the <BODY> tag.

Chapter 13

Fiddling with Forms and Emulating Events

In This Chapter
➤ Forming a form
➤ The elements of a form
➤ "This" object
➤ Let your JavaScript do the clicking: event emulation

Welcome to the end of this semester's JavaScript course. You'll close out the day with some fun stuff—just like the last day of class in grade school, when you cracked the windows, broke out the Yahtzee, and ate pizza on the same desk you took math quizzes on all year. Actually, I'm just fooling. This chapter is about form objects and emulating events, neither of which hold a candle to pizza and Yahtzee.

Behind the Form

The form is a staple of virtually any page that interacts with the user. Forms can take the "form" of several incarnations, from buttons to check boxes to blank text entry boxes. You will probably want to create JavaScript functions that in some way interpret the data produced by these forms.

Because of our close examination of forms in this chapter, you'd better break tradition and refresh yourself with HTML form tags.

You define a form in HTML with the tag <FORM>. This tag may contain several possible attributes, as listed here:

Attribute	Description
METHOD=get or post	Indicates how to submit form data. (get is the default, and it's the usual method.)
ACTION=URL	Indicates where to submit form data.
TARGET=*name of window*	Indicates which window will display responses to the form. (You will usually leave this attribute out unless you want responses to be generated in a new window.)
onSubmit="JavaScript code"	Designates the event handler for a submit event.
onReset="JavaScript code"	Designates the event handler for a reset event. (This event handler is new in JavaScript 1.1.)

You should keep in mind the following information about forms:

➤ Forms are made up of elements (as they are known in HTML-speak), which the user uses to indicate responses. Form elements include generic buttons, radio buttons, check boxes, text entries, and Submit and Reset buttons. A form can have any number of these elements in it.

➤ An element is defined with the <INPUT> tag, which also takes a series of attributes that define the form element. I can't go into detail for each element, but as a refresher, a typical definition for a button element might look like this:

```
<INPUT TYPE="button" name="ad" value="Click to see our Ad"
onClick="showad()">
```

Any elements defined within one set of <FORM> </FORM> tags are considered to be part of one form. Just as there can be any number of elements within one form, there can be any number of forms within one page.

➤ Within the context of JavaScript, each form element is also a JavaScript object. Therefore, each check box, text input area, and so forth has its own set of properties. Although referenced in more detail in Appendix A, "JavaScript: The Complete Overview," the properties of these objects are typically parallel to the HTML attributes of the element.

➤ There are also properties that contain status information about the element; for instance, the checkbox object contains the property "checked," which contains the current logical status of the check box element.

Having established all this, let's begin looking at how the forms object works within JavaScript.

Element and Object

To avoid confusion throughout this chapter, let's clear up the difference between the terms "element" and "object." A form element, such as a check box, is an "element" when you are speaking from an HTML perspective. However, the same check box is an object when you are speaking from a JavaScript perspective. At times, I may seem to use these terms interchangeably because they do ultimately refer to the same "thing." But when I say "element," I'm looking at it from an HTML point of view, and when I say "object," I'm considering it from a JavaScript point of view.

Object of Form

The previous chapter briefly mentioned that forms was a property of document. This is true, but furthermore, document.forms is an object itself. Each form within the document is one property of document.forms. This is important, so let's take this concept again—slowly.

Remember that a form is defined by anything between one set of <FORM> tags:

```
<FORM>
form element definitions
</FORM>
```

Thus, document.forms[0] refers to the first form defined in the document. Likewise, document.forms[1] refers to the second form; that is, any form elements defined within a second set of <FORM> </FORM> tags somewhere else in the document.

Now each form in a document is also an object. Therefore, document.forms[0] is an object whose properties are each an element of that form. The elements are referred to in the manner document.forms[x].elements[y], where x is the form in question, and y is the element within that form.

Imagine that your HTML document contains the following lines:

```
<FORM name=someform>
<INPUT TYPE="button" name="ad" value="Click for Ad" onClick="showad()">
<INPUT TYPE="checkbox" name="married">Are you married?
</FORM>
```

This form contains two elements: a button and a check box. If this is the first form defined in your document, you can refer to its parts in the following manner:

➤ document.forms[0].elements[0] would contain the definition for the button element.

➤ document.forms[0].elements[1] would contain the definition for the check box element.

Alternatively, you can refer to each form element by its name if it is defined in the <INPUT> tag. You can also refer to each form by its name if it is defined in the <FORM> tag. If so, the following statements would be true:

➤ document.someform.ad would contain the button element.

➤ document.someform.married would contain the check box element.

What do I mean when I say, "would contain the definition for the button element?" It means that the value of document.forms[0].elements[0] in this example would be the following string:

```
"<INPUT TYPE="button" name="ad" value="Click for Ad" onClick="showad()">".
```

Shortly, you'll see how to refer to specific portions of each element, so you don't have to use its entire definition.

Properties of Forms

The forms object, like every other object, has a set of built-in properties. Basically, these simply help you to retrieve or modify the main attributes of the form. The following subsections give you all the details.

The action Property

This property allows you to retrieve or alter the value of the action attribute of the form in question. For example, suppose you want to submit the form data to one URL if the user has bought more than a certain number of mugs, or to another URL if he purchased fewer. You might use the classic if...else statement to change the property documents.forms[0].action. This could take place in a function called buymugs(mugs), which accepts the parameter of how many mugs were bought. The function would be called as an event handler from the event trigger onSubmit, an attribute of <FORM>.

Let's play out the code for this scenario:

```
<SCRIPT language="JavaScript">
function buymugs (mugs)
{
if (mugs>=10)
{ documents.forms[0].action = "http://invoice1.htm" }
else
{ document.forms[0].action = "http://invoice2.htm" }
}

<FORM method=get onSubmit="buymugs(this.quantity.value)">
<INPUT TYPE="text" name="quantity" ROWS=1 COLUMNS=3>Quantity of order
</FORM>
```

Looking first at the HTML code, you define a form that contains one element: a text entry box that is three spaces wide. This text entry box is given the reference name "quantity." The FORM definition specifies an onSubmit event handler. It calls the function buymugs() with the parameter this.quantity.value. *this* refers to this whole object (the form) from which you are interested in the property "quantity," which is the specific element within the form named quantity. value is a property of the text entry object, which contains the data the user enters.

The function itself is much the same as previous functions you coded in these chapters. It simply uses an if...else statement to determine a condition and to modify the ACTION= attribute of the first form in your document accordingly.

The method Property

Just like the action property, the method property refers to the METHOD= attribute of the FORM definition. (Don't confuse this property name with the JavaScript function known as a "method"; they are unrelated.) You can similarly use this to change the METHOD of a particular form from GET to POST, or vice versa. A function exactly like the one used above would do the trick:

```
documents.forms[0].method = "get"
```

135

The target Property

This property enables you to retrieve or modify the TARGET= attribute of the FORM. You use it just like the method and action properties.

Elements, Up Close and Personal

I've touched on the fact that the array (or object) elements point to each particular element within a given form. Good. Then recall again the example in the form you defined earlier in this chapter: document.forms[0].elements[0] would contain the definition for the button element. Now the button element in question here also contains several properties of its own. So consider the button element definition again:

```
<INPUT TYPE="button" name="ad" value="Click for Ad" onClick="showad()">
```

The button has a name, which in this case is ad. Thus, you can retrieve or modify its name in JavaScript with a reference like this:

```
document.forms[0].elements[0].name
```

You might assign the value of the preceding line to a new variable, or you might assign a new string to the line. Each particular form element has its own slightly different set of built-in properties. The button object contains a name property, as you've just seen, as well as a value property. In the case of the button, the value property (as well as the value HTML attribute) is the text that appears on the button itself on-screen. Thus, you can also refer to this value:

```
document.forms[0].elements[0].value
```

The checkbox Element

Because each form element serves a slightly different purpose, each object has a slightly different set of built-in properties. Let's consider the checkbox element, which could be defined in this way:

```
<INPUT TYPE="checkbox" name="marstat"
onClick="married(this.marstat.value)">Married?
```

Imagine that the preceding is the second element of the same form that contains the previous button, thus making it documents.forms[0].elements[1]. The name property of this checkbox object works the same way as the name property of the button object.

The checkbox object also contains two unique properties: checked and defaultChecked. These are logical values that, when assigned a true or false value, determine the starting state of the check box (before the user gets his hands on it). Sometimes, you might want a check box to begin in a checked state. You can make it so either by changing the HTML definition of the element or by assigning a true value, as in the following:

```
documents.forms[0].elements[1].checked = true.
```

Note that the value property works differently for the checkbox than for the button. In the preceding checkbox, the property documents.forms[0].elements[1].value is a Boolean that contains the state of the check box. This is what you would refer to if you were processing this form.

In the "Built-In Objects" section of Appendix A, you can find details about the properties available for each particular form element object. Here, you looked at only the button and check box elements.

A New Type of Property

In JavaScript 1.1, the type property has been added to each form element object. Simply, the type property reflects the "type" of form element, as defined in the HTML <INPUT TYPE="elementtype"> tag or the <SELECT> <SELECT MULTIPLE> and <AREA> tags, in the cases of selection boxes or image map areas.

For instance, imagine that your HTML document contained the following form element definition:

```
<form name=formica>
<input type="text" size="3" name="age">
</form>
```

The following JavaScript 1.1 code would yield the value "text":

```
formtype = document.formica.age.type
```

137

Radio Button Matters

In the case of a radio button, the radio button set is an array containing each individual button. For instance, consider this HTML code:

```
<form name=formica>
<input type="radio" checked name="sex" value="m">Male<br>
<input type="radio" name="sex" value="f">Female<br>
</form>
```

To access the type property of the "male" radio button, you use this:

```
formtype = document.formica.sex[0].type
```

More generally, to access any property of the radio button set, use this:

```
variable = document.formica.sex[buttonidx].propertyName
```

The this Object

One of the most important constructions with which you refer to form elements is the this construction. By now, you've seen it pop up several times. Take an official look at it now.

Clearly, a construction such as document.forms[0].elements[1].value is somewhat long and unwieldy. However, when you are referring to form elements from within a particular form definition, you don't have to use such a long construction.

If you are between <FORM> </FORM> tags, the form to which you are referring is a given: this form. Therefore, document.forms[x] can be assumed.

Secondly, you can refer to individual form elements by their name, instead of by elements[y], which makes more sense to the human programmer. Thus, the first element—a button—in your continuing form example from above, could be called elements[0], or it could be called ad. (Recall that you named it ad with the NAME= attribute.)

Therefore, when you refer to a form from within its definition (which you do anytime you define an event handler for the form or element), you can use the simpler construction this.elementname.property. You've seen this in practice a few times. Here's an example that combines a couple of your previous this uses:

```
<FORM onSubmit="evalform(this.email.value)">
<INPUT NAME=email TYPE="text" ROWS=1 SIZE="20">Enter your email
<INPUT NAME="marstat" TYPE="checkbox"
_onClick="married(this.marstat.value)">Married?
```

```
<INPUT NAME=submit TYPE="submit">
<INPUT NAME=reset TYPE="reset">
</FORM>
```

Two event handlers are defined in the preceding form. One handles the onSubmit event and passes to its function the parameter this.email.value. That, then, would be the data entered (value) into the form element email (the text box defined in the second line of the example).

The second event handler occurs in the onClick event of the check box element. It passes to its function the parameter this.marstat.value, which would contain the Boolean state of the check box named marstat.

> **When in Doubt, Be Specific**
> I have found some inconsistencies in the way JavaScript handles this in practice versus how it claims that it should be handled. The simplest solution to any strange errors or difficulties with this is simply to replace the use of this with document.forms[x].

Keep in mind, though, that this works only from within the form definition. If you want to refer to a form other than the one currently being defined, you'll need to use the full document.forms[x].elements[y] construction. That's the only way to explicitly specify which form or element you are talking about to JavaScript. The this construction is basically a shortcut for those instances when it can be assumed which form you're talking about.

The Faked Event

Remember that an "event" usually occurs when a user clicks something. There are a variety of possible events, depending on what the user clicks. In addition, it is possible to emulate a click in JavaScript.

Meaning…? If you have a check box element, you could use JavaScript code to instigate a click on it yourself instead of waiting for the user to click it manually. Why would you want to do this? I don't know. Just kidding…. Actually there are a couple of possible reasons:

> ➤ **To guide the user.** Perhaps on your particular page, you would like to show the user what to do—sort of like a "help" procedure. This way, you can use JavaScript to go around clicking elements as an example for the user's eyes.

> ➤ **To straighten up necessarily related elements.** I'll delve into this possibility below.

Suppose you have the following two elements in your form: a check box that poses the question, "Do you like spicy foods?" and a radio button set that asks the user to choose which spicy food is his favorite. The radio buttons offer three choices: "Mexican," "Indian," and "I said I didn't like spicy foods."

139

Suppose the user deselects the latter check box (which indicates a lack of enthusiasm for spicy foods). In that case, it would be nonsensical for the user to then check one of the regional food types in the radio button set. So how can you prevent the user from saying he doesn't like spicy foods but that his favorite spicy food is Indian?

Using event emulation! (Boy, you knew that was coming, I hope.) This would be the programming logic:

> If the user clicks the radio button, check the status of the check box.

> If the check box is unchecked, emulate a click event to select "I said I didn't like spicy foods" in the radio button.

This way, no matter what the user tries to select in the radio buttons, his selection will be overridden if it conflicts with a previous selection.

You will code the above logic shortly. But first let's see how to emulate an event.

It's All in the Method

Event emulators are methods of the form element objects. Each of the form element objects has a click() method. Simply call this method for the object in question, and it will be clicked. Therefore, to click a check box, you might use the call

```
document.forms[0].checkboxname.click()
```

Important note: A click() method does not initiate an event trigger. Only a "real" click on the check box would trigger the onClick event handler, if defined. If you want to emulate a click and trigger the appropriate event call, simply call the proposed event handler manually after the click() method. For example, let's say your onClick event handler is defined as "married(this.checkbox.value)". If you want to emulate a click and call the event handler, simply use the following JavaScript statements:

```
document.forms[0].checkboxname.click() ;
married(this.value)
```

All you did was call the event handler explicitly following the emulated click because it would not have been triggered by the onClick definition.

Before you run through the example code for the "spicy food" logic, remind yourself how radio buttons work. A radio button is basically a multiple-choice question, from which the user can select only one of the proposed choices. What makes the radio button slightly different from other form elements is that it may contain several subelements; that is, the radio button named "spicetype" could have three subelements, each representing a choice: Mexican, Indian, or Don't like.

The following is the HTML code wherein you define the check box and radio buttons for the spicy foods example.

```
<FORM>
<INPUT NAME="spicy" TYPE="checkbox">Do you like spicy foods?<p>
Please select which spicy food is your favorite:
<INPUT NAME="spicetype" TYPE="radio" value="mexican"
onClick="checkspicy(document.forms[0].spicy.checked)">Mexican
<INPUT NAME="spicetype" TYPE="radio" value="indian"
onClick="checkspicy(document.forms[0].spicy.checked)">Indian
<INPUT NAME="spicetype" TYPE="radio" value="notype"
onClick="checkspicy(document.forms[0].spicy.checked)"> I said I don't like _spicy
foods!
</FORM>
```

Note how each part of the radio button is defined to the same NAME= attribute. This is important. Also, see how each radio button definition contains the same onClick event handler? As a result, anytime a user makes a choice from the radio button, the verification function checkspicy(document.forms[0].spicy.checked) will be called. This is the heart of the logic.

The function's role will be to look at the Boolean (logical) state of the check box named "spicy" (document.forms[0].spicy.value) and either allow the user's radio button selection to remain or force a different selection. You would force a different selection under two conditions:

➤ The user has left spicy unchecked, in which case he must select "I said I don't like spicy foods!" from the radio button.

➤ The user has checked spicy, in which case he cannot select "I said I don't like spicy foods!" from the radio button. Because one of the radio buttons must be selected, in this case, you'd have to select one of the others by default. So you choose Mexican simply because it's first on the list.

Here is the function code in JavaScript:

```
<SCRIPT language="JavaScript">
function checkspicy (likes)
{
if (likes == true)
{ if (document.forms[0].spicetype[2].checked == true)
{ document.forms[0].spicetype[0].click() } }
else
{ if (document.forms[0].spicetype[2].checked == false)
```

```
    { document.forms[0].spicetype[2].click() } }
  }
</SCRIPT>
```

Use the construction spicetype[x] to refer to an individual choice x within the radio button set. Here, first consider whether spicy is checked true. If so, look to see if the last radio button choice (button number 2 because they start counting from 0) is selected. If so, it should not be (because the user indicated that he does like spicy foods). Therefore, you emulate a click event to check "Mexican" (radio button choice 0).

If the user has indicated a distaste for spicy foods, look at the else clause above and determine if the final radio button choice has been selected. If not, emulate a click event to select it because it must be selected in this case.

The reset() method

Here's another addition to JavaScript 1.1 that you can now call:

```
document.forms[x].reset() or document.formname.reset()
```

This emulates a reset event for the form, which would clear the data currently input into the form. Although emulating actions via methods does not usually trigger event handlers, the reset() method is an exception: It does generate a reset event, which is handled by the event handler defined in <FORM onReset="*JavaScript code or function*">.

The Least You Need to Know

➤ The elements of a form are an array of properties of the form object. The object document.forms[x] contains the properties document.forms[x].elements[y], where y is each element defined within a single set of <FORM> tags.

➤ You can also refer to elements[y] by the name of the element as defined in the NAME= attribute of the HTML <INPUT> tag that defines that element.

➤ Each form element is an object with its own properties. For example, the property of the check box element that contains the current Boolean state of the check box is called checked and would be referred to as document.forms[x].elements[y].checked or document.forms[x].checkboxname.checked.

➤ this.property can be used to refer to the current form being defined.

➤ Form elements can emulate clicking themselves by using the method document.forms[x].elementname.click().

➤ Emulating an event does not trigger any event handler specified for that event; only "real" events can be triggers. However, the formname.reset() method is an exception: It does trigger the onReset event handler.

Navigating with Navigator

Back when I was a nervous youth, our board of education, possibly motivated by revenge, felt that it was necessary to provide three strata of physical education classes. Each strata was oriented towards a different Phys. Ed. capacity: budding professional, middling-but-mobile, and victim. Several weeks into the semester, we'd be run through a battery of quasi-legal "tests," several of which probably violated the Geneva Convention. Result cards in hand, we'd stand in queue as the gym instructor (officially, "herr gym instructor") looked us over and pointed us toward a collection point for one of the three strata.

Fortunately, those extended years of trauma now yield a poignant analogy: the Navigator Object, which identifies the Web browser being used to load the Web page, can be used to tailor a Web site toward a particular browser. It enables you to detect the presence of certain plug-ins or to redirect the user to new pages created for his browser's capabilities.

Identity, Please

Built into JavaScript 1.0 and enhanced in JavaScript 1.1, the Navigator Object reports several variants on the identity and capability of the browser being used to load the current page. By cleverly using this information, you can tailor the behavior of a Web page. For example, you can display a Shockwave plug-in if a Shockwave plug-in is installed, or you can send the visitor to a page designed for Microsoft Internet Explorer 3.0 if that's his browser.

What's in a Name?

Understanding and using the Navigator Object is fairly simple. So there's no point in "prevaricating around the bush." Let's begin!

Under both JavaScript 1.0 and JavaScript 1.1, the Navigator Object supports the properties described in the following sections.

appCodename

The "codename" is the internal name by which the Web browser identifies itself. Netscape Navigator, for instance, identifies itself as *Mozilla*. (Curiously, Microsoft Internet Explorer 3.0 also identifies itself as *Mozilla*; this is a compatibility trick, which allows some pages and servers to offer the same content to Internet Explorer as it would to Netscape Navigator.)

Thus, the JavaScript expression

```
navigator.appCodename
```

will yield "Mozilla" if the visitor is using either Netscape Navigator or Microsoft Internet Explorer.

appName

As opposed to the browser's internal identification, this property reflects the external name of the browser. Thus, this expression

```
navigator.appName
```

yields "Netscape" when using Netscape Navigator, or yields "Microsoft Internet Explorer" when using said browser. You'll use this property later to determine which browser a visitor is using and to redirect him to a suitable page.

Mozilla?

"Mozilla" is sort of a joke—one that Netscape has encouraged to live on. For several years in history, when Netscape Navigator was first released, it was not called "Navigator." In fact, it was called simply "Netscape," which later became the name of the company. *Actually*, Netscape was called "Mozilla." Huh?? In written form, the first versions of Netscape were written as "Mozilla," but pronounced "Netscape." This, apparently, was the result of some strange sense of humor on the developers' part. However, as Netscape morphed into a rising corporate star and their browser began to reach the limelight, they realized that spelling "Mozilla" and pronouncing "Netscape" was a confusing marketing scheme (and it's also not that funny). Hence, Mozilla was dropped in favor of the more sober "Navigator."

appVersion

This property yields the version number and platform of the browser. In some cases, such as with Internet Explorer, it also yields the Netscape version with which it is compatible. Thus, if the user is using the 32-bit Netscape Navigator 3.01 under Windows 95, this expression

```
navigator.appVersion
```

yields "3.01 (Win95; I)." And if the user is using Microsoft Internet Explorer 3.01 under Windows 95, the above yields "2.0 (compatible; MSIE 3.01; Windows 95)." This is Internet Explorer's way of saying "I'm just like Netscape 2, but I'm actually MSIE 3.01."

userAgent

Technically, the userAgent is what the browser sends to the Web server as a form of identity. For our purposes, though, this property is basically a concatenation of appCodename and appVersion. This certainly doesn't make it useless; if you want to parse the browser identity for some reference, you can use the userAgent property to get an all-in-one string. For instance, a visitor using 32-bit Netscape Navigator 3.01 under Windows 95 would generate a value of "Mozilla/3.01 (Win95; I)" if you checked the value of navigator.userAgent.

Who Goes Where?

Conceptually, making use of the above properties of the Navigator Object is easy. For instance, imagine that your site contains two home pages, one designed for Netscape

145

users and one for Internet Explorer users. You could create a "false" home page, which actually contains JavaScript that determines the visitor's browser. It then automatically loads the correct page.

Another idea: Because JavaScript 1.1 is currently supported only in Netscape Navigator 3.0, you could test for that browser. If present, you proceed with executing certain JavaScript 1.1-specific functions (such as using an array or replacing images with the Image Object). If Navigator 3.0 is not present, you stick to only JavaScript 1.0 code and forego the added capabilities of 1.1. At the least, this allows users of both types of browsers to receive some functionality from the page.

Speaking of JavaScript 1.1, three additions to the Navigator Object are introduced in that version, which further expand your ability to sniff out features of the user's browser.

javaEnabled()

This method returns a value of true if the user's browser has Java capabilities enabled; otherwise it returns false. Using an expression such as this

```
if ( navigator.javaEnabled() ) { … } else { … }
```

you can execute a Java applet only if the user has Java enabled. Alternatively, if Java is disabled, perhaps you could write a message alerting the user to enable Java to fully experience this page.

plugins Array

This array, named plugins, contains information on each plug-in installed for the browser (such as Shockwave, Quicktime, and so on). In using it most simply, you can check for the presence of an installed plug-in as shown here:

```
isplugin = navigator.plugins["Quicktime"]
if (isplugin)
 { document.writeln ("<EMBED SRC='jurassic.mov' HEIGHT=100 WIDTH=100>" }
else { document.writeln ("You cannot view the film preview without the Quicktime
plug-in.") }
```

Using the above code snippet, you can tailor the page's behavior to the presence or absence of a particular plug-in.

mimeTypes Object

Also a part of the Navigator Object, mimeTypes is an array containing each of the mime types configured for the user's browser. Mime types are types of files as configured either for plugins or for Helper Apps in the browser. For instance, a commonly configured mime type is "image/jpeg," which then calls a defined jpeg image viewer.

To see this in action, you could verify the existence of a configured image/jpeg mime type with this code:

```
if (navigator.mimeTypes["image/jpeg"])
  { some code which loads a jpeg image }
else { document.writeln ("You do not have jpeg image viewing configured.") }
```

He Went That-a-Way

Using some of the knowledge in this chapter, you can use the Navigator Object to instantly and automatically redirect a visitor to the page designed for his browser.

Imagine, for instance, that you're a very industrious sort. You've designed two versions of your home page: one with layout optimized for Netscape Navigator and one optimized for Microsoft Internet Explorer. For example, Internet Explorer 3.0 supports graphic backgrounds within table cells, but Navigator 3.0 does not. You've saved your two home pages as *nspage.html* and *msiepage.html*, respectively.

Thus, you now code the redirection page (saved as *home.html*). It is this page, home.html, that users will initially visit (having jumped there from a link at another site). From there, they'll automatically be taken to the "real" home page designed for their browser. The redirection page need not contain any content, only a small bit of JavaScript code. Logically, it's simple: determine whether the user is using Navigator or Internet Explorer, and then send him to the appropriate home page.

```
<html>
<head>
<title>Browser Redirection</title>
</head>
<body bgcolor="#FFFFFF">

<script>
if (navigator.appName.indexOf("Explorer")==-1)
  { url ="nspage.html" }
else { url = "msiepage.html" }
</script>
```

```
</body>
</html>
```

That's all! In this example, you merely check for the string "Explorer" anywhere in the appName property of the Navigator Object. If it's not present (–1), the user is not using Internet Explorer, and he is sent to the Netscape page (url = "nspage.html"). (Of course, he may not be using Navigator either, but that is your only alternative page.)

On the other hand, if the string "Explorer" *is* found within the appName property, the string indexOf() method returns its position (anything other than –1), and you know that the user is browsing with Internet Explorer. Thus, he is sent to *msiepage.html.*

Similarly, you can use any of the Navigator Object properties and methods discussed in this chapter to tailor the behavior of a Web page.

The Least You Need to Know

➤ The Navigator Object can help you identify the user's browser and which plug ins and mime types are installed for that browser.

➤ navigator.appCodename contains the internal code name of the browser ("Mozilla" for both Netscape Navigator and Microsoft Internet Explorer).

➤ navigator.appName contains a more accurate reflection of the browser name ("Netscape" or "Microsoft Internet Explorer").

➤ navigator.appVersion contains the version number of the browser and possibly the version number of Netscape with which the browser is compatible.

➤ navigator.userAgent contains the user agent header sent to the Web server. This is a string concatenation of the appCodename and appVersion.

➤ In JavaScript 1.1, the Navigator Object supports the method navigator.javaEnabled(), which returns true if the user has enabled Java support and returns false otherwise.

➤ Also new to JavaScript 1.1 is the plugins array, which contains data on each plug-in currently installed. For example, navigator.plugins["Quicktime"] returns true if the Quicktime plug-in is installed and returns false otherwise.

➤ The mimeTypes object in JavaScript 1.1 contains data on the configured mime types. For example, navigator.mimeTypes["image/jpeg"] returns true if the image/jpeg mime type is configured and returns false otherwise.

"Array" (A Ray) of Organization

Consider the file cabinet: Psychologically speaking, one can learn a great deal about a person by looking at the person's cabinet (if he even *has* one). Nonetheless, many can get by in life with a seemingly random pile of papers, documents, and old bills piled in a corner. Not so for the computer. In some ways, it's a crusty old man who wants things the way he wants them, darnit! Which means that data needs to be neatly ordered. The array is the JavaScript 1.1 object that enables you to keep your data organized.

Getting to Know Array

Like the file cabinet, an array is a set of sub-elements. It is a way of organizing data into groups. An array can contain any number of elements, and each element can be any type of data (including another array). We use arrays in real life every day without thinking twice about it: for instance, my "clothing array" consists of a pair of blue pants, a pair of black pants, a striped shirt, eight white socks, etc. My clothing array even consists of shoes, which itself is an array containing the elements sneakers, casuals, Birkenstocks, etc.

Conceptually speaking ("Oh daaarling, speak conceptually to me again!"), the array is not a new object to us in JavaScript-Land. This is because the array is merely an object, in the JavaScript sense. Recall that a JavaScript object is also a set of elements, be they properties or methods.

In the old days of JavaScript 1.0, we created arrays by creating new objects. This worked, but it required extra steps and was a hassle. In JavaScript 1.1, the new Array object allows us to create arrays quickly and easily, without any hassles.

Arrays in JavaScript are quite straightforward to implement. Imagine, for instance, that you have an array that has been named automodels. This array can contain any number of elements such as Toyota, Honda, Ford, and Lexus. (No product endorsements expressed or implied, although the author wouldn't refuse any free samples). Each element has an index number, such as 0, 1, 2, and so on, which marks its ordered position in the array. The syntax for describing an array is:

```
array[idx]=value
```

Thus, an array could be written as:

```
automodels[0]="Toyota"
automodels[1]="Honda"
automodels[2]="Ford"
```

...and so on.

In this respect, the array is like a filing cabinet whose contents are associated with index numbers. This allows you to easily access the data within the filing cabinet. Within a Web page (depending upon its application), you may code several arrays into your JavaScript programs, which contain data relevant to the function of the page.

For example, say you have a form that asks a series of questions of the user—first name, last name, age, address, phone number, and e-mail address. You could store each of these pieces of data in an array such as userinfo, which might look like this:

```
userinfo[0]="Henry"
userinfo[1]="Kissinger"
userinfo[2]=68
userinfo[3]="2001 Accent Ave."
userinfo[4]="(555) 976-9760"
userinfo[5]="kisser@oldstatesman.com"
```

That array could later be accessed in your JavaScript program for any number of purposes—perhaps to create a cookie (Chapter 17) or to store the information in a database that you manage to keep track of registered users of your site.

In JavaScript code, you define an array as follows:

```
arrayname = new Array ()
```

Quite simple. Optionally, you can even define the elements of the array at the same time you create it:

```
arrayname = new Array ("Toyota", "Camry", 1990)
```

Of course, the above only applies if you know in advance what values the array will contain.

The length of an array is a property defined by how many elements it contains. In the earlier Kissinger example, userinfo.length would contain a value of 6.

Methods Without Madness

The Array object possesses three methods, each of which enables you to manipulate the elements in the array. Each method is fairly straightforward, so let's take a moment to consider each.

join( ) method

A method of convenience, the join() method will concatenate each element in the array into one string value. For instance, consider again the following array which contains three elements:

```
car = new Array ("Toyota", "Camry", 1990)
```

If you then called upon car.join() in an assignment statement such as this:

```
model = car.join()
```

the string variable model would contain the value "Toyota,Camry,1990". By default, the join() method uses commas to separate the elements within the string. You can easily specify a different delimiter. For instance, this example:

```
model = car.join(" ")
```

would separate elements with a space rather than a comma, resulting in the string value "Toyota Camry 1990".

reverse( ) method

This one's a no-brainer. Simply, calling the reverse() method for an array will reverse the positions of each element. Suppose you have this four-element array named classes:

```
classes[0] = "Freshman"
classes[1] = "Sophomore"
classes[2] = "Junior"
classes[3] = "Senior"
```

You can call the reverse() method in this way:

```
classes.reverse()
```

As a result, the array would look like this:

```
classes[0] = "Senior"
classes[1] = "Junior"
classes[2] = "Sophomore"
classes[3] = "Freshman"
```

sort( ) method

This method, as its name implies, can be used to sort the elements in an array. Instead of simply reversing them, as the reverse() method does, the sort() method re-orders the elements in the array based upon certain sorting criteria.

The simplest usage of the sort() method is as follows, using the same original classes array from the previous example:

```
classes.sort()
```

The above expression will sort the array's elements alphabetically. If an element in the array is a number, it is also sorted alphabetically (e.g. "500" comes before "95"). The resulting element sequence would look like this:

```
classes[0] = "Freshman"
classes[1] = "Junior"
classes[2] = "Senior"
classes[3] = "Sophomore"
```

Techno Talk

Roll Your Own Sort

For the advanced JavaScript programmer, it's also possible to devise a custom sorting algorithm for the sort() method to use. Using the function call arrayName.sort(sortfunc), you can sort the array using the algorithm coded into your function sortfunc() (or whatever you choose to name it).

The sort() method will re-index the array elements in a manner dependent upon the values your custom sort function returns:

➤ If sortfunc(a, b) returns a value less than zero, sort b to a lower index than a.

➤ If sortfunc(a, b) returns zero, leave a and b unchanged with respect to each other, but sorted with respect to all different elements.

➤ If sortfunc(a, b) returns a value greater than zero, sort b to a higher index than a.

Thus, you should code your custom sorting function to receive two parameters, which the sort() method will automatically send to it. In the body of the function, perform whatever comparison operations you need and return the appropriate value as indicated in the bulleted list above to report the result to the sort() method.

Double-Dipping: A Two-Dimensional Array

In and of itself, the array is a simple concept. This is partially because the basic array is one-dimensional: its elements are indexed only as 0, 1, 2, 3, and so on. One way to increase the flexibility of an array is to build it two-dimensionally.

In a two-dimensional array, each element may also be an array in its own right. Thus, each element in an array can be an array with its own elements. Confusing? It takes some re-reading to get the mental hang of it. Recall a basic array declaration:

```
cars = new Array ()
```

As usual, then, you could say this:

```
cars[0] = "Toyota"
```

The latter is a typical one-dimensional array. Suppose, though, that you'd like to store the types of Toyota models within the cars array. Instead of assigning a string value (such as "Toyota") to cars[0], you can assign a new array!

```
cars[0] = new Array ()
```

Now cars[0] is its own array, with a set of elements. Next, assign the automobile make to index 0 of cars[0] and assign each model name to succeeding elements:

```
cars[0][0]="Toyota"
cars[0][1]="Camry"
cars[0][2]="Celica"
cars[0][3]="4Runner"
```

Moving along, you can add another make and other models to your cars array:

```
cars[1][0]="Ford"
cars[1][1]="Mustang"
cars[1][2]="Taurus"
```

What you've done is create an array-within-an-array! This tends to cause some people's brains to hurt at first glance, but it just takes some practice.

Read this section on two-dimensional arrays several more times if necessary, until you feel you have at least a reasonable idea of what's going on. It's important because you're going to use this type of array in your main programming example for this chapter: the mini JavaScript database.

The Mini JavaScript Database

Although it's certainly nothing to rival Microsoft Access or Borland Paradox, you'll use JavaScript code and the Array object to create a small Web-based database. In fact, this is just the beginning of a database, but it will illustrate the relevant points.

On the surface, the mini database should operate according to these guidelines:

➤ The user can fill out several form fields: name, age, sex, and income level. When he finishes, he clicks a button labeled Add Record. The form is then cleared so that new data can be entered and then added as another record.

➤ A Clear Record button is provided to erase the current data in the form without adding it to the database.

➤ A View Records button gives the user the option of opening an addition browser window, in which the contents of each record are displayed.

First, then, you'll create the HTML code for the page, including the forms and event handlers (although you have yet to write the actual event handler functions).

```
<html>
<head>
<title>The Mini JavaScript Mini-Database</title>
</head>

<body bgcolor="#FFFFFF" onLoad="init()">
<p><H2>The Tiny JavaScript Mini-Database</H2></p>
<p>To add a record, please complete the following fields and then click Add Record.
To view all current records, click View Records.</p><p>

<form name=bio>
<p>First Name<input type="text" size="10" name="firstname">
Last Name<input type="text" size="10" name="lastname">Age
<input type="text" size="3" name="age"></p><p>
<input type="radio" checked name="sex">Male<br>
<input type="radio" name="sex">Female</p>

<p>Income Range:<br>
<select name="income" size="5">
 <option>Scraping By (<$10,000)</option>
 <option>Enjoys Ketchup ($10-20,000)</option>
 <option>Average Jane ($20-40,000)</option>
 <option>Can't Complain ($40-80,000)</option>
 <option>Outta My Way ($80,000+)</option>
</select></p><p>

<input type="button" name="add" value="Add Record" onClick="addrec()">
<input type="reset" name="clear" value="Clear Record">
<input type="button" name="view" value="View Records" onClick="viewrec()"></p>
</form>

<p><p>Thanks for using the mini database!</p>

</body>
</html>
```

In the above HTML, you create a reasonably straightforward Web page. It contains one
form, named bio, with three text form fields (firstname, lastname, and age), a pair of

radio buttons (sex), and a selection box (income). Lastly, the form contains these three buttons:

➤ A button named add, which has an onClick event handler calling the JavaScript function addrec().

➤ A button named clear, which is defined as a reset button and clears the current form data. This button has no event handler because reset buttons are a built-in feature of HTML and JavaScript.

➤ A button named view, which has an onClick event handler calling the JavaScript function viewrec().

In addition, call your attention to the fifth line in the above code, which reads

```
<body bgcolor="#FFFFFF" onLoad="init()">
```

Notice the onLoad event handler specified in the <BODY> tag. It calls the function init().

Although non-functional, the above page would look like the following figure when loaded into a Web browser.

The mini JavaScript database looks good, but it's non-functional until you write the JavaScript code.

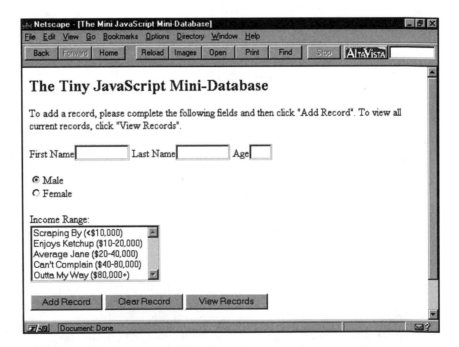

Having created the HTML, you now need to write three JavaScript functions to make this page come alive: init(), addrec(), viewrec().

init( )

The init() function, which is called upon loading of the page into the Web browser, simply prepares the necessary variables for the database.

```
function init()
{
 recidx=0
 record = new Array ()
}
```

In the first line of this function body, you initialize the record counter, recidx, to zero. Next, you create the main array, record.

Later, recidx will be used to keep track of which record is currently at issue, and record will be a two-dimensional array within which the form data is stored.

addrec( )

Now you want to code the addrec() function, which places the data in the form fields into the array.

```
function addrec()
{
 record[recidx]=new Array ()
 record[recidx][0]=document.bio.firstname.value
 record[recidx][1]=document.bio.lastname.value
 record[recidx][2]=document.bio.age.value
 record[recidx][3]=document.bio.sex[0].checked
 record[recidx][4]=document.bio.income.selectedIndex
 recidx++
 document.bio.clear.click()
}
```

After the user has filled out the form, he clicks the Add Record button, which triggers this function. In the first line of the function body, you create the second dimension of the two-dimensional array. You do that by assigning a new array to the recidx element of the record array.

In the next five lines of the function, you assign the data in each form field to successive elements of the second-dimension array (record[recidx]). This is the heart of the database, as the input data is stored in the array. To re-iterate, the form data is stored into the array record[recidx], which itself is an element of the array record.

Next, the record counter recidx is incremented by one to prepare for the next record (in case the user adds another). Lastly, the current form is cleared by calling the click() method of the clear button. The user will now be in a position to enter new data into the form, should he want to create another record.

viewrec( )

When the user clicks the View Records button, this function is launched.

```
function viewrec( )
{
 viewwin=window.open("","View_Records","scrollbars=yes,width=640,height=400")
 viewwin.document.writeln("<H2>View of "+recidx+" Current Record(s)</H2><p>")
 for (var j=0; j<recidx; j++)
  { if (record[j][3]==true) {sex="male"} else {sex="female"}
   viewwin.document.write("<H3>"+record[j][0]+" "+record[j][1]+"</H3>")
   viewwin.document.write("<H4><i>Age:</i> "+record[j][2]+"<br><i>Sex:</i>
"+sex+"<br><i>Income Level:</i> " +record[j][4]+"<p>")
  }
 viewwin.document.writeln("<p><form><input type=button value='Close Record View'
onClick='window.close()'></form>")
}
```

Even though it's the most complex-looking function of the three, viewrec() isn't as tangled as it appears. In the first line of the function body, you open a new browser window, which has the name viewwin, has dimensions of 640×400 pixels, and can display scroll bars if necessary.

In the second line, you write some HTML code to the new window, creating a title and displaying the total number of records being viewed.

Next, you create a for loop that begins with zero and increments by one until it reaches one-less-than the value of recidx. Within this for loop, you write the HTML code to display the contents of each record. This begins with an if...else statement to determine which sex was selected in the radio buttons. You then incorporate the appropriate array elements into HTML code, which is then written to the new window. In doing so, you display the full name, followed by the age, sex, and income level stored in each record.

Finally, when the for loop finishes, you write an additional line of HTML code to the new window, creating a form button the user can click to close the View Records window.

Take a look at the mini JavaScript database in action. This figure shows the page after a user has entered several records into the form and clicked View Records.

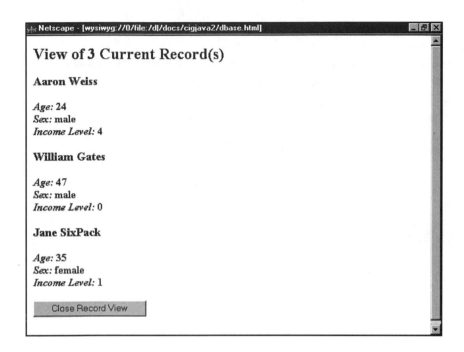

After entering several records into the page, the user clicks the View Records button, which launches the JavaScript function viewrec().

This, then, is the entirety of your page—HTML and JavaScript code combined:

```
<html>
<head>
<title>The Mini JavaScript Mini-Database</title>
<script>

function init()
{
 recidx=0
 record = new Array ()
}

function addrec()
{
 record[recidx]=new Array ()
 record[recidx][0]=document.bio.firstname.value
 record[recidx][1]=document.bio.lastname.value
 record[recidx][2]=document.bio.age.value
 record[recidx][3]=document.bio.sex[0].checked
 record[recidx][4]=document.bio.income.selectedIndex
 recidx++
 document.bio.clear.click()
}
```

159

```
function viewrec()
{
 viewwin=window.open("","View_Records","scrollbars=yes,width=640,height=400")
 viewwin.document.writeln("<H2>View of "+recidx+" Current Record(s)</H2><p>")
 for (var j=0; j<recidx; j++)
  { if (record[j][3]==true) {sex="male"} else {sex="female"}
    viewwin.document.write("<H3>"+record[j][0]+" "+record[j][1]+"</H3>")
    viewwin.document.write("<H4><i>Age:</i> "+record[j][2]+"<br><i>Sex:</i>
"+sex+"<br><i>Income Level:</i> "
record[j][4]+"<p>")
  }
 viewwin.document.writeln("<p><form><input type=button value='Close Record View'
onClick='window.close()'></form>")
}

</script>
</head>

<body bgcolor="#FFFFFF" onLoad="init()">
<p><H2>The Tiny JavaScript Mini-Database</H2></p>
<p>To add a record, please complete the following fields and then click Add Record.
To view all current records, click View Records.</p><p>

<form name=bio>
<p>First Name<input type="text" size="10" name="firstname">
Last Name<input type="text" size="10" name="lastname">Age
<input type="text" size="3" name="age"></p><p>
<input type="radio" checked name="sex">Male<br>
<input type="radio" name="sex">Female</p>

<p>Income Range:<br>
<select name="income" size="5">
 <option>Scraping By (<$10,000)</option>
 <option>Enjoys Ketchup ($10-20,000)</option>
 <option>Average Jane ($20-40,000)</option>
 <option>Can't Complain ($40-80,000)</option>
 <option>Outta My Way ($80,000+)</option>
</select></p><p>

<input type="button" name="add" value="Add Record" onClick="addrec()">
<input type="reset" name="clear" value="Clear Record">
```

```
<input type="button" name="view" value="View Records" onClick="viewrec()"></p>
</form>

<p><p>Thanks for using the mini database!</p>

</body>
</html>
```

The Least You Need to Know

➤ An array is an object that contains any number of elements. Each element may contain a value or be defined as another array.

➤ To create a new array in JavaScript, use this expression:

```
arrayname = new Array ()
```

➤ An array element is referred to by its index:

```
arrayname[0] = elementvalue
```

➤ The length property contains the number of elements currently in the array:

```
numelements = arrayname.length
```

➤ The Array object has three methods:

join("separator") concatenates all element values into a single string value, separating the values by "separator" (which is a comma if nothing else is specified).

reverse() flips the order of elements.

sort() re-orders the elements alphabetically. Numbers are converted to strings and are also sorted alphabetically (not numerically).

➤ You can create a two-dimensional array by assigning a new Array () to an element of an existing array:

```
arrayname[0]=new Array ()
```

You then refer to two-dimensional arrays using both index numbers:

```
arrayname[0][1] = value
```

161

Chapter 16

Image-ine That!

In This Chapter

➤ Out with the old image, in with the new

➤ The truth about the Image object

➤ Glamorous enhanced menus

➤ Wow! Illustrated catalogs!

1.1 Among the modest delivery of new features that have arrived on the JavaScript 1.1 ship, image manipulation has been one of the more popular. This chapter explores the new Image object, which enables you to replace images on a Web page without reloading the entire page. In doing so, you can achieve several nice, although less-than-vital, page enhancements. Consider this chapter a handful of rainbow sprinkles (or "jimmies," depending on your longitude) with which JavaScript 1.1 can add some extra bite to your Web pages.

Inside the Image Object

Traditional HTML coding allows you to place images at specified positions on a Web page—nothing new here. But what if you'd like to *change* one of the images on the page without loading a whole new HTML document? That's the mission of JavaScript 1.1's new Image object.

At its heart, the Image object provides a way for JavaScript code to change the source file of an image. Imagine, for instance, that you have a Web page that contains an image of a dog in the upper-left corner. Using the Image object and the right JavaScript code, you can change this dog image into, say, a cat image. The rest of the page remains unchanged.

Several applications of the Image object have become popular among JavaScript authors:

➤ **Animations**   Authors are creating animations by rotating several image files in one position on the page.

➤ **Enhanced menus**   When the user passes his mouse over an image, it changes into another image. This can be used to highlight selection buttons, for instance, as the user passes over each.

➤ **Illustrated catalogs**   A user can select an item, and an image of that item appears in a specific location on the page. Selecting a different item changes the image. The page never needs to be re-loaded, nor does a form need to be submitted to activate the new selection.

More experienced (read: jaded) Web authors may recognize that the above enhancements have been possible for some time, but they required more complicated programming methods. However, JavaScript 1.1 helps speed development for the experienced author and offers these enhancements even to novice Web programmers.

In this chapter, you'll learn to use the Image object through an examination of two examples: the enhanced menu and the illustrated catalog. There are some good reasons why the animation application isn't particularly wonderful; I'll dish you that dirt towards the chapter's close.

Let's begin, though, with a look at creating an enhanced menu.

Glitz with Ease: Enhanced Menus

As simple and straightforward as text hyperlinks are, many Web designers prefer to add graphical menus to their pages. A common graphical menu, like the one shown here for instance, consists of a series of adjacent images. The user clicks one of these images, which presumably leads to some further activity.

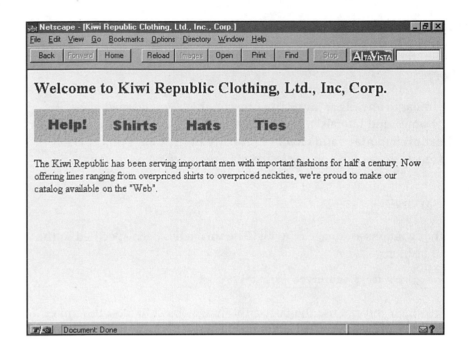

A typical button menu, composed of several adjacent images.

Using JavaScript 1.1's Image object, you can add some glitz to the above menu. Imagine that as the user passes his mouse pointer over each button, it becomes highlighted. In addition to adding aesthetic appeal, this also provides helpful feedback to the user, indicating which button is ready to respond to a click.

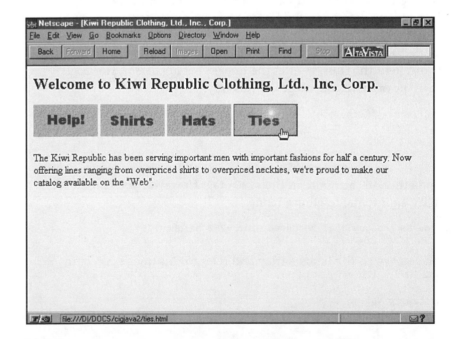

The enhanced button menu, which highlights each button as the mouse pointer passes over it. Note the change in border thickness and the minor spotlight effect on the selected button. Slick!

Before we get down and dirty with the enhanced menu JavaScript code, let's talk specifics about the Image object.

Image Objectified

The Image object is similar to any other JavaScript object (which you learned about in Chapter 5, "Objects, Names, and Literals"). Thus, it has its own set of properties. As far as we're concerned, the most important and effective property of the Image object is its source property, written as src, which you use to specify the image file you want to display, as in:

```
image.src = "kitty.jpg"
```

Picture a Web page that contains an image of a dog. The image has been specified in the HTML code in typical fashion:

```
<IMG SRC="doggy.jpg" border=0 width=200 height=175>
```

There are two ways in which you can use the JavaScript Image object to alter the image that appears where the dog image currently resides on the page. You can reference the image by its index or by its name.

By Index

The document object for the page contains an array known as images (also new to JavaScript 1.1). Each element of document.images[*x*] refers to an image on the page, in the order in which they were defined in the HTML code. For instance, in the page containing only the dog image, document.images[0] is the Image object that refers to it. If the page contained another image after the dog, its Image object would be document.images[1], and so forth. Thus, to alter the image that appears in the dog's place, you could change the order of the images in this way:

```
document.images[0].src = "kitty.jpg"
```

By Name

Often, you don't include the NAME attribute in the <IMG> tag. However, you can do so, thereby giving the image an internal reference name:

```
<IMG name=dogimage SRC="doggy.jpg" border=0 width=200 height=175>
```

Having done that, you can bypass the images array and refer to this Image object in JavaScript by its name:

```
document.dogimage.src = "kitty.jpg"
```

166

Check This Out...

Naming Names

Important note: If the image is defined within a form, and you want to refer to it by name, you must specify that form in the JavaScript expression, as in:

```
document.formname.dogimage.src = "kitty.jpg"
```

Ready to Code!

Now you're ready to consider the code for your enhanced menu. Recalling how to use the src property of the Image object to change the image on a page, let's walk through the logic of your proposed Web page and JavaScript program.

The Web page will be a mock clothing catalog. Its main page features a menu of four adjacent images: Help, Shirts, Hats, and Ties. Suppose you've saved these images as button1a.jpg, button2a.jpg, button3a.jpg, and button4a.jpg.

When designing these images in your image processing software, you also created "highlighted" versions of each image. As you can see in the next figure, each highlighted version has a higher brightness level, a black border, and a spotlight effect (thanks to Adobe PhotoShop!). Suppose these highlighted images are saved as button1b.jpg, button2b.jpg, button3b.jpg, and button4.jpg.

Watch Your Dimensions!
Ideally, when using the JavaScript Image object to replace images on a page, the new image should possess the same physical dimensions as the original. If it does not, the Web browser will scale the new image to fit the dimensions of the image defined in the original <IMG> tag.

The JavaScript logic, then, goes as follows:

➤ Detect the mouse passing over an image (onMouseOver). When it does, change that image to the highlighted version.

➤ Detect the mouse passing away from an image (onMouseOut). When it does, change that image to the non-highlighted version.

Simple enough? Basically, yes, although there is one trick to point out. MouseOver and MouseOut events cannot be triggered for standalone images. Rather, they apply only to hyperlinks and to defined areas in an image map (the latter of which is too complicated for this book). The trick: For each image, create a hyperlink that has no text and insert the <IMG> tag within the hyperlink definition. It might look like this:

```
<a href="help.html" <img src="button1a.jpg" border="0" width="100" height="50"></a>
```

Each of the menu images you've prepared for this page. No great artistic skill necessary!

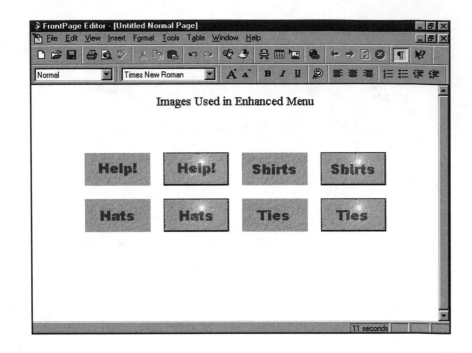

The previous HTML code creates a hyperlink that consists only of the specified <IMG> and leads to "help.html." If you do not want the image to link anywhere, you can simply include a null href, as in:

```
<a href="" <img src="button1a.jpg" border="0" width="100" height="50"></a>
```

Using this trick, you can trigger MouseOver and MouseOut events when the mouse pointer passes over the image!

Taking that into account, the full HTML code for your page would look quite a bit like this:

```
<html>
<head>
<title>Kiwi Republic Clothing, Ltd., Inc., Corp.</title>
</head>
<body bgcolor="#FFFFFF">
<p><H2>Welcome to Kiwi Republic Clothing, Ltd., Inc, Corp.</H2></p><p>

<a href="help.html" onMouseOut="unselect(1)" onMouseOver="select(1)">
 <img src="button1a.jpg" border="0" width="100" height="50"></a>
<a href="shirts.html" onMouseOut="unselect(2)" onMouseOver="select(2)">
 <img src="button2a.JPG" border="0" width="100" height="50"></a>
```

```
<a href="hats.html" onMouseOut="unselect(3)" onMouseOver="select(3)">
 <img src="button3a.JPG" border="0" width="100" height="50"></a>
<a href="ties.html" onMouseOut="unselect(4)" onMouseOver="select(4)">
 <img src="button4a.JPG" border="0" width="100" height="50"></a>

</p>
<p>The Kiwi Republic has been serving important man with important fashions
for half a century. Now offering lines ranging from overpriced shirts to
overpriced neckties, we're proud to make our catalog available on the "Web".</p>

</body>
</html>
```

Function Fun

As illustrated above, you've created four images—each within a hyperlink definition—for each of button1a.jpg, button2a.jpg, and so on. As you might have noticed, you've also set two event handlers for each hyperlink: onMouseOut, which calls the JavaScript function unselect(), and onMouseOver, which calls select(). So now it's time to code these two JavaScript functions!

First, unselect():

```
function unselect(butnum)
{ document.images[butnum-1].src = "button"+butnum+"a.jpg"}
```

Quite a compact little function, isn't it?! This function takes one parameter, butnum, which specifies which button to change to the un-highlighted image. The function also contains a single line of code, which changes the image in question. And notice the document.images[x].src expression: In this case, x is butnum–1 because JavaScript considers the first image to be index zero (even if we humans prefer to call it button number one).

In the second half of the statement, you simply assign a string to the Image object, which represents the correct file name for the un-highlighted button, as in "button2a.jpg."

Now for select():

```
function select(butnum)
{ document.images[butnum-1].src= "button"+butnum+"b.jpg"}
```

Hmm, sure looks familiar. In fact, select() is virtually the same function as unselect() except that it assigns the "b" file name to the Image object, as in "button2b.jpg."

169

Thus, to change button one to its un-highlighted image, you simply need to call unselect(1). To highlight it, you call select(1). And *that* is exactly the logic behind this expression:

```
<a href="help.html" onMouseOut="unselect(1)" onMouseOver="select(1)">
 <img src="button1a.jpg" border="0" width="100" height="50"></a>
```

That's all there is to it! You've created your images within hyperlinks, mixed in some event handlers, and added your JavaScript functions. Loading this page into your browser, you see the enhanced menus in glorious action.

When you slide the mouse pointer over an image, your JavaScript enhanced menu kicks in, replacing the plain image with a snazzy highlighted version.

For your reference, I've included the fully intact HTML code for this page, complete with the JavaScript functions described above.

```
<html>
<head>
<title>Kiwi Republic Clothing, Ltd., Inc., Corp.</title>
<script>

function unselect(butnum)
{ document.images[butnum-1].src = "button"+butnum+"a.jpg"}
```

```
function select(butnum)
{ document.images[butnum-1].src= "button"+butnum+"b.jpg"}

</script>
</head>
<body bgcolor="#FFFFFF">
<p><H2>Welcome to Kiwi Republic Clothing, Ltd., Inc, Corp.</H2></p><p>

<a href="help.html" onMouseOut="unselect(1)" onMouseOver="select(1)">
 <img src="button1a.jpg" border="0" width="100" height="50"></a>
<a href="shirts.html" onMouseOut="unselect(2)" onMouseOver="select(2)">
 <img src="button2a.JPG" border="0" width="100" height="50"></a>
<a href="hats.html" onMouseOut="unselect(3)" onMouseOver="select(3)">
 <img src="button3a.JPG" border="0" width="100" height="50"></a>
<a href="ties.html" onMouseOut="unselect(4)" onMouseOver="select(4)">
 <img src-"button4a.JPG" border="0" width="100" height="50"></a>

</p>
<p>The Kiwi Republic has been serving important man with important fashions
for half a century. Now offering lines ranging from overpriced shirts to
overpriced neckties, we're proud to make our catalog available on the "Web".</p>

</body>
</html>
```

Slick: Illustrated Catalog

The Image object can also be used to change an image based upon user selection in a form. For instance, consider the Necktie Shopping page offered by Kiwi Republic, in which a selection box displays a list of available necktie styles. When the user selects any one style, its image appears on the right side of the page.

By and large, the basic concepts of this example remain unchanged from the enhanced menus. You begin your work by gathering the collection of necktie images to use. In this case, you've acquired five images, each of the same dimensions, with the file names *tie0.jpg*, *tie1.jpg*, *tie2.jpg*, and so on.

Next, you create the HTML code for the selection box form. Using this form, the user will select which tie to view.

```
<form name=tieform>
<select name="tiebox" size="5" onChange="ShowTie()">
```

```
<option selected>Plain Jane </option>
<option>Hearty Red </option>
<option>Green w/Envy </option>
<option>Power Blue </option>
<option>Crazy! </option>
</select>

<img name=tiephoto src="tie0.jpg" hspace="100" width="50" height="150"></p>
</form>
```

Pop-Up Image

In the previous script, you created the form and named it tieform. You then defined the selection box with the name tiebox, and you specified each necktie option. Following the selection box definition, you placed the initial necktie image and named it tiephoto. Because Plain Jane is the initially selected item (<option selected>Plain Jane), *tie0.jpg* will be the initial image displayed.

Re-focusing on the selection definition tag, you see that an event handler is specified: onChange="ShowTie()". As a result, whenever the user changes the selected item, the JavaScript function ShowTie() is called. Let's take a peek:

```
function ShowTie()
{
 tieidx=document.tieform.tiebox.selectedIndex
 document.tieform.tiephoto.src="tie"+tieidx+".jpg"
}
```

This is a mere two-statement function. In the first, you determine which item is currently selected. You do this by assigning the selectedIndex property of tiebox to the variable tieidx. Next, you use tieidx to construct the file name of the necktie image to assign to the src property of the tiephoto Image object. Making this assignment causes the tie image to change to reflect the currently selected item (see the following figure). Voilà!

Here's a complete rendition of the page's code:

```
<html>
<head>
<title>Shopping for Neckties at the Kiwi Republic</title>
<script>
function ShowTie()
{
 tieidx=document.tieform.tiebox.selectedIndex
 document.tieform.tiephoto.src="tie"+tieidx+".jpg"
```

```
      }
      </script>
      </head>
      <body bgcolor="#FFFFFF">
      <h2>Shopping for Neckties at the Kiwi Republic</h2>
      <p>From the list below, select a necktie. An image of the tie appears to the right.
      If none of the neckties in our catalog suit your taste, there is something quite
      dubious about your tastes.</p>
      <form name=tieform>
      <select name="tiebox" size="5" onChange="ShowTie()">
       <option selected>Plain Jane </option>
       <option>Hearty Red </option>
       <option>Green w/Envy </option>
       <option>Power Blue </option>
       <option>Crazy! </option>
      </select>

      <img name=tiephoto src="tie0.jpg" hspace="100" width="50" height="150"></p>
      </form>
      </body>
      </html>
```

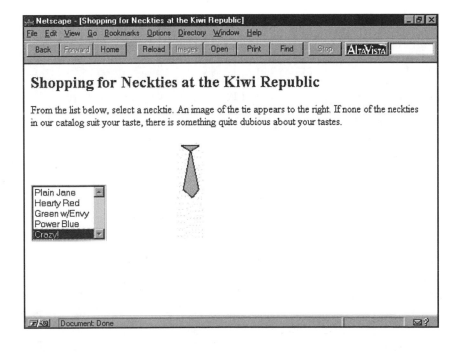

Capitalizing on the Image object, you change the necktie image that's displayed to match the item selected in the form.

173

Future Projects

At the outset of this chapter, I implied that the Image object could be used to create animations. After having seen the Image object in action, you can probably imagine how an animation would be constructed:

➤ Gather a series of image frames, each in a separate file.

➤ Using the image.src= assignment, replace an initial image with each successive frame image.

It certainly works, but there are some real drawbacks. For one, the result isn't much different from a typical animated GIF. What's more, with an animated GIF, all the frames are stored in one file, which cause much less network delay than loading each individual image file does.

On the other hand, if you create an animation using JavaScript code, you could program interactiveness that GIF animations lack. For instance, form buttons could be tied to a delay variable, which would speed up or slow down the rotation of image frames.

The Least You Need to Know

➤ JavaScript 1.1 introduces the Image object, whose properties enable you to replace images on a page without reloading the page.

➤ The images on a page are indexed in the order in which they appear in the HTML code; the first image on the page is number zero.

➤ Each image on a page may also be named using the NAME= attribute of the <IMG> tag.

➤ To replace an image on the page, you can assign the path of the new image to the src property of the Image object you want to change.

➤ Image objects can be referred to by index number in the document.images[ ] array, as in document.images[0].src="kitty.jpg."

➤ Image objects can be referred to by a name defined in the <IMG> tag, as in document.petphoto.src="kitty.jpg." Images that reside within a form must also specify the form name, as in document.someform.petphoto.src="kitty.jpg."

Care for a Cookie?

It's one of the tastiest of morsels. That's why most of us experience a specific pleasant sensation when we think of the word *cookie*. With that in mind, we placidly consider the Web-based cookie, which—though coined with the driest of technogeek humor—has absolutely nothing to do with the aforementioned snack food. In fact, there's no good reason why the subject of this chapter is called a *cookie*. Nonetheless, what it lacks in taste, the Web cookie possesses in style: It's a useful little critter, despite its non-sequitir name.

Using Web cookies, you can personalize Web pages and keep track of information about a user. In this chapter, I'll introduce the concept of a cookie, and you'll learn to create and access them with JavaScript.

Behind the Ball of Dough: Cookie Basics

Cookies allow a Web page to "track" information about a particular visitor. Introduced with the release of Netscape Navigator 2.0, cookies have become widely used on Web sites in the months and year(s) since.

To better illustrate the function of a cookie, let's look at a typical, but simple, example. You own a Web page. A user, whom we'll call Mark Harmon (for no particular reason), visits your Web page. He might have reached it by typing its URL into his Web browser, or he might have simply clicked on a link from a different page. But it makes no difference *how* he got there.

When Mark Harmon visits your page, you assign him a specific identification number *behind the scenes*; Mark Harmon is not aware of this (unless he's configured his browser to alert him of cookie requests). Using a cookie, you then save this identification number to Mark Harmon's hard drive. The next time Mark Harmon visits your Web page, you know it's him—or, more accurately, you know that it's the same computer from which Mark Harmon first visited your page.

The above concept is an example of one use of a cookie: You have stored information to track a particular visitor to your page. You can expand on that concept in a variety of ways. You might use cookies to record past options that Mark Harmon has selected on your site so you can personalize your site and show only information that is relevant to Mark Harmon, based on his past selections.

Cookies have been applied to a wide variety of Web sites, from mail order catalogs to search engines. Using cookies in an ethical manner, you have the potential to mold your Web pages to fit each visitor by remembering their past preferences, and so forth.

In this chapter, I'm going to show you how you can use JavaScript to create some simple cookies. Then you'll retrieve these cookies and customize your Web page to reflect the cookie. While the potential applications and implementations of cookies can grow quite complex, I'll stick to the basics. (Or should that read "non-stick"!?)

Cookie Crumbs: Ethical Issues

The widespread use of cookies has raised the hackles of paranoia among a growing segment of Web users. For many, the mere notion that a Web page can "track" their actions conjures up frightening implications. Others dissent from this view, believing that cookies are by-and-large a harmless convenience. In reality (as usual), both sides have valid points.

It is true that a cookie can be used to keep a record of a fair amount of information about your visit to a site. The cookie can "remember" which links you've selected, which products you've ordered, and so forth. Using this data, many Web marketers hope to collect demographic statistics that they can use to target promotions.

However, there *are* certain limitations to exactly how much information a cookie can track and how personal that information can be. Consider these restrictions on cookies:

➤ Only the domain that created the cookie can access it. For example, cookies created by a Web page at dominos.com cannot be changed or referenced by a Web page at pizzahut.com.

➤ Netscape Navigator allows only 20 cookies to be stored per domain. Thus, dominos.com can save a maximum of 20 cookies.(Of course, they can still store a fair amount of tracking information in those 20 cookies.) In contrast, Microsoft Internet Explorer 3.0 allows only one cookie to be stored per domain.

➤ While a cookie can track the behavior of the user at a particular computer, it can't know who the person using the computer is. At most, the cookie can recognize that a particular computer is visiting a Web page again, but it has no way of knowing which specific human being is at the other end!

➤ Perhaps most importantly, a cookie *cannot* acquire any information from your computer's data. The cookie itself is only a piece of data that has been stored on your computer and retrieved by a Web page. The cookie cannot "spy" into your personal files—or any files at all for that matter.

While the above points make a strong case for the safety of data security with regards to cookies, they do not necessarily prevent cookies from being used unethically. One question is this: Is it ethical to e-mail reams of promotional messages based on the selections of a visitor on a Web page? Many would say no; some would say yes. There is much subjectivity to ethical judgments, but the main point is that cookies simply track information; what other people do with that information and how they use it is where social ethics begin and technology ends.

The Vanilla Cookie

To begin this culinary lesson, let's start with a very basic cookie: merely tracking the date and time of the user's last visit to the Web page.

The mechanics behind a cookie are simple enough. When the user opens your page, you read any data that exists in the currently stored cookie for this user. You use this data in whatever way you want, and then you update the cookie—which contains a name, a value, and other possible information—to reflect the current visit.

In this particular example, you'll check the existing cookie for the last time the user visited this page (if there is any), display that information on the page, and then update the cookie to reflect the current date and time of this visit.

Keep the above process in mind, or refer back to it if necessary as I explain each step in the cookie making process. While the basic concept is simple, there are a lot of details that can become confusing. I'll start simply.

What Are the Ingredients of a Cookie?

Glad you asked. Literally, a cookie is a piece of data that is stored either in the computer's memory or on the hard drive. This piece of data may contain such information as:

➤ A name for the cookie (such as lastvisit).

➤ A value for the cookie (such as Fri Dec 06 18:35:48 Atlantic Standard Time 1996).

➤ An expiration date for the cookie. After this expiration date, the cookie will no longer function, and a new one would have to be created. (If you do not specify an expiration date, the cookie expires as soon as the Web browser is closed, and the cookie is never saved to the hard drive.)

➤ A domain name and path for the cookie. These help determine which Web pages are allowed to access the cookie.

➤ Whether or not the cookie must operate on secure encrypted Web connections only.

How Do I Create a Cookie?

Another excellent question. By combining the ingredients, of course! Specifically, using JavaScript, you assign a string value to the cookie property of the current document:

```
document.cookie = "name = value; expires = date_to_expire"
```

Ingredients

Suppose, then, that you want to store a cookie that tracks the current date and time of the user's visit to this Web page. You'll name the cookie lastvisit; the variable today will contain the current date and time; and the variable expdate will contain the date on which the cookie expires.

```
document.cookie = "lastvisit = today; expires = expdate"
```

The above is fine and good, but here come the details. As it is, cookie syntax requires that the expiration date be in a very specific format: Wdy, DD-MMM-YYYY HH:MM:SS GMT.

Wdy can be any valid three-letter abbreviation for a day name (such as Sun); DD represents a two-digit reflection of the day of the month (such as 09); MMM represents any of the valid three-letter abbreviations for the month (such as Sep); YYYY is the four-digit year (such as 1996). Hours, minutes, and seconds are represented by two digits each (such as 22:15:00). And finally, GMT is the only valid time zone. So if you are calculating an expiration time, don't neglect to account for the time difference between GMT and your own time zone.

> **Valid Day Abbreviations:** Mon, Tue, Wed, Thu, Fri, Sat, Sun

> **Valid Month Abbreviations:** Jan, Feb, Mar, Apr, May, Jun, Jul, Aug, Sep, Oct, Nov, Dec

Fortunately, you'll soon learn about a JavaScript function that can construct the proper date format for you in many cases. However, if you want to specify a specific expiration date that is not calculable in a JavaScript function (in other words, if you want the cookie to expire on "January 1, 1998" as opposed to the calculable "30 days from today"), you still have to refer to the syntax rules above.

Unlike the expiration date, the variable today (which contains the date of the user's lastvisit) can be stored in any format you want. After all, that's your data, which you can use however you want.

Procedure

Now you're ready to write your first function. Combining the ingredients discussed so far, you'll code a small function named BakeCookie(), which creates the above-described cookie. First, the code, and then the explanation.

```
function BakeCookie()
{
var today = new Date ();
var expdate = new Date ();
expdate.setTime(expdate.getTime() + (1 * 24 * 60 * 60 * 1000 * 365));
expdate=expdate.toGMTString();
document.cookie="lastvisit="+escape(today)+";expires="+expdate+";"
}
```

Following your function definition, you define two variables—today and expdate—and assign the current date to each of them. Next, you use a somewhat complicated call to the setTime() method of expdate, setting it to 24 hours ahead of the current time. In doing so, you're preparing to bake your cookie to expire in 24 hours (or one day). To set expdate 30 days ahead, for instance, simply change the initial 1 to 30 in line 5 (where it begins `1 * 24`).

After assigning the expiration date to expdate, you call its toGMTString() method, which converts the date into the syntax needed for the cookie. Lastly, and most importantly, you make the assignment to document.cookie, which bakes the cookie.

Notice that you add the expression escape(today) to the string value assigned to document.cookie, instead of merely adding today. This is because the value of the cookie cannot contain white space or punctuation marks, and calling escape(today) will insert the value of today without any such characters (by saving each illegal character as a special code). Later, when you read the value of the cookie, you'll reverse this effect so that any white space and punctuation marks can be returned to the cookie's value.

Hands Off! Domain Restrictions

Matters can become a little more complicated here. By specifying a domain name in your cookie, you limit which Web pages have access to that cookie. For instance, if in your cookie creation, you appended the specification domain=mysite.com, only Web pages that reside on mysite.com could access this cookie.

The example above assumes that your original Web page *does* reside on mysite.com; remember that you cannot specify a domain other than the one the Web page currently resides in! In other words, you cannot tell a Web page located at beagledog.com that it can access cookies only at terrier.com. That would violate all attempts at cookie privacy.

Every subdomain of the specified domain can access the cookie. To clarify, if you restrict a cookie's domain to mysite.com, all Web pages on bob.mysite.com and mary.mysite.com can access the cookie because those are both subdomains of mysite.com. If you wanted to be even stricter, you could restrict the cookie to mary.mysite.com, in which case pages on bob.mysite.com or mysite.com could *not* access the cookie.

Furthermore, you can also restrict *which* pages within a domain can access the cookie. This is done using the path= specification in the cookie definition. For instance, if your Web pages reside within http://mary.mysite.com/marypages/, you could specify path=/marypages. And if you combine that with the domain restriction, you might wind up with a cookie assignment that looks something like this:

```
document.cookie = "lastvisit = today; expires = expdate; domain = mary.mysite.com;
path=/marypages"
```

This would restrict access to the cookie to Web pages that are within /marypages on the server mary.mysite.com. Whew, this can become quite a mouthful!

In the interest of shortcuts, I should note that leaving out the domain or path specifications does *not* leave your cookie completely vulnerable. If you do not specify a domain restriction, a default restriction will be used (which consists of the domain within which the Web page resides). Therefore, if your page is on a server at mary.mysite.com, and you don't specify the above domain restriction, access to the cookie will be restricted to pages on mary.mysite.com anyway! Thus, in many cases, you can omit the domain restriction, as you did in the earlier example function BakeCookie(). However, in certain unusual server configurations, you might find that your page functions better if you do include the domain and/or path restrictions. When it comes to circumstances where security matters, specifying restrictions is always safer than not doing so.

How Many Cookies in a Batch?

While creating a cookie from a Web page is simple enough (document.cookie="cookie_attributes"), you might be wondering how many cookies you can create from a page. The answer, in fact, lies not with JavaScript but with the Web browser.

Netscape Navigator 2.0 and 3.0, for instance, honor up to 20 cookies per domain. This means that across all of the pages that reside in the same server domain, you can create a maximum of 20 cookies. Dramatically different, however, is Microsoft Internet Explorer 3.0, which supports only one single cookie per domain!

As the JavaScript author, you should keep the above limitations in mind. If your pages are primarily intended for Netscape users, you can bake a 20-cookie batch. But if you want to remain compatible with Microsoft Internet Explorer users, you should pack as much information as you need to into a single cookie (Internet Explorer will silently refuse to create a new cookie if a valid cookie from the same domain already exists).

Setting the Table

Now that you've created your BakeCookie() function, you're ready to incorporate it into a very simple Web page. Consider the HTML code below:

```
<html>
<head>
<script>
function BakeCookie()
{
var today = new Date ();
var expdate = new Date ();
```

```
expdate.setTime(expdate.getTime() + (1 * 24 * 60 * 60 * 1000 * 365));
expdate=expdate.toGMTString();
document.cookie="lastvisit="+escape(today)+";expires="+expdate+";"
}
</script>
</head>
<body bgcolor="#FFFFFF">
<p align="center"><H1><strong>Welcome to the Cookie Monster!</strong></H1></p><br>

<script>
BakeCookie()
</script>
</body>
</html>
```

Now you've created a simple page, which contains only the centered text "Welcome to the Cookie Monster!". Within the <HEAD> tags is your first function, BakeCookie(), and at the end of the document is a simple JavaScript call to the function.

When a user loads this page for the first time, he sees only the welcome text; but the current date and time cookie is stored. In this case, because you specified an expiration date, the cookie is stored to his hard drive. Had you not specified an expiration date, the cookie would remain in RAM and would expire as soon as the user shut down his Web browser.

That's just wonderful, right? But how, then, do you make use of this cookie? Conceptually, it's simple: When the user loads this page, you read the value of the cookie and use it to customize the message on the page. Following that, you update the cookie with the new date and time.

The First Bite: Reading the Cookie

To read the value of the cookie, you need to create a function. This function will search the user's cookie list for the named cookie of your choice. If it finds that cookie, and if the page has access to the cookie (as explained in the earlier section on domain and path restrictions), it returns the value of that cookie. The skeleton of such a function would look like this in pseudo-JavaScript:

```
function ServeCookie (cookie_name)
{statements which search for and retrieve value of cookie}
```

You could then incorporate a call to ServeCookie() into some other JavaScript code, which would use the value of the cookie as in:

```
document.writeln ("Hi again! Your last visit to this page was on " +
ServeCookie("lastvisit"))
```

The above code would add a message to the current Web page, greeting the user with the exact date and time of his last visit, as recorded in the cookie. Of course, if the cookie has expired since the user's last visit, the situation will be as if the person had never visited before and has no pre-existing cookie for this page.

Before you, then, lies the matter of coding the ServeCookie() function. The truth is, this function is a bit complicated. Needless to say, I don't want to burden an audience new to JavaScript with a complex, long, and possibly confusing explanation. Fortunately, this function is very portable: You can use it, as is, in any Web page, without having to understand exactly how it works. All you have to do is call it with the name of the cookie to serve, and it delivers that cookie's value. If the cookie does not exist or has expired, this function returns the value null. Here is the function ServeCookie():

```
function ServeCookie(name)
{
 var namestr = name + "="
 var namelen = namestr.length
 var cooklen = document.cookie.length
 var i = 0
 while (i < cooklen)
  { var j = i + namelen
    if (document.cookie.substring(i, j) == namestr)
     { endstr = document.cookie.indexOf (";", j)
       if (endstr == -1) {endstr = document.cookie.length}
       return unescape(document.cookie.substring(j,endstr))
     }
    i = document.cookie.indexOf(" ", i) + 1
    if (i == 0) break
  }
 return null
}
```

The Confessions of ServeCookie()

A technically curious sort, eh? You really want to know what is going on inside the ServeCookie() function? Well, I'm not going to spell it out line by line, but here's a basic summary.

Using a combination of string properties, such as length, and string methods, such as substring() and indexOf(), as well as several if statements, this function locates the first character to the right of the equal sign following the cookie name and extracts the string of characters from that position to the character immediately preceding the first semicolon. If the cookie name cannot be found, a value of null is returned. Well, now look, I've gone and spilled all the secrets. Happy now?

Got Milk? Washing It Down

All of the essential elements have been covered: you know the functions for creating the cookie, as well as for reading its value. You have the basic HTML for your Web page, and you've seen how to incorporate a call to ServeCookie in a document.writeln JavaScript statement. Now, then, you dunk:

```
<html>
<head>
<script>
function BakeCookie()
{
var today = new Date ();
var expdate = new Date ();
expdate.setTime(expdate.getTime() + (1 * 24 * 60 * 60 * 1000 * 365));
expdate=expdate.toGMTString();
document.cookie="lastvisit="+escape(today)+";expires="+expdate+";"
}

function ServeCookie(name)
{
 var namestr = name + "="
 var namelen = namestr.length
 var cooklen = document.cookie.length
 var i = 0
 while (i < cooklen)
  { var j = i + namelen
```

```
      if (document.cookie.substring(i, j) == namestr)
        { endstr = document.cookie.indexOf (";", j)
          if (endstr == -1) {endstr = document.cookie.length}
          return unescape(document.cookie.substring(j,endstr))
        }
      i = document.cookie.indexOf(" ", i) + 1
      if (i == 0) break
    }
  return null
}
</script>
</head>
<body bgcolor="#FFFFFF">
<p align="center"><H1><strong>Welcome to the Cookie Monster!</strong></H1></p><br>

<script>
if (ServeCookie("lastvisit") == null)
  {document.writeln ("<H2>Hello stranger! Enjoy your first visit to this page.
</H2><HR>")}
  else {document.writeln("<H2>You're back! Last visit to this
page:<BR>"+ServeCookie("lastvisit")+"</H2><HR>")}
BakeCookie()
</script>
</body>
</html>
```

The only new bit above is the logic added to the end of the document between the final set of <SCRIPT> tags (seven lines up from the last line). You test to see if the value for the lastvisit cookie is null, in which case the user has not visited this page before (or his cookie has expired). If his cookie is null, you write an appropriate first-time greeting to the page. If his cookie does contain a value, you welcome him back and display the time and date of his last visit. Finally, you call the BakeCookie() function and update the cookie.

An initial visit to this page, then, would result in a screen resembling the one shown in the next figure.

Either this is the user's first visit to this page, or his cookie has expired.

Someone who's re-visiting this page and has a valid cookie would receive the familiar greeting shown in the following figure.

This is no stranger; he's been to this page before! Cookies remember.

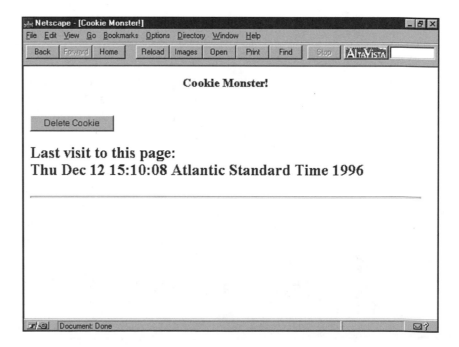

Chips, Almonds, and Assorted Cookie Magic

In this chapter, we've looked in detail at constructing a relatively simple cookie. The basic procedure, however, can be applied to any level of complexity. For instance, you could do any of the following:

➤ Design a text form, wherein the user submits his name. You then store the value of this form in a cookie and greet the user by name upon his next visit.

➤ Create an online catalog so that whenever the user adds an item to his shopping cart, a cookie stores that information. When the user chooses to advance to the cashier, an invoice appears, showing the user's name and each item in the cart.

➤ Manipulate a search engine so it stores a user's preferred options, such as how many hits to display at once, which criterion to sort hits by, and so forth. When the user re-visits the page, his preferred options are already selected.

You can do any of these things by building on the JavaScript concepts and code shown in this chapter. Certainly, the code will grow more complex as you send the values from form fields to cookie-baking functions. To repeat a standard recommendation, learn by watching others! When you come across a Web page which is "remembering" your choices, it's using cookies. Spend some time studying the source code for that Web page to see how the author created it.

Remember, though, that not all Web pages use JavaScript to track cookies. Obviously, look for Web pages whose source code indicates that they are using JavaScript!

All Together Now

The tools provided throughout these chapters should serve as a good overview of JavaScript and its applications. I've avoided delving into highly complex programming examples in part because this is an introduction to the language and in part because such examples are more about programming science than the JavaScript language itself.

The best way to learn a programming language is, as my irritating piano teacher used to say, through "practice, practice, practice." And experimentation, although she didn't ever mention that. You'll need to read these chapters multiple times, in different manners. For the first read-through, you might look to pick up the general concepts behind JavaScript programming. On a second read-through, try focusing on the specific syntax of the JavaScript statements and expressions.

Then, at each example, attempt to throw together your own code that varies slightly from the example. See if it works, and if so, vary it further with new ideas. Eventually, you work toward combining concepts from multiple examples, and before you know it, you're constructing your own programs from scratch. Be sure to read through the script example chapters in Part 4, "Scripting the Whole Bean." They provide full examples of JavaScript programs, with explanations, which pull together all the concepts from throughout this book.

One word of advice is not to be beset by frustration when programs don't work the first time through. Errors and malfunctions are the stuff that programs and programmer's lives are made of. Sometimes, the error is caused by something silly, such as forgetting a closing bracket or parenthesis. Other times, you haven't a clue why the program is not working. In those cases, it's a good idea to try other approaches to the end, and see if they work. Or just scream. There is a whole science to debugging—which is of great value to learn if you become heavily involved in programming—but when all else fails, I always recommend the "clear head" approach. That is, walk away. Come back another day. Many dastardly bugs are resolved this way. The rested, clear mind can solve some problems in minutes that the haggard mind struggles with for hours. A perusal through Chapter 23, "What to Do When It Won't Work: Debugging Your Scripts," might be beneficial, as well. There you'll find some further consideration given to script debugging and pest extermination.

Now that you've had that not-exactly-a-pep talk, you're off and programming!

The Least You Need to Know

➤ Cookies are used to track information about a particular visitor to a Web page, such as the last time of visit or which links he selected.

➤ A cookie is a bit of data that is stored in either the user's RAM or hard drive; the cookie contains a name and a value, and possibly an expiration date and other access restrictions.

➤ You create a cookie in JavaScript by assigning its specifications to document.cookie, the template of which looks like this:

```
document.cookie = "name=value; expires=expiry_date; domain=domain_restriction;
path=path_restriction; secure"
```

➤ By coding functions to create a cookie and read a cookie, you have the two elements necessary to use and manipulate cookies from the Web page.

➤ Using the value contained in a cookie (obtained via the cookie reading function), you can customize Web pages or process the value in any way you want.

Part 4
Scripting the Whole Bean

If you've made it this far (and your head hasn't exploded), you've made it through the worst part: learning JavaScript. By now, you might have an idea or two brewing in the back of your brain. If so, you can't wait to get scripting to see your idea come to "CyberReality." For those of you who need a little more encouragement, you'll find a collection of examples to help you get started.

The example scripts you'll find in this section showcase a variety of JavaScript behavior: controlling the page, changing page attributes, randomly selecting things, and responding to the user clicking a button. Feel free to observe, analyze, and adapt these scripts to meet your own needs. Toss 'em in your tool kit—you just might find a use for them somewhere down the line.

Inside, you'll find some example scripts, including a graphical BlackJack game (make wagers with the neighbors!).

BRIAN'S CAR ALARM ERROR PROMPT DIDN'T GO OVER TOO WELL AT THE OFFICE.

Chapter 18

Script Example 1: Hello World

In This Chapter

➤ A simple template for creating JavaScript scripts

➤ Positioning the <SCRIPT> tag to control output

➤ Writing HTML tags from within the <SCRIPT>

➤ Providing "controlled access" to parts of the document

Putting It All Together

If you've made it this far, you've probably been wondering when the background information, command lists, statement explanations, and other groundwork would stop and the real fun—creating your own real JavaScript Web pages—would begin. Wait no longer! The fun starts now! Because no introduction to a new computer language would be complete without the requisite "Hello World" application, that's where you'll start. Your little "Hello World" script will also give you a basic HTML framework that you can use for the rest of the examples in this book.

Hello World?

Every discipline has its traditions, and programming is no exception. One long-standing ritual found in almost every introductory book on any computer programming language is to have the first program be one that displays the phrase "Hello World" on the screen.

The Basic Template

You can use the following template as a framework for all of your JavaScript files. From time to time, you may want to move things around a bit, but that's what templates are for: to give you a starting point. Don't consider them to be the only way to script—they're just one possibility.

```
<HTML>
<HEAD>

<TITLE>Your Title Here</TITLE>

<SCRIPT LANGUAGE="JavaScript">
<!-- Hide script from non-JavaScript browsers

// your script statements go here

//-->
</SCRIPT>

</HEAD>

<BODY>

// Your HTML display statements go here

</BODY>

</HTML>
```

As I mentioned in Chapter 3, the `<SCRIPT>` tag serves as a wrapper around JavaScript statements, and you can place it anywhere within the HTML file. For the sake of consistency, place it in the `<HEAD>` tag.

Hello World 1

Suppose you want to present a simple page that displays a JavaScript dialog with the phrase "Hello World from the Land of JavaScript!" when the user clicks a button. If you remember back a bit, you can accomplish this through the use of an event handler that runs a function. The event handler you need to use is onClick, and the function is a simple one:

```
function HelloWorld()
{
alert("Hello World from the Land of JavaScript!")
}
```

So, putting it together, you get:

```
<HTML>
<TITLE>Hello World</TITLE>
<HEAD>
<SCRIPT LANGUAGE="JavaScript">
<!-- Hide script from non-JavaScript browsers
function HelloWorld()
{
alert("Hello World from the Land of
JavaScript!")
}
//-->
</SCRIPT>
</HEAD>
<BODY>
<FORM>
Click on the button below to receive a _special message:
<P>
<INPUT TYPE="submit" VALUE="Click Me!" _ONCLICK="HelloWorld()">
</FORM>
</BODY>
</HTML>
```

> **Run Script, Run**
> "Running" a JavaScript program is as simple as loading the HTML document into the Web browser. If you've created the script file on the same computer on which the browser is installed, you will load a "local file." Do this opening the **File** menu and choosing an option named something like **Open file** or **Open local file**.

When you fire up Netscape Navigator and run this script, you should get something like what you see in the next figure.

Hello World!

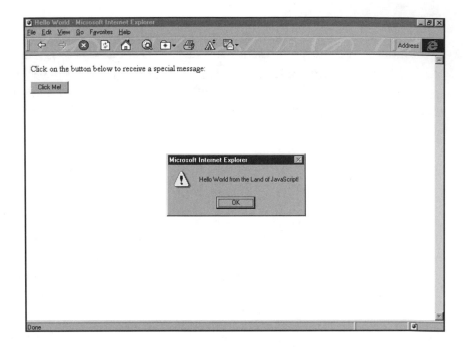

There are a couple of things to note here. First, the JavaScript code for buttons needs to go inside a <FORM> tag; otherwise, it's simply ignored (you can test this by removing the <FORM> tag from the above script and running it again). One of the most common mistakes beginning Web writers make is forgetting to use the <FORM> tag; and then they wonder why their buttons and check boxes aren't being displayed.

Note that, in the previous example, you're using a Submit button (as defined by the <INPUT> tag attribute TYPE="submit"). The Submit button also generates an onSubmit event, which you could have used to equal effectiveness as the onClick event in this case. However, the onSubmit event handler is defined in the <FORM> tag, not the <INPUT> tag. You can check this out for yourself by replacing the previous example with the following one, which will yield the exact same results:

```
<FORM ONSUBMIT="HelloWorld()"><INPUT TYPE="submit" VALUE="Click Me!"> </FORM>
```

Congratulations, you're now a JavaScripter!

Hello World 2

Okay, so your first little example wasn't all that elaborate. Well, you have to start somewhere! Now you're ready to deviate from your template a little and look at a more significantly useful way to place text on the screen. Now you will generate new messages directly into the on-screen document.

You may remember (from Chapter 12) that one of the objects JavaScript gives you is the document object, which provides a way to program the currently displayed document. Normally, when you load a Web page, the HTML statements within it are interpreted and displayed by the browser. With JavaScript, you can write HTML statements directly into the document at any time, as generated on-the-fly by your JavaScript program. To see what I mean, consider the following example:

```
<HTML>
<TITLE>Hello World</TITLE>
<HEAD>
<SCRIPT LANGUAGE="JavaScript">
<!-- Hide script from non-JavaScript browsers
document.write("<H2>Hello World from the Land of JavaScript!</H2>")
//-->
</SCRIPT>
</HEAD>
<BODY>
<P>
 (the previous message compliments of JavaScript)
</BODY>
</HTML>
```

Running this document produces the same output as the following non-JavaScript page:

```
<HTML>
<TITLE>Hello World</TITLE>
<HEAD>
<H2>Hello World from the Land of JavaScript!</H2>
</HEAD>
<BODY>
<P>
 (the previous message compliments of JavaScript)
</BODY>
</HTML>
```

Interactive Style

Given the previous two examples, you might be thinking, "So what was the point of that?" Consider, though, that in the JavaScript version, you could have output that message at any time as a result of certain conditions having been met or a certain type of user interaction. In the HTML version, the message is plopped onto the screen, and it's there for good. Thus, JavaScript enables you to generate on-screen messages via HTML code in reaction to conditions or user events.

A New Spin

Now let's rework the first example so that you wind up with something truly JavaScripty. The following program will be a mini "tour guide" front-end to a display on the history of spices. Two buttons will appear in the window, each containing the name of a spice. When the user chooses the spice, a JavaScript function is called that generates new HTML code on-the-fly for display on the screen. This new code will display two appropriately phrased links that lead toward new (hypothetical) documents: one containing recipes that use the spice, and the other containing a history of trade for that spice. This sounds complicated, but it is, in fact, simple with JavaScript.

```
<HTML>
<TITLE>Spice Tours 96</TITLE>
<HEAD>
<SCRIPT LANGUAGE="JavaScript">
<!--Hide script from non-JavaScript browsers
function tour(spice)
{
var recipes="<A HREF=" + spice + ".html>See recipes using " + spice + "</A><p>";
var trading="<A HREF=" + spice + "trade.html>See history of the " + spice +
" trade</A><p>" ;
document.write("<H2>Please select one of the guided tours below<H2>") ;
document.write(recipes) ;
document.write(trading) }
//-->
</SCRIPT>
</HEAD>
<BODY>
Please click on the desired spice below:
<FORM>
<INPUT TYPE="button" VALUE="Garlic" ONCLICK="tour('garlic')">
<INPUT TYPE="button" VALUE="Cinnamon" ONCLICK="tour('cinnamon')">
</FORM>
</BODY>
</HTML>
```

The following two figures illustrate what the user would see when interacting with the this program.

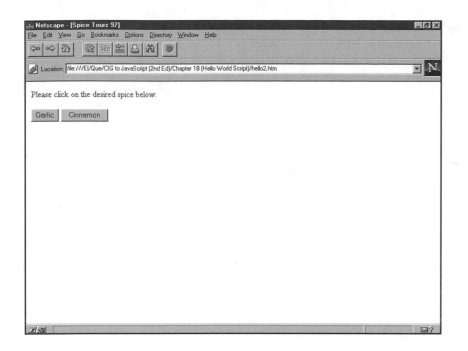

Here, the salivating user can select which spice to learn more about.

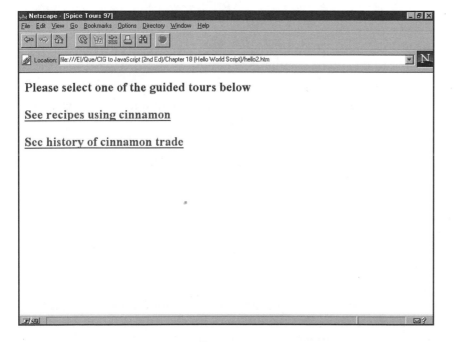

The JavaScript function then generates new HTML code to display the spice-appropriate hyperlinks.

After the user has selected a spice trail to follow, the JavaScript program generates some new HTML code on-the-fly, reflecting the user's choice and displaying a suitable page. As pictured here, the new page refers to the spice the user has chosen. As well, the hyperlinks lead to pages specific to the chosen spice.

Let's consider the previous program. It basically contains two segments. The JavaScript function definition comes first, and the HTML code defining the button options comes second. First consider the HTML code. It should look familiar by now: You created a form in which there are two button elements, and you labeled each button with a spice name. You could have coded as many buttons as you wanted. Both buttons contain an onClick event handler, calling the function tour(). Notice how you pass a string literal, representing the spice in question, as the parameter to tour().

Now consider the tour() function. The first line of statements, an assignment to the variable recipes, looks complicated but is actually simple. The purpose of this line is to paste together a string containing the full HTML code for a hyperlink. It then assigns that whole string to the variable recipes. You can assume, for example, that the document containing garlic recipes will be called "garlic.html," and so you use a combination of concatenations to construct this string. Recall that the variable spice contains either the string "garlic" or "cinnamon," depending on which button the user clicked. Therefore, according to JavaScript, the following string winds up being assigned to recipes:

```
"<A HREF=garlic.html>See recipes using garlic</A><p>"
```

This is HTML for a hyperlink and will momentarily be output to the browser window.

The second statement line constructs a similar link for the history of trading. This is followed by three document.write() statements, which simply output all of this HTML to the browser window, as shown in the previous figure.

Web Etiquette

If you've done a bit of Web surfing, no doubt you've encountered many pages that have links "for text-based browsers" or "for non-Netscape browsers." Because there are several "standards" on the Web today, not all browsers can handle all things. Thoughtful Web authors try to accommodate this by creating different collections of pages that are tailored to different types of browsers.

Although the most popular browsers (Netscape Navigator 2.0 or greater and Internet Explorer 3.0 or greater) support JavaScript, some other browsers are still in use out there. For those who do not use JavaScript-capable browsers, it's nice to still be able to view your pages, even if the pages' features and functionality are reduced in some way. You can do this quite neatly by taking advantage of what you just learned.

Because you can generate HTML using the document.write() method, you can create the following JavaScript-aware page:

```
<HTML>
<TITLE>Welcome to My JavaScript</TITLE>
<BODY>
<H1>So...you're interested in JavaScript?</H1>
Hello World! Well, you've come to the right place for JavaScript.
But, if you don't have <A HREF="http://home.netscape.com/">Netscape
Navigator</A> or <A HREF="http://www.microsoft.com/ie/default.asp">
Microsoft Internet Explorer</A>, you won't be able to see any of the fun!
<SCRIPT LANGUAGE="JavaScript">
<!-- Hide from non-JavaScript browsers
document.write("<HR>")
document.write("<P>")
document.write("To proceed to my JavaScript pages,")
document.write('<A HREF="myjavascript.html">Click here</A>.')
//-->
</SCRIPT>
</BODY>
</HTML>
```

The following figure shows the resulting page. With this little trick, you can keep people from trying to view your JavaScript pages if they don't have a browser that can handle it. That way, they won't be disappointed by the gibberish they see on-screen.

Check This Out...

Clarify Your Marks

Note that when you have to use double quotation marks for something else in the display line (such as an URL), you can use single quotation marks to bracket the entire display string. Or you can use double quotation marks to bracket the entire string and single quotation marks within it. Either way works, as long as you are consistent: If you start the string with a double quotation mark, be sure to bracket the end of the string with a double quotation mark and use single quotation marks when necessary within. (And vice versa.)

199

Only a JavaScript-enabled browser will display the last line.

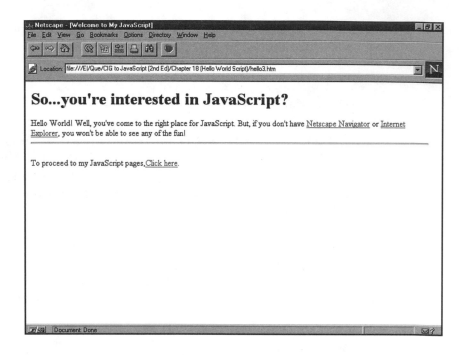

There's More on the Web!

You can download the script examples in Chapters 18 through 22—as well as find other useful JavaScript material—from the Que Web site. Point your browser to:

http://www.mcp.com/que/new-users/cig_jscript/!start_here.html

There you'll find a complete HTML version of this book, graphic files to go along with some of the script examples used in the book, and links to other cool JavaScript-related material!

The Least You Need to Know

Having seen all that makes up JavaScript in the earlier chapters of this book, you now embark on the adventure of creating your own pages. In your first example, you displayed a simple "Hello World" message in two ways: from within the document through the document object and from the JavaScript alert( ) function. You then constructed a user-interactive program that generated context-appropriate messages on-screen. Finally, you saw that you can hide URL links inside a script to keep non-JavaScript browsers from displaying things that wouldn't work for them.

Chapter 19

Script Example 2: Random Chatter

In This Chapter

➤ Generating "random" numbers with JavaScript

➤ Easily creating an array of things

➤ Making changes to the page itself (randomly)

When Is Random Not Random?

Computers are "linear" machines, very logical and precise. Humans have no problem picking a number between 1 and 10, but computers don't have the capability to randomly select things. And yet, card games, dice games—just about any game you can think of—involves some sort of random selection. And we do love to play games on computers. So how, then, do computers take a "shot in the dark"? By using a formula that's dependent on something that is always changing: the time of day.

Using military time (where hours are numbered from 0 to 23 instead of "a.m." and "p.m."), you can create a pseudo-random number, or a number that seems random because it changes every second. Simply speaking, take the hour of the day, the minute of the hour, and the second of the minute and multiply them together. In the first edition of this book, the above is exactly how we acquired random numbers in JavaScript. It worked well, but it involved an understanding of the Date() object and modulus math to massage the hours, minutes, and seconds into a random number within our desired range.

The Rebirth of random()
Actually, the random() method of the Math object is not new to JavaScript 1.1. In fact, the same method was available in JavaScript 1.0; however, it only worked on UNIX-based computers. Therefore, for most of us using our browsers in Windows, the random() method was of no help. The new feature introduced with JavaScript 1.1 is the compatibility of random() across all platforms. Yay, progress!

Fortunately, JavaScript 1.1 introduces a new method, random(), which is a method of the Math object. While the random number is still based on the date and time as I just described, the calculations are automatic. Using the random() method, you'll see how generating random numbers with JavaScript 1.1 is a snap.

Random numbers are used commonly in computer programs, especially games. Lottery-style games, gambling games, and so forth tend to be common beginners' programs. Perhaps if you were designing an online "store" for your wares, you might offer customers a chance at a discount via a lottery or slot-machine style game. Using the random() method, it's just a short hop to implementing a random-number generator into your JavaScript programs.

Random Numbers with the random() Method

As I alluded to earlier, random() is a method of Math, a built-in JavaScript object. Generating a basic random number, then, is as simple as this:

```
rnumber = Math.random()
```

Note the capitalization of Math in that expression. The Math object must begin with the capital "M." That code will generate a random number between 0 and 1 and assign the result to the variable rnumber.

Notice what I just said, though: It "will generate a random number between 0 and 1." Under many circumstances, this is too narrow a range to deal with. Usually, when you want a random number, it needs to fall within certain bounds. For example, there are only 52 cards in a deck (unless you count the jokers), so a card game should choose random numbers within the range of 1 to 52. You need to be able to scale the range of numbers, a feat which is easily accomplished with a little multiplication. For example, to generate a random number between 0 and 52, you simply multiply the result of the random() method by 52:

```
rnumber = Math.random() *  52
```

Of course, for the deck of cards example, you actually want a number between 1 and 52, not zero. An easy fix: simply generate the random number between 0 and 52-minus-1 and then add 1 to the result:

```
rnumber = Math.random() * (52-1))+1
```

One last hitch: That last expression can generate any real number between 1 and 51, including 4.532, 8.991, and so on. When choosing from a deck of cards (or in many similar examples), you want only integers within the range—for example, between 1 and 52, which could be 10, 15, or 23. To do that, you use the round( ) method of the Math object to round the result to the nearest integer value:

```
rnumber = Math.round(Math.random() * (52-1))+1
```

Perfect! Based on the above, you can imagine a basic formula for generating any random integer between a lowerbound and an upper bound:

```
rnumber = Math.round(Math.random() * (upperbound-lowerbound))+lowerbound
```

Now that you can randomly generate a number within a particular range, you need to have a selection of things to randomly pick from—and that's next.

Internet Explorer and Random-ness

Earlier in this chapter, I stated that the random() method was essentially introduced with JavaScript 1.1. Remember that only Internet Explorer 3.0 supports JavaScript 1.0. In an earlier sidebar, though, I also noted that random() was a feature of JavaScript 1.0 but is only usable on UNIX-based computers. That was true of Netscape. But with Internet Explorer, the random() method does work correctly, even in Windows. The moral of this story? Both Internet Explorer 3.0 and Netscape Navigator 3.0 support the random() method as discussed in this chapter!

The Random Chatter Example

Let's create a simple example that randomly picks a phrase from an array of sentences. You saw how to create and use arrays in Chapter 15, "'Array' (A Ray) of Organization." Every time the user clicks the button, something new appears on the screen. Here's the JavaScript page.

```
<HTML>
<TITLE>Random Chatter</TITLE>
<HEAD>
<SCRIPT LANGUAGE="JavaScript">
<!--Hide from non-JavaScript browsers
function getrandom(maxValue)
{
rnumber = Math.round(Math.random()*(maxValue-1))+1
return rnumber
}
function showRandom(field)
{
textArray = new Array(10);
textArray[1] = "JavaScript is Fun!";
textArray[2] = "Let's Browse the Web in Style!";
textArray[3] = "We're now JavaScript-powered!";
textArray[4] = "Click again, I don't like this choice.";
textArray[5] = "And now ... something completely different.";
textArray[6] = "So far ... so good.";
textArray[7] = "Ok ... now what?";
textArray[8] = "A nice choice, if I do say so myself.";
textArray[9] = "Only one more to go ...";
textArray[10] = "That's it!";
field.value = textArray[getrandom(10)];
}
//-->
</SCRIPT>
</HEAD>
<BODY>
<H1>Random Chatter</H1>
<HR>
JavaScript can be quite a talker, and can even randomly pick things to say.
<P>
<FORM>
<HR>
Click on the button, I'll think of something to say
<INPUT TYPE="button" VALUE="Take a chance!"
ONCLICK="showRandom(this.form.randomOut)">
<CENTER><INPUT TYPE=text NAME="randomOut" size="60"></CENTER>
</FORM>
</BODY>
</HTML>
```

204

There's your random-number function, getrandom( ). In this case, it's returning a number between 1 and 10. Notice that you pass the parameter 10 (your maxValue) to getrandom( ) in the function call in the final statement of showRandom( ). The value that random( ) returns (rnumber) is used by the showRandom( ) function to pick a text line from textArray. The selected text is then loaded into the value property of the form field that is passed to showRandom( ). In the BODY of the page, you'll find the "Take a chance!" button that fires showRandom( ) whenever you click it, as well as the randomOut form field that receives the text selected by showRandom( ).

Color Me Random

To see another mini-example of random numbers, you can add another button to your page that causes the background color to change each time the button is clicked. To do so, follow these steps:

1. Build an array of the color codes. As you know from your HTML experience, color codes are stored in hexadecimal triplet format (which specifies the amounts of red, green, and blue used in each color).

2. Pick a color randomly from this array.

3. Set the bgColor property of the JavaScript document object to this new value.

For a list of 138 of the most common colors, their RGB values, and their hexadecimal triplets, see Appendix A, "JavaScript: The Complete Overview" at the end of this book. For a quicker reference, use this table of hexadecimal triplets for some basic colors.

Color	Hexadecimal Triplet	Color	Hexadecimal Triplet
black	000000	maroon	800000
blue	0000FF	orange	FFA500
brown	A52A2A	pink	FFC0CB
cyan	00FFFF	purple	800080
gold	FFD700	red	FF0000
gray	808080	silver	C0C0C0
green	008000	white	FFFFFF
lime	00FF00	yellow	FFFF00
magenta	FF00FF		

Here's your function to pick a background color:

```
function SetBkgndColor()
{
colorArray = new Array(7);
colorArray[1] = "#FF0000";
colorArray[2] = "#00FF00";
colorArray[3] = "#FFFF00";
colorArray[4] = "#0000FF";
colorArray[5] = "#FF00FF";
colorArray[6] = "#00FFFF";
colorArray[7] = "#FFFFFF";
document.bgColor = colorArray[getrandom(7)];
}
```

Notice that all you need to do to cause the background color to change is set document.bgColor. Remember that document is a predefined JavaScript object that gives you direct access to the current document and how it's being displayed. (See Chapter 12, "The Document Shuffle," for more information on the document object.)

Putting it all together, here's your new random chatter page:

```
<HTML>
<TITLE>Random Chatter</TITLE>
<HEAD>
<SCRIPT LANGUAGE="JavaScript">
<!--Hide from non-JavaScript browsers
function getrandom(maxValue)
{
rnumber = Math.round(Math.random()*(maxValue-1))+1
return rnumber
}
function showRandom(field)
{
textArray = new Array(10);
textArray[1] = "JavaScript is Fun!";
textArray[2] = "Let's Browse the Web in Style!";
textArray[3] = "We're now JavaScript-powered!";
textArray[4] = "Click again, I don't like this choice.";
textArray[5] = "And now ... something completely different.";
textArray[6] = "So far ... so good.";
```

```
textArray[7] = "Ok ... now what?";
textArray[8] = "A nice choice, if I do say so myself.";
textArray[9] = "Only one more to go ...";
textArray[10] = "That's it!";
field.value = textArray[getrandom(10)];
}
function SetBkgndColor()
{
colorArray = new Array(7);
colorArray[1] = "#FF0000";
colorArray[2] = "#00FF00";
colorArray[3] = "#FFFF00";
colorArray[4] = "#0000FF";
colorArray[5] = "#FF00FF";
colorArray[6] = "#00FFFF";
colorArray[7] = "#FFFFFF";
document.bgColor = colorArray[getrandom(7)];
}
//-->
</SCRIPT>
</HEAD>
<BODY>
<H1>Random Chatter</H1>
<HR>
JavaScript can be quite a talker, and can even randomly pick things to say.
<P>
<FORM>
<HR>
Click on the button, I'll think of something to say
<INPUT TYPE="button" VALUE="Take a chance!"
ONCLICK="showRandom(this.form.randomOut)">
<CENTER><INPUT TYPE=text NAME="randomOut" size="60"></CENTER>
<HR>
Or ... click here and I'll change color!
<INPUT TYPE="button" VALUE="Color Me!" ONCLICK="SetBkgndColor()">
</FORM>
</BODY>
</HTML>
```

The following figure shows you what that page looks like when it's running.

Randomly selecting text and changing document properties.

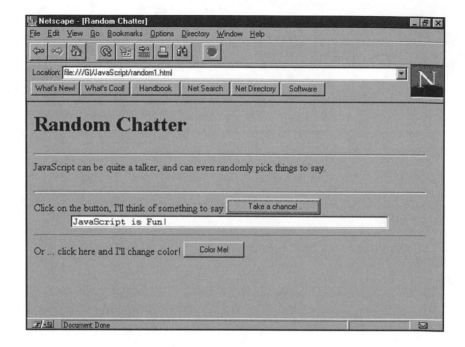

The Least You Need to Know

In this chapter's example, you learned how to:

➤ Get a JavaScript program to randomly pick from a list of selections.

➤ Create a function that you can use for a variety of things, such as the random() function, which can select a random number within specified bounds.

➤ Pick up a nifty little function that makes creating arrays a snap.

➤ Create a Web page that randomly displays various strings and changes color at the click of a button.

Chapter 20

Script Example 3: Which Way Do We Go?

In This Chapter

➤ The question of audience

➤ Separate and equal

➤ Automatic redirection

Making the Grade

In this example, we're going to look at a simple but important technique: browser-sensitive site navigation. Even though JavaScript is supported by the major Web browsers Netscape Navigator and Microsoft Internet Explorer, some users out there may be using a browser that does not support JavaScript (such as Lynx, Opera, or Ibrowse).

When you're creating a Web site, it's important for you to consider whether you want it accessible to all Web surfers or only those who use JavaScript-capable browsers. Of course, this depends in large part on the function of the site: If the site is a BlackJack game that's written in JavaScript (like the one in Chapter 21), it clearly is useful only to visitors with JavaScript-capable browsers. In fact, in the case of our BlackJack program, only JavaScript 1.1-capable browsers can play it.

On the other hand, perhaps you're using JavaScript to "jazz up" a site. Yet, its basic content (information about you, your company, and so on) may be relevant to anyone. In this case, it's sometimes best to create two versions of your content pages: one version for users without JavaScript and one for users with.

Parallel Universes

Imagine that your site consists of two "parallel universes": one set of pages with graphics and JavaScript code and one set without JavaScript code (whether or not they contain graphics is up to you). We'll say that each version of the site's home page is named as follows:

home_js.html is the page that contains JavaScript code.

home_nojs.html is the page that does not contain JavaScript code.

All of the hyperlinks within home_nojs.html also lead to non-JavaScript versions of pages, and the hyperlinks within home_js.html lead to JavaScript versions of pages where appropriate.

The trick, then, lies in how to come up with a single URL that any surfer can visit and that will automatically sweep the user to the correct version of the home page.

He Went That-a-Way!

Solving this proposition requires the creation of a "dummy" page, which performs the redirection to the appropriate "real" home page, depending on the visitor's browser.

Suppose your dummy page is named home.html. The logic behind the redirection is based on these points:

➤ You create a one-statement JavaScript program, which assigns a new URL to the location variable. Hide this program, as usual, from non-JavaScript browsers.

➤ After the JavaScript code, add a <META> tag to the page to refresh the page with a new URL.

When a JavaScript-capable browser loads this page, it executes the single line of JavaScript code and loads the new page into the window. A non-JavaScript browser can't see this code and, therefore, continues down until it hits the <META> tag, which causes it to load a new specified page.

```
<html>
<head>
</head>
<body bgcolor="#FFFFFF">
<script language="JavaScript">
<!-- Hide from non-JavaScript browsers
location = "home_js.html"
//-->
</script>
<META HTTP-EQUIV="REFRESH" CONTENT="0; URL=home_nojs.html">
</body>
</html>
```

When a visitor loads this page (which we've named and publicized as home.html, so the user doesn't realize he's actually opening a redirection page), a JavaScript browser will immediately open home_js.html. Alternatively, a non-JavaScript browser will immediately open home_nojs.html, and the deed is done. From that point on, everything else is taken care of by virtue of having employed the correct hyperlinks in each version of the home page.

You can easily test this example, even with Netscape Navigator or Internet Explorer. To do so, create the above dummy page and open it in Netscape. It should attempt to load home_js.html (or whichever URL you decide to code). Then disable JavaScript in Navigator using the **Network**, **Preferences**, **Language** command and revisit the page. This time, it should try to load home_nojs.html (or whichever URL you code for the non-JavaScript page).

Easy!

The Least You Need to Know

In this short chapter, you learned the importance of audience-friendly Web sites. When offering content that is relevant to readers with any browser, it's often wise to offer said content in non-JavaScript forms for users who don't have capable browsers. By creating and publicizing a "dummy" home page, you can automatically redirect visitors to the JavaScript-enabled or -disabled true home page. All it takes is a one-statement JavaScript program and a <META> tag to redirect non-JavaScript browsers.

Chapter 21

Script Example 4: BlackJack

In This Chapter

➤ More randomness

➤ Updating the data in FORM fields

➤ Using the JavaScript while loop

Game Time

After last chapter's return-to-algebra and the headaches that go with it, it's time for some fun and games! Let's play a few hands of cards and prove that JavaScript is an effective environment for game creation. To this end, you'll cook up a little script that plays a simple game of BlackJack.

First, let's define the ground rules for the game:

➤ For this demonstration, Aces have the value of 11.

➤ All "face" cards (Jack, Queen, and King) have the value of 10.

➤ All cards will be dealt "face up." This means you'll know what the dealer (house) has from the start.

➤ The deck is "infinite," meaning you can draw more than one Ace of Spades in a row. (For those of you fond of Las Vegas or Atlantic City, this is called a multiple-deck shoe.)

➤ The user will click a Hit or Stand button, depending on whether he wants another card.

➤ After the user clicks Stand, the dealer starts drawing cards. The dealer continues to draw until either the house's hand totals more than 17 or the house busts. In other words, the house stands on 17.

➤ When both the dealer and the user have stopped taking cards, the winning hand is the one closest to 21 without going over (busting).

➤ If the dealer and the user have the same total at the end of a hand, they "push" (tie), and no one wins or loses.

Okay, so we cut a few corners with the rules. If you want to extend the game to handle such things as splits, doubles, betting, and Aces that are 1 or 11, please feel free to experiment.

Browser Caution

This particular BlackJack example is functional and attractive, but it does make use of the JavaScript 1.1 images[ ] array to display the playing cards on the page as each hand is drawn. However, don't forget that only Netscape Navigator 3.0 or greater supports JavaScript 1.1 (as of the time of this writing). Therefore, this program will not work as-is on Internet Explorer 3.0, because IE doesn't support the image replacement functions.

To revise this example for Internet Explorer, you'd have to strip the image-related functions from the program and replace them with a less-advanced feedback system (such as window alerts) in order to report the results of each card drawn.

Pick a Card

In Chapter 19, "Random Chatter," you learned how to generate a random number between some minimum value and maximum value using the JavaScript Math.random( ) method. Recall that you could, for instance, generate a random number between 1 and 4 using this expression:

```
rnumber = Math.round(Math.random() * (4-1))+1
```

This works quite nicely for your purposes here, because you need to randomly pick two things for each card "drawn" from the deck:

➤ The suit: Spades, Clubs, Diamonds, or Hearts (one selection out of four)

➤ The face value of the card: Ace, number from 2–10, Jack, Queen, or King (a face value selection between 2 and 11 because Aces are given a value of 11).

Because there are four suits, you can easily write a function to pick a suit by randomly generating a number between 1 and 4:

```
function pickSuit()
{
suit = Math.round(Math.random() * (4-1))+1;

if(suit == 1)
return "Spades";

if(suit == 2)
return "Clubs";

if(suit == 3)
return "Diamonds";

return "Hearts";
}
```

You really need to check suit only to see if it's 1, 2, or 3. If it isn't one of those, it must be 4 and you don't have to use an if statement to make sure. This is an "old programmer's trick" that saves a few keystrokes and a couple of steps when the program is running. (If you want to drop a buzzword at your next party, this is called *program optimization*.)

The next step is to pick the card from the suit. There are 13 cards in each suit: Ace, 2 through 10, Jack, Queen, and King. You need your card picker to return two things: the value of the card, which is a number from 2 to 11 (remember, Aces are 11) and the name of the card, which is either the card number or the word "Jack," for instance. This causes a bit of a dilemma: "Jack", "Queen", "King", and "Ace" are all strings, but "2", "3", "5", and so on are numbers. You need both.

Because you need two distinct things from your card picker, make two distinct functions: one to return the value and one to return the name. The value function simply takes the number of your card (a number from 1 to 13) and returns a value from 2 to 11:

```
function cardValue(card)
{    .
if(card == 1)
return 11;
```

```
if(card > 10)
return 10;

return card;
}
```

If the card is 1 (an Ace), you say it's worth 11. If the card is a face card, its number will be 11, 12, or 13, so you say it's worth a value of 10. Otherwise, it's worth the number that's passed in.

Figuring out the card name is similar:

```
function cardName(card)
{
if(card == 1)
return "Ace";

if(card == 11)
return "Jack";

if(card == 12)
return "Queen";

if(card == 13)
return "King";

return new String(card);
}
```

Each face card has a different name, so you can't just say "If it's greater than 10...." Therefore, you need a separate if statement for each face card. Finally, the number cards are simply returned, but you convert the value to a string (using the "new String" expression).

Here's how you construct your PickACard() function:

```
function PickACard(strWho)
{
card = Math.round(Math.random() * (13-1))+1;
suit = pickSuit();

ShowCard(strWho, cardName(card), suit);
```

```
    return cardValue(card);
    }
```

Return the card's value from PickACard() so you can use this function to add to the totals in the dealer's and user's hands. Notice, though, the function call to ShowCard().You haven't created this function yet, so let's discuss it.

Graphic Gaming

Remember from Chapter 16, "Image-ine That!," that you can dynamically replace graphic images on a page using the Image object and the images[ ] array of JavaScript 1.1. This applies perfectly to the BlackJack games—or any card game for that matter. Here's the basic theory behind adding card images to the page:

➤ You prepare a full set of 52 card images all of the same dimensions.

➤ In the HTML code for the page, you place a bunch of blank transparent GIF images where actual cards may appear. For the BlackJack game in particular, you'll place six blank images in a horizontal row to represent the dealer's hand, and six more blanks to represent the user's hand.

➤ After each card is drawn, change the image source of the appropriate blank image to show the appropriate playing card image.

Conjuring the Code

To accomplish the above, you'll need to create the following items in the JavaScript program:

➤ Two counters, each of which keeps track of which card is being drawn for either the dealer or the user (e.g. whether the card drawn is the first, second, third, etc. in his hand).

➤ A function ClearCards(), which simply replaces all card images with blank ones when the user starts a new game.

➤ A function ShowCard(), which checks the currently drawn card (number and suit) and calculates the correct filename. For this to work, the filenames for the card images must follow some determinable pattern. In this example, you'll save the card images as "2h.gif" for the 2 of Hearts, "kd.gif" for the King of Diamonds, and so forth. After the filename has been calculated, ShowCard()replaces the appropriate blank image (determined by the counter) with the card image.

217

You're almost ready to code. First, however, you should create a small function named init(), which will initialize the counters.

```
function init()
{
 dealidx=0;
 useridx=0;
 gameon=true
}
```

In this function, you zero the two counters (dealidx and useridx), which keep track of which number card in the hand is being drawn. In addition, you set the variable gameon to true. This variable will be used in other functions to control game flow, preventing the user from hitting "Hit" or "Stand" if a game is not currently in session.

Now you're ready to code the ClearCards() function.

```
function ClearCards ()
{
 for (i=0; i<12; i++)
   { document.images[i].src="cards/blank.gif" }
}
```

This is also a simple function. It sets up a for loop that counts from 0 to 11 (the blank placeholder cards placed on the page) and sets each image's source file to the blank card.

Finally, you create the most complex of these functions: ShowCard().

```
function ShowCard (who, name, suit)
{
 //Construct filename for the card image
 if (name.length > 2)
   { name1=name.substring(0,1) }
 else { name1=name } ;
 name1=name1.toLowerCase()
 name2 = suit.substring(0,1);
 name2 = name2.toLowerCase();
 filename = "cards/"+ name1 + name2 + ".gif";

 //Load filename into correct image slot
 if (who=="Dealer")
```

```
  { document.images[0+dealidx].src = filename; dealidx++ }
else { document.images[6+useridx].src = filename; useridx++ }


}
```

This function takes three parameters: who has drawn the card (either "dealer" or "user"), the name of the card (2 through 10 for number cards or "Jack", "King", "Queen", "Ace" for name cards), and the suit of the card ("Hearts", "Diamonds", "Clubs", or "Spades"). After the card is drawn, these parameters are sent to ShowCard() by whichever function calls it.

In the first half of ShowCard(), the filename for the card image is constructed. The first if statement determines whether the card name is longer than 2 characters, in which case it strips the first letter from the name and converts it to lowercase. This results in a number between 2 and 10 or j, k, q, or a. Next, the first letter of the suit is stripped and converted to lowercase. Finally, the two parts are concatenated into a string conforming to the card image filename, as in cards/5h.gif (the 5 of hearts).

In the second half of ShowCards(), an if statement determines whether this card was drawn by the dealer or user. In either case, it then uses the JavaScript 1.1 images[] array to change the source file of an image on the page. To determine which image, it adds the current index (dealidx or useridx) to the proper offset. Because the first six blank cards on the page represent the dealer's hand, his offset is zero. The sixth placeholder card on the page is the first card in the user's hand, so the useridx is added to an offset of 6. After that, the correct image file is loaded into the correct placeholder on the page, and the index counter is incremented by one.

Dealer Takes a Card

The user takes a card only when he clicks the Hit me button. However, after the user clicks Stand, the dealer must repeatedly take cards until the house's hand goes over 16. This means you have to set up a function that repeats the pickacard() process until 17 is reached or exceeded. If you think this sounds like a job for a while loop, you're right.

Recall the basic form of the while loop: "While {something} is 'true', keep doing something else." In this case, you want to keep picking cards while the total in the dealer's hand is less than 17.

```
function Dealer()
{
  if (gameon==false)
   {message ("You must click 'New Hand' first!")}
```

```
   else
    {
    while(form.dealer.value < 17)
     {
      form.dealer.value = eval(form.dealer.value) + PickACard("dealer");
     }
    }
  }
```

Simple, isn't it? Note that the entire function is encased within the positive clause of an if statement. This prevents the function from executing if a game has not yet begun (signaled by the gameon variable). If gameon is false, the user is sent a message stating that he should begin the game by clicking the New Hand button.

Speaking of sending messages, note the call to a function named message(). This is a simple function (as you'll see in the final illustration of the program) that merely alters the value of a form button at the top of the browser. This button is used as a "message board" to inform the user.

The function for when the user picks a card is equally straightforward:

```
function User()
{
  if (gameon==false)
    {message ("You must click 'New Hand' first!")}
  else
    {
    form.you.value = eval(form.you.value) + PickACard("user");
    if(form.you.value > 21)
     {
      gameon=false;
      message("You busted! Game over, man. Click 'New Hand' to play again.");
     }
    }
}
```

And, after the players have taken all the cards they want, figuring out who won is a snap:

```
function LookAtHands(form)
{
```

```
if (gameon==true)
{
  if(form.dealer.value > 21)
  { gameon=false;
    message("House busts! You win! Click 'New Hand' to play again.");
  }
  else   if(form.you.value > form.dealer.value)
  {
    gameon=false;
    message("You win! Click 'New Hand' to play again.");
  }
  else
  if(form.dealer.value == form.you.value)
  {
    gameon=false;
    message("Push! Good match — Click 'New Hand' to play again.");
  }
  else
  {
    gameon=false;
    message("House wins! Click 'New Hand' to try again.");
  }
 }
}
```

To kick off a new game, you call the NewHand() function, which resets the score and board (image indexes, game scores, and card images) and then deals the first card to the dealer and the user.

```
function NewHand(form)
{
  ClearCards();
  message ("New game started — Good Luck!");
  form.dealer.value = 0;
  form.you.value = 0;

  form.dealer.value = eval(form.dealer.value) + PickACard("dealer");
  form.you.value = eval(form.you.value) + PickACard("user");
}
```

221

Using the eval( ) function guarantees that the information in form.you.value is treated as a number, not a string. (JavaScript has a tendency to look at things as strings, whether they are strings or not.)

JavaScript Is Very Fond of Strings

JavaScript will convert any form fields that are nothing but numbers into their string equivalents. Therefore, if you want to change the value of a number in a field, you should first use the eval( ) function to make sure that the field value is treated as a number, not a string. For example, if you have a form field called number and it holds the value 23, you add 5 to it like this:

```
form.number.value = form.number.value + 5;
```

The resulting number has the value "235", as though you were tacking strings together. However, you can use eval( ) to keep this from happening:

```
form.number.value = eval(form.number.value) + 5;
```

In this case, the result will be "28".

Now that you've learned about the important functions in the logic of this game, it's time to "spread the felt." Let's set up the gaming table.

Deal Me In

The game page needs two text form fields (for the house's and user's totals) and three buttons: Hit, Stand, and New Hand. Each button will have its own onClick event handler to process taking a card (for a hit) or having the dealer take cards (if the user chooses to stand). From the functions you've compiled so far, you can see that the following statements are true:

➤ The Hit button should run the User( ) function to see if the user has gone over 21.

➤ The Stand button should run the Dealer( ) function and then the LookAtHands( ) function to see who won.

➤ The New Hand button should reset the dealer's and user's hands to 0, clear the image index counter, clear any card images currently in view, and pick a new starting card for each player.

You create the game buttons with form fields that call the appropriate functions, such as:

```
<input type="button" value="Hit me!" onclick="User(this.form)">
<input type="button" value="Stand"
onclick="Dealer(this.form);LookAtHands(this.form);">
<input type="button" value="New Hand" onclick="init();NewHand(this.form)">
```

These form fields are placed within a table on the page to improve the look of the page.

Knowing that, you're ready for the complete script for the BlackJack game. Watch for the following things, which appear beside all described functions: the message form field at the top of the page, the table containing the scores and game buttons, and finally a table containing the 12 placeholder images for the cards.

```
<html>
<head>
<title>BlackJack</title>
</head>

<body onload="gameon=false;document.forms[1].reset()">
<script language="JavaScript">
<!-- Hide from non-JavaScript browsers
function init()
{
 dealidx=0;
 useridx=0;
 gameon=true
}

function pickSuit()
{
   suit = Math.round(Math.random() * (4-1))+1;

   if(suit == 1)
      return "Spades";

   if(suit == 2)
      return "Clubs";

   if(suit == 3)
      return "Diamonds";
```

```
      return "Hearts";
}

function cardName(card)
{
   if(card == 1)
      return "Ace";

   if(card == 11)
      return "Jack";

   if(card == 12)
      return "Queen";

   if(card == 13)
      return "King";

   return new String(card);
}

function cardValue(card)
{
   if(card == 1)
      return 11;

   if(card > 10)
      return 10;

   return card;
}

function message (msg)
{
 document.forms[0].message.value = msg
}

function ClearCards ()
{
 for (i=0; i<12; i++)
```

```
     { document.images[i].src="cards/blank.gif" }
}

function ShowCard (who, name, suit)
{
 //Construct filename for the card image
 if (name.length > 2)
  { name1=name.substring(0,1) }
 else { name1=name } ;
 name1=name1.toLowerCase()
 name2 = suit.substring(0,1);
 name2 = name2.toLowerCase();
 filename = "cards/"+ name1 + name2 + ".gif";

 //Load filename into correct image slot
 if (who=="dealer")
  { document.images[0+dealidx].src = filename; dealidx++ }
 else { document.images[6+useridx].src = filename; useridx++ }

}

function PickACard(strWho)
{
   card = Math.round(Math.random() * (13-1))+1;
   suit = pickSuit();

   ShowCard(strWho, cardName(card), suit);

   return cardValue(card);
}

function NewHand(form)
{
   ClearCards();
   message ("New game started — Good Luck!");
   form.dealer.value = 0;
   form.you.value = 0;

   form.dealer.value = eval(form.dealer.value) + PickACard("dealer");
   form.you.value = eval(form.you.value) + PickACard("user");
}
```

```
function Dealer(form)
{
  if (gameon==false)
   {message ("You must click 'New Hand' first!")}
  else
   {
    while(form.dealer.value < 17)
     {
      form.dealer.value = eval(form.dealer.value) + PickACard("dealer");
     }
   }
}


function User(form)
{
  if (gameon==false)
    {message ("You must click 'New Hand' first!")}
  else
    {
     form.you.value = eval(form.you.value) + PickACard("user");
     if(form.you.value > 21)
      {
       gameon=false;
       message("You busted! Game over, man. Click 'New Hand' to play again.");
      }
    }
}


function LookAtHands(form)
{
 if (gameon==true)
 {
   if(form.dealer.value > 21)
   { gameon=false;
     message("House busts! You win! Click 'New Hand' to play again.");
   }
   else   if(form.you.value > form.dealer.value)
   {
      gameon=false;
```

```
        message("You win! Click 'New Hand' to play again.");
    }
    else
    if(form.dealer.value == form.you.value)
    {
        gameon=false;
        message("Push! Good match — Click 'New Hand' to play again.");
    }
    else
    {
        gameon=false;
        message("House wins! Click 'New Hand' to try again.");
    }
 }
}
//-->
</script>


<h2><center>BlackJack</h2></center>
<center><form>
    <h5><input type=button name="message" value="To begin gambling, click 'New
Hand'. (Dealer stands on 17)">
    </h5>
</form></center>


<hr>


<form>
    <div align="center"><center><table border="3" width=40%>
        <tr>
            <td>Dealer has</td>
            <td><center><input type="text" size="5" name="dealer"></center></td>
        </tr>
        <tr>
            <td>You have</td>
            <td><center><input type="text" size="5" name="you"></center></td>
        </tr>
        <caption align="bottom">
         <input type="button" value="Hit me!" onclick="User(this.form)">
         <input type="button" value="Stand"
```

```
            onclick="Dealer(this.form);LookAtHands(this.form);">
                <input type="button" value="New Hand"
            onclick="init();NewHand(this.form)">
                </caption>
            </table>
            </center></div>
        </form>


        <table border="0" width="100%">
            <tr>
                <td>Dealer's Hand</td>
                <td><img src="cards/blank.gif" width="73" height="97">
                    <img src="cards/blank.gif" width="73" height="97">
                    <img src="cards/blank.gif" width="73" height="97">
                    <img src="cards/blank.gif" width="73" height="97">
                    <img src="cards/blank.gif" width="73" height="97">
                    <img src="cards/blank.gif" width="73" height="97">
                </td>
            </tr>
            <tr>
                <td>Your Hand</td>
                <td><img src="cards/blank.gif" width="73" height="97">
                    <img src="cards/blank.gif" width="73" height="97">
                    <img src="cards/blank.gif" width="73" height="97">
                    <img src="cards/blank.gif" width="73" height="97">
                    <img src="cards/blank.gif" width="73" height="97">
                    <img src="cards/blank.gif" width="73" height="97">
                </td>
            </tr>
        </table>

        </body>
        </html>
```

When viewed from a browser, your BlackJack game looks like the following figure.

Of course, this game will work best if you actually have the 52 card images to load. You can certainly make your own, but remember to change the dimensions coded into the HTML program to fit your images (the images used in this example were 97 pixels high and 73 pixels wide). However, if you don't want to attempt that on your own, visit the Web site for this book to download the card images used in this example.

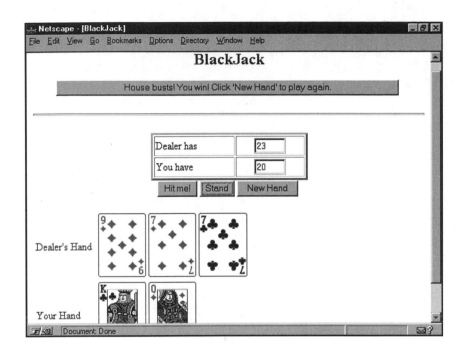

Gambling with JavaScript (it's cheaper than Vegas).

The Least You Need to Know

In this example, you learned how to create a game with JavaScript. Using the tools you've collected from previous chapters, you built a simple BlackJack player. You also saw how using the while statement makes it possible to continue working inside a function until some condition is met. To make sure that the totals you were building in the form were correct, eval( ) makes sure that field values are treated as numbers instead of strings. And with JavaScript 1.1's images[ ] array, you dynamically displayed images for the cards in each hand.

Chapter 22

Script Example 5: Welcome Back

In This Chapter

➤ Cookie recap

➤ Packing data into a cookie

➤ Extracting data from the cookie

➤ Custom content

A Warm Welcome

Everyone enjoys a warm welcome, even from a Web site. Back in Chapter 17, "Care for a Cookie?," you learned how a Web page can "remember" information about a visitor. Cookies make it possible to store information on a user's hard drive (or in his RAM), which can be retrieved when and if that person—or someone else using his computer—revisits the page.

In Chapter 17, you used a basic example of a cookie that "remembered" the time and date of a user's last visit to the page. Let's elaborate on that example in this chapter, and create a Welcome Back page, that meets the following criteria:

➤ Keeps track of a visitor's name, date of last visit, and number of visits in total.

➤ If no cookie is found for the user, he is asked to enter his name into a text form field, and the cookie is then created.

➤ If a cookie is found for the user, a customized welcome page appears, and the cookie information is updated. You'll also add a button with which the user can delete the cookie if he would like to become a "new visitor" again.

The major functions of this program are quite similar to those from Chapter 17; but they do boast a few additional enhancements. As usual, you'll begin by looking at each function of the Welcome Back program.

Constructing the Cookie

The cookie will be saved on two occasions: after the user enters his name (if this is his first visit to the page) and upon visiting the page (if this is not the user's first visit).

Remember that for a single cookie, you can store one string of information. However, you can cleverly pack as much useful data into this string as possible. When you code your GetCookie() function, you'll untangle the data to pull out the information you stored.

In this example, the cookie value actually contains three pieces of data: the date/time, the user's name, and the total number of visits so far. You'll pack this data into the single cookie named lastvisit, as follows:

```
lastvisit = datetime_username#totalvisits
```

By doing this, you can use the GetCookie() function to pull the date (the characters prior to the underscore), the user's name (the characters between the underscore and the pound sign), and the total number of visits (the characters to the right of the pound sign).

Setting Cookie

With that preamble, here is the code for SetCookie():

```
function SetCookie(name)
{
 cookidx++
 today = new Date ()
 expdate = new Date ()
 expdate.setTime(expdate.getTime() + (24 * 60 * 60 * 1000 * 365))
 expdate=expdate.toGMTString()
```

```
document.cookie="lastvisit="+escape(today)+"_"+name+"#"+cookidx+";
expires="+expdate+";"
}
```

Notice that SetCookie() takes one parameter, name, which is the name of the cookie. In this example, calls to SetCookie will pass it the name lastvisit because that's the only cookie this page uses.

Aside from that, this function is not unlike that in Chapter 17. The current date and time is calculated, and then a concatenated string containing the date, the user's name, the visit total (cookidx), and the expiration date is assigned to the cookie. Note also, though, cookidx, which is the counter to keep track of the user's visit total. At the top of this function, cookidx is incremented by one to add the current visit to the total.

Getting Cookie

Moving along, the "opposite" of SetCookie() will be GetCookie(). The object of GetCookie() is clear enough: to retrieve the cookie information and decode it into useful data. Although the following function may look complicated, it's not quite so bad. First it uses a while loop to locate and extract the cookie value from the entire cookie, and then it parses that value for the date, user name, and visit total.

```
function GetCookie (name)
{
 var namestr = name + "="
 var namelen = namestr.length
 var cooklen = document.cookie.length
 var i = 0
 while (i < cooklen)
  { var j = i + namelen
    if (document.cookie.substring(i, j) == namestr)
     { endstr = document.cookie.indexOf (";", j)
       if (endstr == -1) {endstr = document.cookie.length}
       tempstr = unescape(document.cookie.substring(j,endstr))
       //entire cookie value extracted into tempstr, now we can parse for details
       cookdate = tempstr.substring(0,tempstr.indexOf("_"))
       cookname = tempstr.substring(tempstr.indexOf("_")+1,tempstr.indexOf("#"))
       cookidx = tempstr.substring(tempstr.indexOf("#")+1,tempstr.length)

       return tempstr
     }
    i = document.cookie.indexOf(" ", i) + 1
```

233

```
    if (i == 0) break
  }
 return null
}
```

If GetCookie() fails to find a cookie with the specified name (e.g. lastvisit), it returns a null value. Otherwise, cookdate contains the date and time, cookname contains the user's name, and cookidx contains the visit total.

Canceling Cookie

Lastly, you need a function to delete the cookie, in case the user wants to eliminate the record of his visit. Though not vital, this is a courtesy function: Many Web surfers don't appreciate someone keeping track of them without their consent. If you provide a delete cookie function, the user at least has the opportunity to "cover his tracks."

```
function DeleteCookie (name)
{
 var expdate = new Date()
 expdate.setTime (expdate.getTime() - 1000000000)
 document.cookie= name + "=" + GetCookie(name) + "; expires=" +
expdate.toGMTString()
 location=thispage
}
```

Deleting the cookie isn't terribly difficult. Above, the current date is determined, and then a value representing a date in the past is assigned to expdate. The cookie is then re-saved with the new expiration date. Because this expiration date is before the current date, the cookie is now expired and, therefore, cannot be retrieved by the Web browser.

Finishing Touches

Having written the heart of the Welcome Back program, you only need to add some Web page content to make use of those functions.

In this case, you don't know for certain which Web page content to display. After all, if this is the user's first visit to the page (in which case, GetCookie() returns null because the cookie is non-existent or expired), you want to display a formal greeting and a request that the user enter his name to create the cookie. On the other hand, if this is a repeat visit, you want to display some customized content such as "Welcome back, Bill! This is visit #3, your last being on September 9, 1996." It's not unlike the well-known letter from Publisher's Clearing House, but the key is not to overdo the custom content (as in "Welcome to my page, BILL. Here, BILL, you will find information of interest to BILL.") You know what I mean.

To achieve that goal, you write some JavaScript code outside of a function. Instead, it simply resides between the <BODY> tags, where normal HTML code usually goes. As a result, this JavaScript code will automatically execute whenever the page is loaded.

```
<body bgcolor="#FFFFFF">
<SCRIPT Language="JavaScript">
<!-- Hide from non-JavaScript browsers
thispage="welcomeback.html"
cookidx=0
if (GetCookie("lastvisit") != null)
 { SetCookie(cookname)
   document.clear()
   document.writeln("<H2><center>Welcome back, "+cookname+"!</H2></center><p>")
   document.writeln("Thanks for returning to my home site. This is visit
#"+cookidx+" to this page, the last
   visit being on "+cookdate)
   document.writeln("<br><form><input type=button value='Delete Cookie'
   onClick=DeleteCookie('lastvisit')></form>")
 }
else
 { document.clear()
   document.writeln("<H2><center>Welcome to my home site!</H2></center><p>")
   document.writeln("Since this is your first time visiting my site, please enter
your name below. It will be used to identify you on future visits to this
page.<p>")
   document.writeln("<form><input type=text name=cookname width=15><br><input
type=button value='Submit!'
   onClick='SetCookie(this.form.cookname.value); location=thispage'></form>")
 }
//-->
</SCRIPT>
</body>
```

The above code revolves around a basic if statement: if GetCookie() does not return null (therefore the cookie exists, and this is not a first visit), a series of document.writeln statements constructs the "Welcome Back, so-and-so" greeting. Also note that a button is created with an onClick event handler to call the DeleteCookie() function, as a courtesy to the user. Alternatively, if GetCookie() does return null, a different series of document.writeln statements constructs another greeting page, which contains a text field for the user to submit his name.

In cases where the user either hits the Delete Cookie button or Submits his name to create the first-time cookie, the page is automatically reloaded with the "location=thispage" statement to reflect the change (thispage having been earlier assigned the true URL of this page).

Cookies Are Served!

Here it is: The entire Welcome Back page.

```
<html>
<head>
<title>My Home Site</title>
<SCRIPT Language="JavaScript">
<!-- Hide from non-JavaScript browsers
function SetCookie(name)
{
 cookidx++
 today = new Date ()
 expdate = new Date ()
 expdate.setTime(expdate.getTime() + (24 * 60 * 60 * 1000 * 365))
 expdate=expdate.toGMTString()
 document.cookie="lastvisit="+escape(today)+"_"+name+"#"+cookidx+";
expires="+expdate+";"
}
function GetCookie (name)
{
 var namestr = name + "="
 var namelen = namestr.length
 var cooklen = document.cookie.length
 var i = 0
 while (i < cooklen)
  { var j = i + namelen
    if (document.cookie.substring(i, j) == namestr)
     { endstr = document.cookie.indexOf (";", j)
       if (endstr == -1) {endstr = document.cookie.length}
       tempstr = unescape(document.cookie.substring(j,endstr))
       //entire cookie value extracted into tempstr, now we can parse for details
```

```
        cookdate = tempstr.substring(0,tempstr.indexOf("_"))
        cookname = tempstr.substring(tempstr.indexOf("_")+1,tempstr.indexOf("#"))
        cookidx = tempstr.substring(tempstr.indexOf("#")+1,tempstr.length)

        return tempstr
      }
    i = document.cookie.indexOf(" ", i) + 1
    if (i == 0) break
  }
 return null
}
function DeleteCookie (name)
{
 var expdate = new Date()
 expdate.setTime (expdate.getTime() - 1000000000)
 document.cookie= name + "=" + GetCookie(name) + "; expires=" +
expdate.toGMTString()
 location=thispage
}
//-->
</SCRIPT>
</head>
<body bgcolor="#FFFFFF">
<SCRIPT Language="JavaScript">
<!-- Hide from non-JavaScript browsers
thispage="welcomeback.html"
cookidx=0
if (GetCookie("lastvisit") != null)
 { SetCookie(cookname)
   document.clear()
   document.writeln("<H2><center>Welcome back, "+cookname+"!</H2></center><p>")
   document.writeln("Thanks for returning to my home site. This is visit
#"+cookidx+" to this page, the last visit being on "+cookdate)
   document.writeln("<br><form><input type=button value='Delete Cookie'
onClick=DeleteCookie('lastvisit')></form>")
 }
else
 { document.clear()
   document.writeln("<H2><center>Welcome to my home site!</H2></center><p>")
```

237

```
    document.writeln("Since this is your first time visiting my site, please enter
your name below. It will be used to identify you on future visits to this
page.<p>")
    document.writeln("<form><input type=text name=cookname width=15><br><input
type=button value='Submit!' onClick='SetCookie(this.form.cookname.value);
location=thispage'></form>")
 }
//-->
</SCRIPT>
</body>
</html>
```

When loaded into your Web browser for the first time, the Welcome Back page appears as pictured here.

The Welcome Back page upon first visitation.

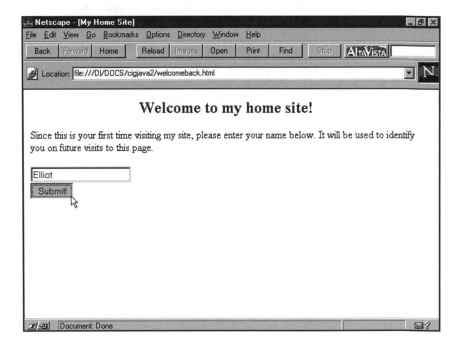

Future visits to the page recall the saved cookie and generate the friendlier greeting shown in the next figure.

When you return to the Welcome Back page, you see that you haven't been forgotten!

The Least You Need to Know

In this chapter, we returned to the theme from Chapter 17, "Care for a Cookie?," and took it to the "next level" (as they say in sports clichés). You learned how to pack several pieces of information into a single cookie and how to extract them later. You also saw how to use JavaScript to create custom content by writing HTML code directly to the page, using the data retrieved from the cookie. Publisher's Clearing House, look out!

Chapter 23

What to Do When It Won't Work: Debugging Your Scripts

In This Chapter

➤ Who the bugs are

➤ Spelling, grammar, and an apple for the teacher

➤ Capitals count

➤ Logic and Design

Bugs! Bugs! Bugs!

Whether it's ants at a picnic or cockroaches in the closet, bugs aren't most people's favorite critters. They get in things, spoil things, and generally cause a great deal of consternation. Their appearance usually gets a standard response: insecticide, a fly swatter, or a call to the exterminator. Bugs just aren't popular—unless maybe you're a bug collector. (Any bug collectors out there, please accept my apology; I'll use the proper term: entomologist.)

Computer programs are often much like life: Programs don't always work, and when they don't, it is said (in another humorous adaptation by programmers of yore), "This program has a bug." Whether you have termites in your walls or errors in your code, a bug is a bug, and a bug isn't good.

As you embark down the path to JavaScript enlightenment, you'll no doubt encounter a few bugs of your own. In the next few pages, you'll take a look at some of the more common causes of bugs and how to exterminate them.

The End Result

A bug can occur in two forms, one of which is sometimes more insidious than the other. The first sort of bug makes itself quite obvious—like a cockroach in the middle of the kitchen. These bugs prevent the program from executing beyond a certain point due to some illegal statement. JavaScript can recognize these and attempt to scold you, as you will learn shortly.

The more insidious bugs, perhaps not unlike termites deep in the foundation, are those that are not illegal statements but are based on incorrect logic. Your program executes because the statements are "legal," but the results are incorrect because your programming logic was flawed at some point. These can be extremely difficult to exterminate. We'll discuss such nasties second.

BZZT! The ERROR

When your bug is the result of an illegal statement, JavaScript will holler at you with a big pop-up alert box like the one shown here.

A JavaScript error message.

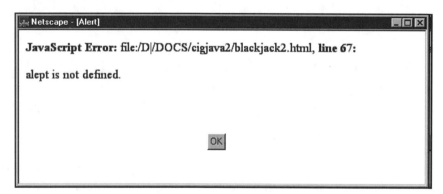

```
Netscape - [Alert]                                          _ □ X

JavaScript Error: file:/D|/DOCS/cigjava2/blackjack2.html, line 67:

alept is not defined.




                          OK
```

The first line of the error window identifies the file (or URL) where the bug occurred, while the second line tries to identify the bug. In this figure, the real problem was that a built-in JavaScript function was misspelled—but the error states that the function (as it was misspelled) was "not defined." This is the browser's way of saying, "I can't find a function by that name," and it makes an important point: errors that you may get in JavaScript will help tell where the bug occurred, but they may not tell you exactly what the error was. Therefore, figuring out what caused an error will sometimes require a bit of sleuthing.

Another thing you might notice is that the first line ends with the word "line" and a number. This is the line number in the HTML document where the error was found, which should at least help you find its location. Note that every line of the HTML file is counted as one line (not just those containing JavaScript code). Sometimes the URL is longer than the error window, and a scroll bar will appear so you can scroll within the error window to see the whole message.

Because illegal statement errors are often the easier bugs to get rid of, the previous information is half the battle if not more. JavaScript has already told you where and in which statement the problem lies. Thus, you can spelunk into the code to where the bug resides with some accuracy. From there, your final mission (which you should choose to accept) is to determine why the noted statement is illegal. There are several possibilities you should consider; they are detailed in the following sections.

Tpyo...er...Tipo...uh...Spelling Errors

By far, the most common source of bugs is the typographical error. In a word: that darned misspelling. Unlike humans, who can still get the general idea of what you're trying to say (whether you remember to put the "i" before the "e" or not), computers aren't so flexible. If it isn't spelled exactly right, the computer doesn't have a clue what you mean. The problem with "typos," as they're called, is that (as you saw in the previous section) the browser isn't smart enough to say, "Ahh, you didn't spell it right." If it were, the browser would know what the right value was...right?

Instead, a typo can cause one of several things to happen:

➤ **Nothing is displayed.** This happens, for example, when you misspell an HTML tag. By definition of HTML, if a browser encounters a tag it doesn't recognize, it ignores it. This is especially a problem when you get really fancy with JavaScript, as you can use document.write() and string construction to dynamically build HTML statements to display (and because the HTML tags are being generated, they are harder to see).

➤ **The HTML tag is displayed**, even though you want it to format text and not show itself. Again, this is a side effect of the browser's interpretation of HTML. Sometimes, when a browser can't identify a tag, it assumes that the tag is actually text to be displayed.

➤ **A property value is not set or changed.** The JavaScript-enabled browser will obediently set the "property" to the specific value. But because this isn't the same property you wanted to adjust, the result will be different than you expected.

➤ **A "??? is undefined" message is displayed.** This is most common with functions because JavaScript must be able to find the function code whenever it encounters a function call.

And the list goes on…and on…and on. In a nutshell, spelling something wrong is a lot like trying to order food in a French bistro when you don't speak French: Depending on what word you get wrong, you could end up with anything from a scoop of sorbet to a boiled shoe. Check your spelling!

A Capital Idea

FYI…
Appendix A lists all the components of JavaScript. In addition, Chapters 5 through 17 show the proper capitalization for JavaScript functions, objects, and properties.

"Kissin' cousins" to spelling errors are errors in capitalization. The JavaScript documentation notes that JavaScript is case-sensitive (upper- and lowercase matter). Case is important, and capitalization is critical.

Many functions, methods, and properties in JavaScript are "compound words" made up of multiple words slapped together (for example, getDate()). In most cases, the second word is capitalized while the first word is not. If you try to type in a JavaScript component and don't capitalize the second (or third, or fourth) word, you'll probably generate an error.

Matching Mates

On many occasions in JavaScript programming, you use paired bookends, such as brackets { }, parentheses ( ), and both single- and double-quotation marks. As with socks in the laundry, improperly matched pairs will result in a statement of problematic fashion. It is vital that every open bracket and parenthesis have an appropriate closing mate somewhere further down in the code. People most often lose track when they are nesting parentheses or brackets, such as when they are using a loop statement within a loop statement.

It is not uncommon to find multiple closing parentheses or brackets at the end of a series of statements; each one pairs up with an opening mate that appears earlier. It might look strange, but an eye for an eye and a bracket for a bracket, as they say (don't they?). Well, it's something to watch for.

JavaScript Errors

If you're still stumped and you're positive you spelled everything correctly, move on to Phase 2: Interpreting the JavaScript error message. JavaScript has a handful of errors that it kicks up for a variety of situations. Take a look at each and note what to check for if you encounter one. For purposes of the "error lineup," look at the second line of text displayed in the error window. Any parts of the message that may change will be represented by a string of question marks (?????).

????? Is Not Defined

You've already met this guy. He's trying to tell you that either you misspelled something or you have forgotten to include the function body (the guts of the function) in the script. It might also mean that the function requires an uppercase letter or two, so you might want to check the function against what you find here in the book.

????? Is Not a Function

You tried to call an object's function (for example, document.write()), but the function doesn't exist. Check the spelling and capitalization.

????? Is Not a Numeric Literal

You attempted to perform some sort of math operation on a string. For example, if you wanted to take the numeric value 2 and display "2nd" on the screen, something like this

```
document.write(2 + "nd");
```

will generate the error. This is because, as JavaScript evaluates the expression inside the parentheses, the type of the expression is whatever variable type JavaScript encounters first when reading from left to right (or whatever way is the default for evaluation; using more than one pair of parentheses can change this order). In this example, JavaScript assumes that you want to print out a numeric value, but then you try to tack a string on the end (which is a no-no).

To get around this, you need to "convert" the expression to a string before you start evaluating it. You can easily do this by adding a "null" or "empty" string in front of the number like this:

```
document.write("" + 2 + "nd");
```

The Dreaded Crash

Sometimes things get really hairy, and you're presented with the infamous "illegal operation" dialog box.

This message means that something's seriously wrong!

After you see this message, Netscape or Internet Explorer itself shuts down. First rule: don't panic. Chances are you've made some simple mistake, and although the browser *should* have a better way of handling it, instead it charges forward blindly until it gets hopelessly stuck.

A common way to cause this error (if you really like creating bugs instead of fixing them) is to try to treat a numeric value like a string and manipulate it. For example, this code

```
var n = 264;
document.write(n.substring(0, 1));
```

will definitely cause a crash. However, if you convert the number to a string first, like this

```
var n = 264;
var strN = "" + n;
document.write(strN.substring(0, 1));
```

then everything's fine.

Along the same lines, calling a method of a numeric variable (even if it's not a string method) may cause the browser to explode. There isn't any "solution." Rather, the best thing to do is to live by the punch line to that old joke: don't do it. Actually, the fault isn't yours, it's the browser's—it should generate an error in such circumstances, not crash. Presumably, future browser revisions will weed out these landmines. On the other hand, they may also introduce others. Fortunately, at least, you won't be the only one to discover the problem, and if a browser has a true defect, it will become well known in the JavaScript support areas (newsgroups, mailing lists, Web pages, etc).

Design Errors (or "Why Did My House Just Collapse?")

Often sneakier and much more difficult to track down are *outcome bugs*. These do not result from an illegal statement that JavaScript cannot understand. They are the results of errors in program design, which produce the wrong results when you execute the program.

Think of an entire JavaScript program (or any computer program, for that matter) as a large exercise in logic and grammar. Even if your grammar is impeccable (JavaScript makes no error complaints), your logic may be flawed. It may be flawed in one tiny section of code or in several tiny sections of code, or your entire design might be logically flawed.

Ultimately, the only solution to these problems requires three possible steps:

1. Locate the region of code likely to contain the design flaw.

2. Follow the logic, and then redesign where necessary.

3. Return to step 1 if the problem persists.

Finding the Holes Where the Rain Gets In

Suppose you've written a JavaScript program that calculates a loan payment schedule. The program contains no syntax errors, but the alleged payment amount it reports is clearly incorrect. You have a design flaw (don't feel too depressed; virtually every program contains some design flaw the first time around).

To locate the region of code where the flaw most likely is, you have to consider the program itself. Presumably, you have several functions in such a program, each of which performs some calculation. Therefore, any of those would make good suspects at this point; after all, a wrong final tally is probably caused by an erroneous calculation.

Look at the sections of code you might suspect. Read them over carefully and follow the logic in your mind. If no flaw is immediately apparent, dip into the programmer's toolbox for handy debugging tool number one: the inside scooper.

One of the most revealing ways to track down design bugs is to gain some insight into what is going on "behind the scenes" while the program executes. A very common way to do this is to stick new lines of code here and there that display the current values of particular variables. This way, when you execute the program again, you have a better idea of what is going on "in there." In JavaScript, you can do this using the window.alert() method. For example, imagine that the suspect code looks like this:

```
function evalform (address) {
   crucial = address.indexOf("@");

   if(crucial == -1) {
      window.alert ("Your e-mail address is invalid! " +
                    "You are an abject liar!");
      return false;
   } else {
      message = "You entered " + address + " — is this correct?";
      return window.confirm(message);
   }
}
```

To check behind the scenes, you need to find out just what JavaScript thinks the values of address and crucial are. So you could stick the following two lines just after the second line above:

```
window.alert ("Value of address is "+address);
window.alert ("Value of crucial is "+crucial);
```

When the program executes again, the values for those variables are displayed, giving you a clue as to whether they are at least what you were expecting them to be. If they aren't, you must begin your investigation again, but at least you've narrowed it down. (Do remember, though, to remove these lines of code once the program is working, because they're not intended to be part of the final program.)

In addition to variable values, another common test is for program flow. Did the execution even reach your function? Perhaps your function was never even executed because of some other design flaw in your logic. You can easily test for this just as you did before: somewhere within the questionable function, stick a line that you're sure will generate some action if the function is, in fact, being executed. You could insert the line `window.alert ("Hi function bob was just called")`, for instance.

Sigh and Rebuild

Using some combination of the previous example—perhaps many times, if necessary— you will eventually track down the region of code that is logically flawed. From there, you must identify the flaw and rebuild to correct it. Once you're certain you have the right portion of code, the only sure way to identify the flaw, is to step through it mentally, bit by bit. In a Zen-like way, imagine that you are the computer, and attempt to interpret the code exactly as the computer would. You might even grab a pencil and paper and write down the values of variables as you progress through your mental exercise. This can be very tough work. Sometimes the logic flaw will pop out at you quickly. In a most difficult case, however, you might be completely stumped. This is the "art" of programming.

A clear head always helps, so time away from the screen can be a benefit. Equally useful are smart people—or at least experienced ones; there are many places on the Internet where people exchange programming hints and pose questions to others. Check out the UseNet newsgroup `comp.lang.javascript` for just such chatter and support.

The Mighty Debugger

Internet Explorer users are often on the short end of the stick when it comes to JavaScript support, but when it comes to bug extermination, you're in for a treat. Microsoft has recently released a free JavaScript debugger utility, which you can download from:

http://www.microsoft.com/ie/activex/debug.htm

Once you download and install the debugger, it hooks into Internet Explorer's View, Source feature. Additionally, it will also pop up anytime Internet Explorer runs into an error when executing a JavaScript program.

But what *is* this debugger? In short, it is a small utility that helps you follow the logic and flow of the JavaScript program. Like a programmer's VCR, when the debugger is launched you can "freeze frame" or "step forward" and "step back" through the JavaScript code. The debugger shows which line of code is currently being executed. In this way, you can see where if…then clauses are leading to, how loops are functioning, and so on. This is an excellent way to find out when a program is skipping a bit of code or going to a different bit of code than you anticipated. And once you find the problem, you can fix your program so that it flows correctly.

Remember, though, that the Microsoft Debugger only works with Internet Explorer, not Netscape Navigator. This does limit its usefulness, because Netscape Navigator is the better browser for running JavaScript programs. Perhaps a debugger will be released for Navigator as well. Perhaps one already has been by the time you read this!

The Least You Need to Know

Bugs are a common problem when you're creating any type of program, and a JavaScript program is no exception. JavaScript tries to provide information on where the bug is and what it is, but it doesn't always offer the most accurate analysis of the problem. Furthermore, some bugs can generate errors that makes no sense whatsoever—unless you understand a few tricks.

For the most part, mistakes in spelling or capitalization are the worst culprits when it comes to bugs. The three questions you, as a JavaScripter, should ask are:

➤ Is everything spelled correctly?

➤ Is everything capitalized correctly?

➤ Do all my open parentheses and brackets have accompanying closed parentheses or brackets?

If your code is free from grammatical errors, it might be suffering from design flaw. You need to examine the logic of your code. For that purpose, you might try these suggestions:

➤ Insert window.alert() methods in various places to reveal the values of variables. This gives you behind-the-scenes insight.

➤ Use window.alert() methods to indicate whether a function is even being called at all.

249

➤ If your JavaScript program is compatible with Internet Explorer, download and install Microsoft's script debugger. It's like a programmer's VCR: It enables you to follow the logical flow of the JavaScript code as it is executed and spot problems as they happen.

Chapter 24

Ideas

In This Chapter

➤ Things to try with JavaScript

Document Madness

Take the first example (your "Hello World" script in Chapter 18) and extend it to do other things to the page. Remember that you can access the document object from inside or outside of a JavaScript function. Experiment with:

➤ Writing HTML tags inside the <SCRIPT> tag.

➤ Changing other attributes of the document (text color, link color, and so on).

➤ Placing the <SCRIPT> tag in the BODY of the document instead of the HEAD, so that any JavaScript statements that aren't part of a function are executed whenever the script loads.

➤ Use script hiding to create parts of the document that are visible only to people running JavaScript-enabled browsers.

To take one example, imagine that you'd like to present the user with an opening greeting and an important message. You can ensure that the user reads this message before proceeding with the page by inserting a window.alert() method immediately after the <BODY> tag.

This ensures its execution every time the page is loaded. Regardless of what else is in this page, you might write code such as:

```
<BODY>
<SCRIPT language="JavaScript">
<!-- begin hide
window.alert("Thank you for visiting the Spice Tours 97. " +
             "Before you read on, you must be 21 to continue.");
// end hide -->
</SCRIPT>

... rest of page HTML code and possibly more JavaScript ...

</BODY>
```

Whenever a user accesses this page, the first encounter he'll have will look like the following figure.

Disclaimers—the wave of the future.

Custom Pages

Using the random() function you learned about in Chapter 19, create a page that changes its appearance based on:

➤ The time of day

➤ The day of the week

➤ The month

➤ Whether it's a holiday

Or, just cook up something that's different every time a user loads it. Try changing the color, the text that's displayed, or both. Many users create pages that never change again, which results in a certain staleness. You can include the preceding items in your program to spice up a page without requiring a lot of owner maintenance. For example, consider this function, which is called when the page is opened in a browser:

```
function colorday() {
   dateobj = new Date();
   today = dateobj.getDay();

   if (today == 1) {
      document.bgColor="blue";
   }

   if (today == 2) {
      document.bgColor="teal";
   }

   if ((today > 3) || (today == 0)) {
      document.bgColor="salmon";
   }
}
```

Using this function, the current day would be determined and assigned to today (in JavaScript, 0 is Sunday, 1 is Monday, and so on). From there, you simply use a series of if...then statements to assign various colors to the background depending on which day it is. Mondays are blue, Tuesdays are teal.... Clever, huh?!

Web Roulette

The window object has a method that allows you to load another URL. To see how it works, write a script that randomly picks a URL from a list and takes the user there at the click of a button. For this, you'd rely on the method window.open(), which would spawn a new browser window and connect to a URL you specify. Recall that this method is described in detail in Chapter 10, and it is also referenced in the list of objects and functions in Appendix A, "JavaScript: The Complete Overview."

The design behind this should be comprehensible by now. This program would require three key components:

➤ An array of URLs to choose from. You construct this array just as you did in Chapter 19, with the MakeArray() function.

➤ The random() function, which will choose one of the URLs from the array.

➤ The window.open() method.

Given that you covered each of these components in detail previously in the book, a simple Web Roulette script should be quick work—allowing you that much more time to design the nifty roulette wheel graphics!

Tour Guide

Using the window object's URL loading method, create a sequence of pages that automatically take the user from one page to the next. You could do this as a "slide show" of your favorite work or for an automated "kiosk" that displays your company's products.

Games, Games, Games

Extend the blackjack example to handle these elements:

➤ Betting

➤ Aces that can be 1 or 11

➤ The house hitting on "soft 17"

➤ Splits, double-downs, insurance, and so on

Or try your hand at writing a different game. Perhaps Poker, Roulette, Craps, or Hearts. You can include graphics of the cards and actually display the hands.

Would you like to play a game? By Stephen Wassell.

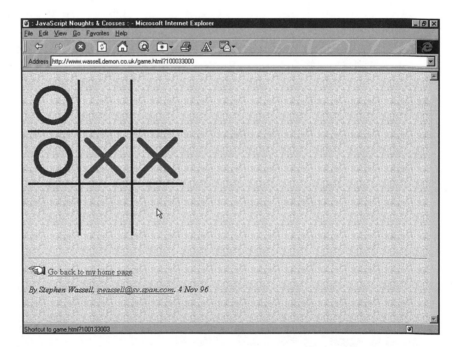

Sell T-Shirts

A basic catalog implementation might revolve around T-shirt sales. You might, for instance, include a series of images or text descriptions representing the clever witticism on each shirt. These images or text may be designed as either HTML links or standard HTML text accompanied by an "Add this item to shopping cart" button. Use an onClick event to catch the order, and then add the price of the shirt to a cumulative total (as you did in Chapter 8 with your mug-selling venture).

You can even construct an invoice that is output to the Web browser using string concatenations and the document.write() method when the visitor clicks on some appropriate "Go to Cashier" link. And you might want to program in the option to remove items from the cart—in case the user has a last minute change of heart.

A Script That Writes Scripts

JavaScript's text handling allows you to build text strings out of parts of strings. Create a script that allows a user to pick options from a table and then generates an HTML document that incorporates those selections. For example, you can create a "build your own home page" or a "list of favorite links" script.

Spreadsheet

A spreadsheet is nothing more than a table that performs operations on the data in its cells. Write a script that makes a table act like a spreadsheet. With the substring parsing capabilities of JavaScript, you can even build "formulas" that are analyzed when the user clicks Compute.

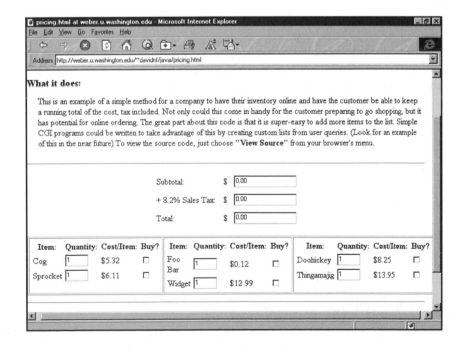

One form of a spreadsheet: a running purchase total, by David Nagy-Farkas.

255

Database Query Front-End

Given a table of options, the user can select various components and have the script build a query (using SQL, for example) that can be submitted to a database. To actually utilize this, you would need access to the Web server's CGI interface because JavaScript can't read information outside its document.

Check This Out...

Groaning over Your Loan?

You can download a handy loan calculator script (among others) from this book's page on the Que Web site at:

http://www.mcp.com/que/new_users/cig-jscript/!start_here.html

Take this script and extend it to compute any data field based on the information provided in the other fields. You can also use the script to compute and display the principal and interest amounts of each payment for the life of the loan.

Tutoring

You can design a JavaScript-based Web site that offers tutoring services in a variety of subjects. Programming the informational text itself would be simple enough, and even customizing it to an individual user could rely on string concatenations and document.write() methods.

To test skills in either flash card or multiple-choice format you could use regular buttons and radio buttons. Questions could either be presented in a relevant sequence or using the random() function. In addition, you could use event handling to interpret the student's answers and provide context-sensitive responses—perhaps even correct answers, explanations, or repeated attempts at the question.

Keep track of cumulative right/wrong totals and output a customized "report card" at the end of each lesson.

And the Scripting Goes On

Here are some other scripting ideas you might want to try:

➤ A "quote of the day" script

➤ A full-blown calculator—simple, financial, or scientific (see the following figure)

➤ A board game such as Monopoly, Mastermind, or Yahtzee

➤ Whatever else you can think of!

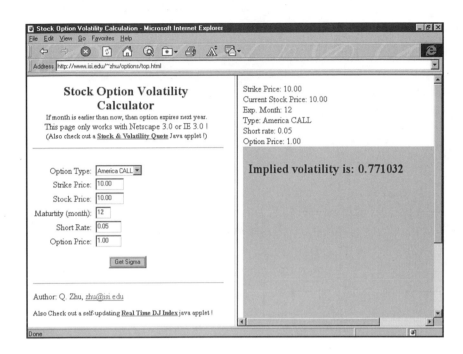

*An inspired
JavaScript calculator,
which also controls a
Java applet for the
advanced calcula-
tions (in the frame
on the right).*

The Least You Need to Know

➤ JavaScript is such a powerful extension to HTML and the Web that you can do almost anything with JavaScript that you can do with Java—but without having to write and compile full-blown programs.

➤ Take a little time to explore on the Web. Check out some of the sites covered in Chapter 4. See what other JavaScripters are up to.

➤ When you've created your script and it is working "perfectly," load it onto your Web site and invite the world to stop by.

Chapter 25

Stepping Up to Straight Java

In This Chapter

➤ What is Java?

➤ The Java Developer's Kit

➤ Integrating Java into HTML

➤ How to get up to speed writing your own applets

➤ Connecting to Java with JavaScript

JavaScript's Big Brother

If you've made it this far in the book, good for you! As you've seen, JavaScript is a very powerful language for extending the capabilities of your World Wide Web pages. No doubt, as you've surfed around checking out other authors' uses of JavaScript (okay, and peeked at their source code to get more ideas), you've encountered talk about a thing called Java. If you're the curious sort, you're probably wondering just what Java is and whether it's worth looking into. In this chapter, I'll explain what Java is and how you can start to develop your own Java applets. Even if full-blown Java programming isn't your "cup of tea," as they say, you might want to use JavaScript to connect with and control Java applets, which you'll see in the final section of this chapter.

Java is a full-blown programming language, designed for the purpose of providing "truly interactive" content through the World Wide Web; Java is the language on which JavaScript is based. Developed by Sun Microsystems, Java attempts to bridge the "multiple platform" gap that exists on the Internet by creating applications (called applets) that will run on any computer of any type—as long as a Java-enabled browser is handy. The same Java applet will run on Windows 95, Windows NT, UNIX, and Macintosh, eliminating the need for customizing the applet to the particular computer.

Java Relies on a "Virtual Computer"

In order to pull off the trick of being useable on a variety of platforms, Java applets actually run on what's called the Java Virtual Machine. Look at it this way: Certain programs available today enable you to run Windows software on a Macintosh, or UNIX software on a Windows computer, and so on. They do this by emulating the behavior of a particular computer type (they "pretend" to be a Mac or Windows or UNIX machine so that the software thinks it's running on the correct computer). The Java Virtual Machine is another type of emulator, but it doesn't emulate Mac, Windows, or UNIX. Rather, it pretends to be a totally different type of system. And by defining what the Java computer can and cannot do, Sun was able to create a program that—no matter what physical hardware it's run on—will always look like a Java computer to the applets.

Confounded Compiling

Because Java is a programming language (like Pascal, BASIC, C, or C++), to work with it, you have to write a program. Java programs are similar to JavaScript scripts, except that they are much more extensive and require a lot of additional material in order to successfully complete the next phase of Java development: compiling. *Compiling* an applet means to take the program you've written and run a special program on it that converts it from "near-human-readable" format to "Java-machine-readable" format (called *bytecode*) so that a Java browser can run the applet.

Java is an "object-oriented" programming language most closely related to C++. "Object-oriented" is a difficult concept to explain clearly, but in essence, it means that the language revolves around manipulating end-results instead of designing the tools for manipulation. An object-oriented sculptor, for instance, would be more concerned with melding together various blocks of clay than with the tools that carve the clay initially. The popular construction toy Legos is a nice example of an object-oriented activity.

In this chapter, you're not going to dig deep into the bowels of Java. Like JavaScript, Java is still evolving, and by the time you're holding this book in your hands, there will no doubt be newer tools available for creating Java applets. Instead, you'll take a quick glance at what it takes to put together an applet and at how to link applets into your HTML pages.

To start, you'll need to do a little surfing and pick up a copy of the collection of utilities Sun puts out to aid Java programmers. It's called the Java Developer's Kit.

Java Browsing

As with JavaScript, you need to use a Java-capable browser to run Java applets. At the time of this writing, the 32-bit versions of both browsers discussed in this book (Microsoft Internet Explorer 3.0 and Netscape Navigator 3.0) support Java. For Windows 3.1 users (16-bit) interested in Java, both Netscape and Microsoft are planning to release Java-capable versions of their browsers in 16-bit form within the year; they may have already done so by the time you read this.

The Java Developer's Kit

Before you dive into Java programming, you need to pick up a copy of the Java Developer's Kit (JDK for short). The JDK includes:

➤ A compiler to turn your applet program code into bytecode, the language the interpreter understands.

➤ An interpreter that runs your applets one line at a time.

➤ An applet viewer for testing and running applets.

➤ A debugger to help track down problems in your applet code.

➤ A collection of example applets to play with.

➤ A huge collection of documentation files in browser (HTML) format.

➤ An upgrade utility to convert any old applets (created before the Java specifications were solidified) to the current standard.

In a nutshell, the JDK has everything the budding Java programmer needs to start.

What? How much does it cost? Well, put your checkbook away! The JDK is available free off the Internet. Simply fire up your browser (any browser will do) and point it at the Sun Java Homesite at the address below. The following figure shows the Sun Java Homesite.

http://www.javasoft.com/

Links to download the Java Developer's Kit.

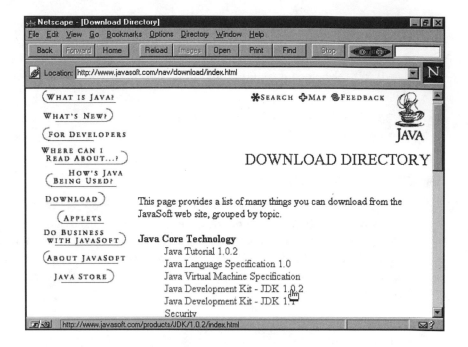

Browse your way into the Download section, and you'll find the links for downloading the JDK for your machine. Note that, as pictured above, there are actually two JDK's currently available: one for Java 1.02 and one for Java 1.1. If you want to create applets compatible with the current crop of Java-capable browsers, stick with 1.02. Java 1.1 is the newest release of Java and contains special features that the 3.0 browsers don't support yet (presumably, the 4.0 versions of Internet Explorer and Netscape Navigator will support JDK 1.1 applets). The file you'll be downloading is rather large (4M or more), so start the download process and then go get a cup of coffee.

When the file has been downloaded completely, follow these steps:

1. Move the file to the root of the drive where you want to install the JDK (C:\ for example). Make sure that you have at least 5 megabytes of free space on the disk before going to the next step (that's 5 megabytes after you copy the file to it).

2. Run the file (from a DOS window, or by selecting **File**, **Run** from Windows NT, or by selecting the **Run** option on Windows 95's Start menu).

Techno Talk

An .EXE File That Unpacks Itself? This is called a self-extracting archive, and all you have to do is "run" it. In Windows 3.x, you can choose **File**, **Run** from the Program Manager; in Windows 95, you choose **Run** from the **Start** menu on the taskbar. The file then decompresses and installs itself.

262

The file will automatically unpack itself, create a \java directory and a bunch of subdirectories, and copy a ton of files into these new directories. When all this is done, you can delete the original file (or store it in a safe place, if you like to keep a copy around just in case).

Where Are the Manuals?

One of the nice things about the JDK is the existence of very thorough documentation. What documentation, you ask? Well, if you fire up your browser and open the \java\progguide\index.html file, you'll be introduced to one of the nicest documentation collections on Java and the JDK available (see the following figure).

JDK online documentation.

Now, scroll down a bit. As you can see in the next figure, below the Getting Started heading, you'll find Duke, the Java mascot (a cute little guy who looks amazingly like the Starfleet insignia). Look at that—he's waving at you! You guessed it. Duke's a Java applet!

All of the documentation that comes with the JDK is available in HTML format, so you might want to browse around a bit right now before going further in the book. One thing to note, though, is that not all the HTML files in the JDK are linked to the other files. The JDK contains a collection of document sets. You can simply list all of the JDK help files with the File Manager or the Windows Explorer and double-click any of the HTML files you like. They will then be opened into your browser.

Duke waves a friendly greeting. Resist the temptation to wave back.

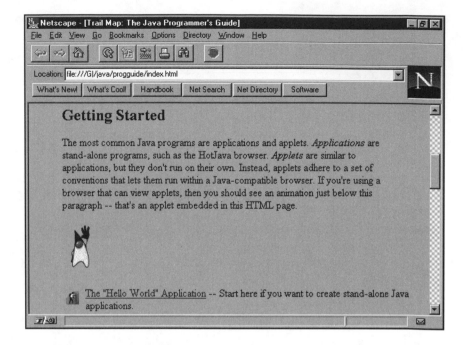

Back from your local surfing? Good! Take a quick detour into HTML to see how Java applets connect to Web pages: the <APPLET> tag.

Introducing the <APPLET> Tag

Just as JavaScript scripts are identified by their own custom HTML tag (the <SCRIPT> tag you learned about back in Chapter 3), Java applets are included in Web pages through their own custom tag: the <APPLET> tag. As with other HTML tags, browsers that don't support Java will simply ignore the tag, so you can safely create Java-enabled pages that don't limit their viewing to Java-enabled users. (However, you will need to do a little more HTML to provide those who haven't caught up with the times something to look at).

The CODE Attribute Must Be Relative Unlike most other HTML tags and attributes that use URLs, the CODE attribute cannot be an absolute URL; it must point to something *relative* to the current directory the HTML files are in.

The <APPLET> tag's structure is relatively simple. Actually, there are two tags that work together: APPLET and PARAMS. The <APPLET> tag looks like this:

```
<APPLET CODE="appletFile" WIDTH=pixels HEIGHT=pixels>
<!-- Alternate HTML code goes here -->
</APPLET>
```

The CODE attribute identifies the applet program and is a file with a ".class" extension located in the same directory as the HTML document. To make your page do something for those poor souls who don't have a Java-enabled browser, you can place any additional alternative HTML statements inside the <APPLET> tag. Java browsers will ignore these statements, and non-Java browsers will ignore the <APPLET> tag (which works out quite well, don't you think?).

The WIDTH and HEIGHT attributes define the size of the applet on the page. An applet's size is specified in pixels. In addition, there are several other optional attributes that you can add to the <APPLET> tag to modify its behavior.

CODEBASE

The CODEBASE attribute lets you specify a URL (directory path) where your applet .class files are located (if they're in a place other than your HTML documents). As I mentioned previously, if you don't specify CODEBASE, the applets are assumed to be in the same directory as the HTML files.

ALT

If, for some reason, a browser understands the <APPLET> tag but can't run applets (for example, if the browser's Java capability has been disabled by the user), you can specify some text to display with the ALT attribute. This is similar to the ALT attribute of the <IMG> tag, which displays the specified text string on browsers that don't show graphics (text-based browsers or browsers with image loading disabled).

NAME

The NAME attribute does the same thing for <APPLET> that it does for other HTML tags: It gives the applet a name, allowing other applets on the same page to locate and talk with each other (in much the same way JavaScript uses NAME to find and talk to different frames or fields in forms).

ALIGN

Just like the <IMG> tag attribute of the same name, ALIGN controls how the applet is lined up. Acceptable values of the attribute are LEFT, RIGHT, TOP, TEXTTOP, MIDDLE, ABSMIDDLE, BASELINE, BOTTOM, and ABSBOTTOM.

VSPACE and HSPACE

These attributes also behave the same way their <IMG> tag counterparts do: They specify the amount of space (in pixels) to leave above and below the applet (VSPACE) and on each side of the applet (HSPACE).

265

Passing Applet Parameters

Those of you who remember the days of DOS (those glory days before Windows, X-Windows, and the Macintosh made pictures out of everything) might recall that you could run some programs by typing the name of the program and adding additional information on the command line before pressing the Enter key. Those additional pieces of information were called parameters.

It's possible to create applets that can take parameters. (In the case of applets, parameters are additional options that are unique to the applet and aren't covered by other <APPLET> attributes.) Passing parameter values to an applet is done with the <PARAM> tag. <PARAM> tags are placed after the <APPLET> tag and before any of the "alternate HTML" statements and the </APPLET> tag. The <PARAM> tag looks like this:

```
<PARAM NAME=appletAttribute VALUE=value>
```

In that expression, NAME identifies the particular attribute, and VALUE identifies its value. If you have more than one parameter, you use more than one <PARAM> tag. The parameters available depend on the particular applet in question and are defined by the applet's programmer in the source code to the Java applet. For Java programmers, inside the applet code, you access the values passed in with <PARAM> with the getParameter() function.

For example, imagine an applet named ScrollText. As advertised, this applet can scroll a text message across the browser window. It's stored in the file ScrollText.class and can take several parameters that customize its behavior:

You Can Spot Old (pre-JDK) Applets Easily
As you surf the Web, if you come across an applet that's implemented in HTML using an <APP> tag instead of the JDK <APPLET> tag, you've found an old applet that was created prior to the standardization of Java. For it to function in today's browsers, it may have to be upgraded via the utilities provided in the JDK.

```
<APPLET CODE="ScrollText.class" NAME="scroller" HEIGHT=100
WIDTH=300>
 <PARAM NAME=text VALUE="Welcome to my Home Page">
 <PARAM NAME=font VALUE="Arial">
 <PARAM NAME=speed VALUE=20>
</APPLET>
```

In the above HTML example, you first specify the applet ScrollText.class, name it scroller, and set its dimensions. Then, having referred to the applet's documentation, you set three parameters: text (with the message to scroll), font (with the font style to render the text), and speed (which controls the pace of the scroll). Remember that these parameters are individually programmed into each applet and are particular to an applet.

Java with Class

Java and JavaScript share many things, including the "objects" or things that give you access to different parts of a Web page. Java extends this by allowing you to create your own types of objects, as well as by offering up a larger collection of "canned" objects. Predefined objects in Java are bundled together in "classes" or collections of objects that share a common purpose.

Classes are at the heart of what makes Java an object-oriented language. A class is like a library of objects, all of which inherit certain characteristics from the class itself. "Class" is a hierarchical concept: One class could be a subset of a higher-level class. In Java, there is an "abstract class," which is a parental class containing many child classes. In this case, though, the abstract class is never directly used. Rather, it is defined solely to provide the "genes" for its children classes.

If any of this seems confusing, that's because it is. That is why entire books are written about object-oriented programming and Java in particular. Now, though, at least you have a taste for what object-orientedness is about: modules that are part of larger modules, which are part of even larger modules.

C++ is a very common object-oriented programming language that also revolves around these class concepts. One major difference between C++ and Java, in terms of how they deal with classes, is that Java programs can more easily withstand changes in class definitions without breaking any programs based on the previous definitions. In C++, on the other hand, if you change any class definitions, every program written using the previous definitions must be recompiled. For this reason, Sun calls Java "dynamic."

Hello World!

Let's close with a quick look at making your own Java applet. As it was in JavaScript, your first applet should be the traditional "Hello World" program. The Java program looks like this:

```
/* HelloWorld.java: Hello World...Java Style */
public class HelloWorld
{
public static void main(String args[])
{
System.out.println("Hello World!");
}
}
```

Save this file as HelloWorld.java. Then, after you type that, you need to compile the applet. Get yourself to a DOS prompt (you'll need to open a DOS window to do this) and type the following:

```
javac HelloWorld.java
```

Finally, you can run your new applet right from DOS by typing this:

```
java HelloWorld
```

Congratulations! You've just taken another big step: Java programming!

Command Line? I'm Running a Mac!

If you're running a Macintosh (or a PowerPC), you're probably a bit confused by the reference to a "command line" because the Mac operating system doesn't have one. Does this mean that Mac users are out of luck when it comes to creating Java applets? Sadly, at this moment, the answer is "Yes—unless you're willing to spend some money." There are no environments or library sets (source code) for Java compiling on the Mac available for free off the Internet. Several companies (Symantec at **http://www.symantec.com/** and Metrowerks at **http://www.metrowerks.com/** to name two) have announced that they will be integrating Java applet creation into their compilers, but their products aren't available yet.

Natural Intelligence, however, does market a package called Roaster that gives Mac users the ability to compile and develop Java applets on the Mac from inside the Mac OS. For more information, check out Natural's web page at this address: **http://www.natural.com/**.

Mating Java and JavaScript

A significant new feature in JavaScript 1.1 is called "LiveConnect." Actually a set of features, LiveConnect allows you, using JavaScript code, to poke into the core of an applet. By doing so, you can gain access to an applet's variables, methods, and classes. You can exploit this to change the way an applet behaves on the page in response to other events.

LiveConnect supports a variety of interactions between JavaScript and Java, but several require a more detailed understanding of Java than I've presented in this book. Therefore, I'll focus solely on controlling applets with JavaScript code.

Imagine, then, that your page contains one applet whose function is to scroll a text message. In JavaScript 1.1, you can refer to this applet in either of two familiar ways:

➤ You can use document.appletName if you specify the NAME attribute in the <APPLET> tag. In this case, say your HTML reads like this:

```
<APPLET CODE="scroller.class" NAME="scroller"HEIGHT=100 WIDTH=250>
```

You can refer to this applet in JavaScript as document.scroller.

➤ You can use document.applets[idx], where the first applet on the page is number 0, the second is 1, and so forth. Looking back at the above scroller applet, you could also refer to it as document.applets[0], assuming it is the first applet on the page.

LiveConnect, for our purposes, allows you to call public methods within the Java applet. This is much like calling a function in your JavaScript code, except that the "function" resides within the Java applet (and is called a method instead of a function). To find out which public methods are available in an applet, you need to look at its source code (not the .class file, but the applet source file, which often ends in the extension .java). If you're creating your own applets, this is easy because the author has the applet source code handy. However, if you're trying to LiveConnect to other author's applets, things may get trickier; even if the author makes the applet source code available, it may take a close reading of it to understand how it works.

Because we haven't delved very deeply into authoring Java source code, let's just consider a relevant snippet of the scroller applet source:

```
public void start() {
            if(thread == null) {
                    thread = new Thread(this);
                    thread.start();
    }
        }
```

If you haven't programmed Java and are familiar only with JavaScript, the snippet of code above may look a bit strange. Nonetheless, you can identify two important characteristics about the above:

➤ It looks like a JavaScript function definition. Although it's not exact, you can at least recognize that this is a method within the Java applet.

➤ This method is defined as "public," as indicated by the word "public" that begins the method definition. Because this method is public, you can access it from your JavaScript code. Methods that are not defined as public (they won't have the word "public" in the method definition) cannot be called from JavaScript.

The lesson in all this is that, using JavaScript, you can call the above Java method with a statement such as:

```
document.scroller.start()
```

This statement will launch the start( ) method in the applet named scroller on the current page.

Similarly, this applet also contains a public method named stop( ). As you can imagine, the statement document.scroller.stop( ) would stop the applet's execution.

Depending upon the particular applet, the above principles can be used to modify all sorts of applet behavior. Suppose, for example, that the applet also had a public method named bgcolor( ).You could perhaps use the JavaScript statement document.scroller.bgcolor("green") to change the applet's background color to green.

To repeat, though, the public methods available in an applet all depend on what the applet's author chose to create. It can sometimes be difficult to understand other author's programs, which is why LiveConnecting to any old applet isn't always easy. If you program your own applets, you can create public methods that interface most successfully with JavaScript.

To close this chapter, take a look at a small sample page that pulls together the LiveConnect principles you've learned. This page contains a text-scrolling applet, as well as two form buttons. By exploiting LiveConnect in onClick event handlers, these form buttons can be used to start and stop the scrolling message.

```
<html>
<head>
<title>JavaScript Meets Java</title>
</head>
<body bgcolor="#FFFFFF">
<center><h2>Java Fun: See the pretty applet ...</h2></center><p>
<center>
<applet code="ScrollingText.class" name="scroller" width="350" height="128">
 <param name="DIRECTION" value="RightLeft">
 <param name="FONTSIZE" value="40"><param name="TEXT" value="This is a scrolling
message ... wheee ...">
</applet>
<p>
<center><h3>JavaScript Magic: Use the form buttons below to modify the applet</
h3></center>
<form>
```

```
<input type=button value="Start" onClick="document.scroller.start()">
<input type=button value="Stop" onClick="document.scroller.stop()">
</form>
</body>
</html>
```

The Least You Need to Know

➤ You learned that Java is a programming language, similar to C++ or Delphi, that is built around objects. Java is similar to JavaScript, but Java also enables you to create your own object and class types, extending the language to do what you need it to.

➤ Java programs are called *applets*. After a program (applet) is written, it must be compiled before it can be incorporated into an HTML document. After it's compiled, the applet is linked into a Web page through the <APPLET> tag.

➤ Using JavaScript 1.1, you can take advantage of LiveConnect, which enables you to access the Java applet from JavaScript code. You can call any public methods in the applet source from JavaScript, with the following syntax:

```
document.appletName.method(parameters)
```

or

```
document.applets[idx].method(parameters)
```

JavaScript: The Complete Overview

For those of you who want everything in one place, here's a complete reference to what makes up JavaScript. All JavaScript objects, object properties, and methods are accessed via this expression:

```
object.xxxxx;
```

where *object* is the particular object and *xxxxx* is the property or method.

The SCRIPT Tag

This indicates that the enclosed text is JavaScript. In addition to using it, it is good practice to hide the JavaScript statements within a <COMMENT> tag.

Syntax

```
<SCRIPT [LANGUAGE="JavaScript"] [SRC="scriptURL"]>
<!--hide from non-JavaScript browsers -->

<!-- JavaScript statements and functions go here -->

//-->
</SCRIPT>
```

Attributes

LANGUAGE   Defines the scripting language—in this case, "JavaScript." This attribute must be included, unless the SRC attribute is used and the extension of the URL defined by SRC is .js.

SRC   Defines a URL (alternate file) where the JavaScript statements are located. JavaScript files should end with .js.

The window Object

The top-level object for each HTML document.

Properties

frames[ ] Array of child frames. Frames are stored in the order defined in the source document.

frames.length Number of defined child frames.

self The current window.

opener The window name of the calling window, if the current window was created with the open( ) method.

parent The parent window (if the current window is a subwindow in a <FRAMESET>).

top The top-most window, which owns all visible frames. Top-most windows are their own parents.

status The message appearing in the browser status window.

defaultStatus The default message appearing in the browser status window, when the status property is not in effect.

name The internal name, if any, defined for the window when opened with a window.open ( ) method.

Methods

alert("message") Displays a "JavaScript Alert" dialog box with the specified message.

blur( ) Removes focus from current window.

confirm("message") Displays a "Confirm" dialog box (one with OK and Cancel buttons) with the specified message. Returns TRUE if the user clicks the OK button; returns FALSE if the user clicks the Cancel button.

focus( ) Brings focus to current window.

prompt("message") Displays a "prompt" dialog box, which queries the user to input data in response to a displayed message.

scroll(x,y) Scrolls the current window to the pixel coordinates x,y. (The upper-left corner of the window is 0,0.)

open("URL," "name") Opens a new client window, gives it the specified name (equivalent to the NAME attribute of a <FRAME> tag), and loads the specified URL.

close( ) Closes the window.

The frame Object

Recall that a frame is a subwindow of the entire browser window. As such, the frame object contains almost all the same properties and methods as the window object.

The frame object lacks only the status, defaultStatus, and name properties of the window object.

The location Object

Contains information on the current URL.

Properties

href The entire URL as a JavaScript string.

protocol A string consisting of the first part of the URL (including the first colon); for example, http:.

host A string consisting of the hostname:port part of the URL; for example, \\www.winternet.com\~sjwalter\.

hostname A string consisting of the hostname part of the URL; for example, www.winternet.com.

port A string consisting of the port (if any) from the URL. The port is a numerical value that (if it exists) is located after the hostname and is preceded by a colon. If there is no specified port, this string is empty.

pathname A string consisting of everything in the URL after the third slash; for example, ~sjwalter\javascript\index.html.

hash A string consisting of any text after the # (CGI parameters).

search A string consisting of any text after the ? (CGI parameters).

275

The document Object

Contains information on the current document.

Properties

title Current document title. If no title is defined, title contains "Untitled."

location Full URL of the document.

lastModified A Date object-compatible string containing the date the document was last modified.

referrer Contains the URL of the calling document; that is, the page from which the user linked to the current page.

bgColor Background color, expressed as a hexadecimal RGB value compatible with HTML syntax (for example, "#FFFFFF" for white). Equivalent to the BGCOLOR attribute of the <BODY> tag.

fgColor Foreground (text) color, expressed as a hexadecimal RGB value compatible with HTML syntax. Equivalent to the TEXT attribute of the <BODY> tag.

linkColor Hyperlink color, expressed as a hexadecimal RGB value compatible with HTML syntax. Equivalent to the LINK attribute of the <BODY> tag.

vlinkColor Visited hyperlink color, expressed as a hexadecimal RGB value compatible with HTML syntax. Equivalent to the VLINK attribute of the <BODY> tag.

alinkColor Activated (after button press, before button release) hyperlink color, expressed as a hexadecimal RGB value compatible with HTML syntax. Equivalent to the ALINK attribute of the <BODY> tag.

forms[ ] Array of form objects in the document, in the order specified in the source. Each form has its own form object.

forms.length The number of form objects within the document.

links[ ] Array objects corresponding to all HREF links in the document, in the order specified in the source.

links.length The number of HREF links in the document.

anchors[ ] Array of all "named" anchors (between the <A NAME=""> and </A> tags) within the document, in the order specified in the source.

anchors.length The number of named anchors in the document.

images[ ] Image objects that correspond to each image on the page.

applets[ ] Java applet objects that correspond to each applet on the page.

embeds[ ] Plugins objects that represent each plug-in on the page.

Methods

write("string") Writes string to the current window. string may include HTML tags.

writeln("string") Performs the same as write( ), but adds a carriage return. This affects only preformatted text (inside a <PRE> or <XMP> tag).

clear( ) Clears the window.

close( ) Closes the window.

The form Object

Corresponds to a <FORM> tag set defined in a document. Each <FORM> tag has its own forms object.

Properties

name String value of the NAME attribute of <FORM>.

method Numeric value of the METHOD attribute of <FORM>: "0" = GET; "1" = POST.

action String value of the ACTION attribute of <FORM>.

target Window targeted for form response after the form has been submitted, as specified in the <FORM> tag.

elements[index] The elements property is an object that contains as its properties the object of each element in the form. Thus, if your form has three elements (a text input box, a submit button, and a checkbox), form.elements is an object that contains three properties, each one a respective object (a text object, a submit button object, and a checkbox object).

length Contains the number of elements in the form.

Methods

submit( ) Submits the form.

reset( ) Resets the form.

Event Handlers

onSubmit( ) Identifies code to run (either JavaScript statements or functions) when the form is submitted (when the user clicks a defined Submit button).

onReset( ) Identifies code to run when the form is reset.

The text and textarea Objects

The text (specified by the <TEXT> tag) and textarea (specified by the <TEXTAREA> tag) elements share the same object components.

Properties

name String value of the NAME attribute.

value String value of the contents of the field.

defaultValue String value of the initial contents of the field.

type Specifies what type of object this form field is (e.g. "text" or "Textarea").

Methods

focus( ) Sets input focus to the object.

blur( ) Removes input focus from the object.

select( ) Selects the object's input field.

Event Handlers

onFocus Executes when input focus enters field (by tabbing in or by clicking but not selecting in the field).

onBlur Executes when input focus leaves the field.

onSelect Executes when the field is input-focused by selecting some of its text.

onChange Executes when input focus exits the field and the value of the field has changed from when onFocus occurred.

The checkbox object

Corresponds to the <INPUT TYPE="checkbox"...> tag.

Properties

name String value of the NAME attribute.

value String value of the contents of the checkbox. If checked, value="on"; if unchecked, value="off".

checked Boolean value of the contents of the checkbox. If checked, status=TRUE; if unchecked, status=FALSE.

defaultChecked Boolean value that reflects the CHECKED attribute (the default state).

type Specifies what type of object this form field is (e.g. "checkbox").

Methods

click( ) Selects the checkbox, causing it to be "on" (or TRUE).

Event Handlers

onClick Executes when the user checks or unchecks the box.

The radio Object

Corresponds to the <INPUT TYPE="radio"...> tag. The form radio[index] is used to refer to a single radio button of the radio object (that is, one of its multiple choices).

Properties

name String value of the NAME attribute.

length The number of radio buttons in the radio object.

value String value of the VALUE attribute.

checked Boolean value. True if pressed; false if not pressed.

defaultChecked Boolean property that reflects the value of the CHECKED attribute.

type Specifies what type of object this form field is (e.g. "radio").

Methods

click( ) Selects the radio button.

Event Handlers

onClick Executes when the radio button is selected.

The select Object

Corresponds to the <SELECT> tag. The JavaScript object consists of an array of option objects, each of which has the following components.

Properties

length Contains the number of objects in the select object.

name The internal name of the select object as defined by the NAME= attribute.

selectedIndex The index number of the currently selected option of the select object.

type Specifies what type of object this form field is (e.g. "select").

options[ ] This property is an object reflecting the contents of the <OPTION> tag used when defining a select object in HTML. It contains the following properties:

> **text** String containing the text after the <OPTION> tag. Assigning a new value to options[*idx*].text will either change the menu item text or add a new item, in the case of an *idx* higher than the current number of items.

> **value** Reflection of the VALUE attribute. This is sent to the server when the Submit button is pressed.

> **defaultSelected** Boolean, which reflects the SELECTED attribute of the <OPTION> tag.

> **selected** Boolean, which indicates the current selected state of the option.

Event Handlers

onFocus Executes when input focus enters the field.

onBlur Executes when input focus leaves the field.

onChange Executes when input focus exits the field and the field value has changed since the onFocus event.

The button Object

There are three types of buttons in a FORM, defined by the TYPE attribute of the <INPUT> tag:

> ➤ Submit (TYPE="SUBMIT")

> ➤ Reset (TYPE="RESET")

> ➤ Custom (TYPE="BUTTON")

All button objects (regardless of type) have the components outlined here.

Properties

value String containing the VALUE attribute.

name String containing the NAME attribute.

type Specifies what type of object this form field is (such as "submit", "reset", or "button").

Methods

click( ) Selects the button.

Event Handlers

onClick Executes when a button is clicked.

The submit and reset Objects

The submit object relates to the button defined by the `<INPUT TYPE="submit">` tag, whereas the reset object refers to the `<INPUT TYPE="reset">` tag. Both contain the same properties, methods, and event handlers. Note that the submit button does not contain the onSubmit event handler; that event handler belongs to the form object.

Properties

name The contents of the NAME= attribute.

value The contents of the VALUE= attribute, which in the case of a submit button is the text displayed on the button face.

Methods

click( ) Selects the button.

Event Handlers

onClick Triggers when the button is clicked.

The password Object

A password form element is a text-entry box that hides the user input by masking typing with asterisks. It is defined with the `<INPUT TYPE="password">` tag. The password object relates to the characteristics of this element.

Properties

defaultValue Contains the contents of the VALUE= attribute.

name The contents of the NAME= attribute.

value The current data entered into the password field.

type Specifies what type of object this form field is (e.g. "password").

Methods

focus( ) Brings focus onto the password element.

blur( ) Removes focus from the password element.

select( ) Selects the current data in the password element, ready to be modified.

The navigator Object

This object is used to determine which version of Netscape Navigator a visitor to your page is using.

Properties

appCodeName Reflects the "codename" of the user's browser. For example, the codename for Navigator is "mozilla."

appName Reflects the real name of the user's browser.

appVersion Reflects the version number of the user's browser.

userAgent This property reflects the full information on the user's browser, including its codename, version number, and platform (such as Win95).

plugins[ ] This array reflects which plug-ins are installed on this user's browser.

mimeType[ ] An array that reflects which MIME types are configured for this user's browser.

Methods

javaEnabled( ) This method returns a value of true if the user's browser has Java enabled, or false if it's disabled.

The string Object

The string object provides a wealth of methods for manipulating the contents of a string. Create a new string using this syntax:

```
strvar = new String(string)
```

Properties

length The length of the string—that is, how many characters long it is.

Methods

big( ), blink( ), bold( ), fixed( ), italics( ), small( ), sub( ), strike( ), sup( ) Methods that add their respective HTML tags to the string. For example, if the variable message currently contains the string "Hello", then

message.big( ) would yield the string "<BIG>Hello</BIG>"

message.italics( ) would yield the string "<I>Hello</I>"

and so forth, for the HTML tags appropriate for the method names above.

fontColor(color), fontSize(size) Adds respective HTML tags to a string, assigning font color or font size as specified in the parameter passed to the method.

charAt(index) Returns the character located at position index within the string.

indexOf (searchValue, [fromIndex]) Searches the string for the first instance of the string searchValue. If fromIndex is specified, it begins the search from that position within the string. Returns value of index of first letter where the string is first found.

lastIndexOf (searchValue, [fromIndex]) Searches for searchValue beginning at the (rightmost) end of the string and working backward. Reports first instance found searching backward from end, or fromIndex if specified.

substring (indexA, indexB) Extracts the substring starting from position indexA to position indexB.

toLowerCase( ), toUpperCase( ) Convert string to all lowercase or all uppercase letters.

The Date Object

To use the Date object, you must first create a new instance of a Date object. Do this by assigning a variable of your choosing to new Date( ), as follows:

```
variablename = new Date();
```

283

The object contains no properties and a plethora of methods, which can be used to extract or set various characteristics of the date.

Methods

getDay( ), **getDate( )**, **getHours( )**, **getMinutes( )**, **getMonth( )**, **getSeconds( )**, **getTime( )**, **getTimeZoneOffset( )**, **getYear( )** Methods that return a value respective to the method name; for example, getMinutes( ) returns the current number of minutes into the current hour.

setDate( ), **setHours( )**, **setMinutes( )**, **setMonth( )**, **setSeconds( )**, **setTime( )**, **setYear( )** Methods that can be used to set the respective values.

toGMTString( ) Returns current date in GMT format, which is exemplified by this:

```
Sun, 11 Feb 1996 13:18:21 GMT
```

toLocaleString( ) Returns the current date in "locale" format, which looks like this:

```
02/11/96 13:18:21
```

parse(date) This method is commonly used in combination with the setTime( ) method. The setTime( ) method requires its parameter in the number of milliseconds since January 1, 1970 at 00:00:00 hours. The parse method can convert a traditional date string (such as "May 23, 1972") into millisecond format for use with the setTime( ) method.

The Math Object

This object contains properties and methods that allow access to common mathematical constants and calculations.

Properties

The following properties represent the following constant values:

LN10	(natural log of 10)	2.302
LN2	(natural log of 2)	0.693
PI		3.1415
SQRT1_2	(the square root of 1/2)	0.707
SQRT2	(the square root of 2)	1.414

Methods

abs (x)	Returns absolute value of x
acos (x)	Returns arc cosine of x
asin (x)	Returns arc sine of x
atan (x)	Returns arc tangent of x
ceil (x)	Returns the least integer greater than or equal to x
cos (x)	Returns the cosine of x
exp (x)	Returns e (Euler's constant) to the power x
floor (x)	Returns the greatest integer less than or equal to x
log (x)	Returns the natural log of x
max (x, y)	Returns the greater of x and y
min (x, y)	Returns the smaller of x and y
pow (x, y)	Returns x to the yth power
round (x)	Returns x rounded to the nearest integer (.5 cutoff)
random()	Returns a random real number between 0 and 1
sin (x)	Returns sine of x
sqrt (x)	Returns square root of x
tan (x)	Returns tangent of x

The Image Object

The Image object reflects the attributes of an image on the current page. An image on the page can be referred to either via the images[ ] array or by the image name, as shown here:

```
document.images[2].propertyName

document.dogimage.propertyName
```

Properties

border Reflects the BORDER attribute.

complete Boolean value indicating whether Navigator has completed its attempt to load the image.

285

height Reflects the HEIGHT attribute.

hspace Reflects the HSPACE attribute.

lowsrc Reflects the LOWSRC attribute.

name Reflects the NAME attribute.

prototype Lets you add properties to an Image object.

src Reflects the SRC attribute (can dynamically change the image on a page).

vspace Reflects the VSPACE attribute.

width Reflects the WIDTH attribute.

The images[ ] array also contains this property:

length Reflects how many images are in the page (e.g. *document.images.length*).

The Array Object

You can create a new array using this syntax:

```
arrayvar = new Array(length)
```

Properties

length Reflects the number of elements in the array.

Methods

join(*separator*) Joins all elements in the array into one string, each separated by the character specified in *separator* (default separator is a comma).

reverse( ) Reverses the index order of all elements in the array.

sort(*sortfunc*) Sorts the index order of elements in the array. By default, sort is done lexicographically, unless a custom *sortfunc* is specified.

Reserved Words

The following words are *reserved words*, which means that you cannot give your variables, functions, methods, or objects any of these names. Some of these words are already used for different purposes in JavaScript, and others are reserved for future use, such as further expansion of the JavaScript language.

abstract	extends	int	super
boolean	false	interface	switch
break	final	long	synchronized
byte	finally	native	this
case	float	new	throw
catch	for	null	throws
char	function	package	transient
class	goto	private	true
const	if	protected	try
continue	implements	public	var
default	import	return	void
do	in	short	while
double	instance of	static	with
else			

Predefined JavaScript Colors

Here is a list of JavaScript's built-in color names. Instead of using a hexadecimal triplet to specify the colors on your page, you can assign a string literal to specify one of the following built-in color names (see Chapter 13 for details on how to do this):

Color	Red	Green	Blue	Hexadecimal Triplet
aliceblue	240	248	255	f0f8ff
antiquewhite	250	235	215	faebd7
aqua	0	255	255	00ffff
aquamarine	127	255	212	7fffd4
azure	240	255	255	f0ffff
beige	245	245	220	f5f5dc
bisque	255	228	196	ffe4c4
black	0	0	0	000000
blanchedalmond	255	235	205	ffebcd
blue	0	0	255	0000ff

continues

continued

Color	Red	Green	Blue	Hexadecimal Triplet
blueviolet	138	43	226	8a2be2
brown	165	42	42	a52a2a
burlywood	222	184	135	deb887
cadetblue	95	158	160	5f9ea0
chartreuse	127	255	0	7fff00
chocolate	210	105	30	d2691e
coral	255	127	80	ff7f50
cornflowerblue	100	149	237	6495ed
cornsilk	255	248	220	fff8dc
crimson	220	20	60	dc143c
cyan	0	255	255	00ffff
darkblue	0	0	139	00008b
darkcyan	0	139	139	008b8b
darkgoldenrod	184	134	11	b8860b
darkgray	169	169	169	a9a9a9
darkgreen	0	100	0	006400
darkkhaki	189	183	107	bdb76b
darkmagenta	139	0	139	8b008b
darkolivegreen	85	107	47	55662f
darkorange	255	140	0	ff8c00
darkorchid	153	50	204	9932cc
darkred	139	0	0	8b0000
darksalmon	233	150	122	e9967a
darkseagreen	143	188	143	8fbc8f
darkslateblue	72	61	139	483d8b
darkslategray	47	79	79	2f4f4f
darkturquoise	0	206	209	00ced1
darkviolet	148	0	211	9400d3
deeppink	255	20	147	ff1493

Color	Red	Green	Blue	Hexadecimal Triplet
deepskyblue	0	191	255	00bfff
dimgray	105	105	105	696969
dodgerblue	30	144	255	1e90ff
firebrick	178	34	34	b22222
floralwhite	255	250	240	fffaf0
forestgreen	34	139	34	228b22
fuchsia	255	0	255	ff00ff
gainsboro	220	220	220	dcdcdc
ghostwhite	248	248	255	f8f8ff
gold	255	215	0	ffd700
goldenrod	218	165	32	daa520
gray	128	128	128	808080
green	0	128	0	008000
greenyellow	173	255	47	adff2f
honeydew	240	255	240	f0fff0
hotpink	255	105	180	ff69b4
indianred	205	92	92	cd5c5c
indigo	75	0	130	4b0082
ivory	255	255	240	fffff0
khaki	240	230	140	f0e68c
lavender	230	230	250	e6e6fa
lavenderblush	255	240	245	fff0f5
lawngreen	124	252	0	7cfc00
lemonchiffon	255	250	205	fffacd
lightblue	173	216	230	add8e6
lightcoral	240	128	128	f08080
lightcyan	224	255	255	e0ffff
lightgoldenrod-yellow	250	250	210	fafad2
lightgreen	144	238	144	90ee90

continues

continued

Color	Red	Green	Blue	Hexadecimal Triplet
lightgrey	211	211	211	d3d3d3
lightpink	255	182	193	ffb6c1
lightsalmon	255	160	122	ffa07a
lightseagreen	32	178	170	20b2aa
lightskyblue	135	206	250	87cefa
lightslategray	119	136	153	778899
lightsteelblue	176	196	222	b0c4de
lightyellow	255	255	224	ffffe0
lime	0	255	0	00ff00
limegreen	50	205	50	32cd32
linen	250	240	230	faf0e6
magenta	255	0	255	ff00ff
maroon	128	0	0	800000
mediumaquamarine	102	205	170	66cdaa
mediumblue	0	0	205	0000cd
mediumorchid	186	85	211	ba55d3
mediumpurple	147	112	219	9370db
mediumseagreen	60	179	113	3cb371
mediumslateblue	123	104	238	7b68ee
mediumspringgreen	0	250	154	00fa9a
mediumturquoise	72	209	204	48d1cc
mediumvioletred	199	21	133	c71585
midnightblue	25	25	112	191970
mintcream	245	255	250	f5fffa
mistyrose	255	228	225	ffe4e1
moccasin	255	228	181	ffe4b5
navajowhite	255	222	173	ffdead
navy	0	0	128	000080
oldlace	253	245	230	fdf5e6

Color	Red	Green	Blue	Hexadecimal Triplet
olive	128	128	0	808000
olivedrab	107	142	35	6b8e23
orange	255	165	0	ffa500
orangered	255	69	0	ff4500
orchid	218	112	214	da70d6
palegoldenrod	238	232	170	eee8aa
palegreen	152	251	152	98fb98
paleturquoise	175	238	238	afeeee
palevioletred	219	112	147	db7093
papayawhip	255	239	213	ffefd5
peachpuff	255	218	185	ffda69
peru	205	133	63	cd853f
pink	255	192	203	ffc0cb
plum	221	160	221	dda0dd
powderblue	176	224	230	b0e0e6
purple	128	0	128	800080
red	255	0	0	ff0000
rosybrown	188	143	143	bc8f8f
royalblue	65	105	225	4169e1
saddlebrown	139	69	19	8b4513
salmon	250	128	114	fa8072
sandybrown	244	164	96	f4a460
seagreen	46	139	87	2e8b57
seashell	255	245	238	fff5ee
sienna	160	82	45	a0522d
silver	192	192	192	c0c0c0
skyblue	135	206	235	87ceeb
slateblue	106	90	205	6a5acd
slategray	112	128	144	708090

continues

continued

Color	Red	Green	Blue	Hexadecimal Triplet
snow	255	250	250	fffafa
springgreen	0	255	127	00ff7f
steelblue	70	130	180	4682b4
tan	210	180	140	d2b48c
teal	0	128	128	008080
thistle	216	191	216	d8bfd8
tomato	255	99	71	006347
turquoise	64	224	208	40e0d0
violet	238	130	238	ee82ee
wheat	245	222	179	f5deb3
white	255	255	255	ffffff
whitesmoke	245	245	245	f5f5f5
yellow	255	255	0	ffff00
yellowgreen	154	205	50	9acd32

Speak Like a Geek: The Complete Archive

absolute address   An URL that includes the full Internet address of the machine on which the HTML file resides; for example, **http://www.machine.com/~*username*/index.html**.

address   An URL that includes the full Internet address of the machine on which the HTML file resides; for example, **http://www.machine.com/~*username*/index.html**.

alert   A pop-up window that displays a message to the user. The user must click the OK button to proceed.

anchor   A location within an HTML document that is invisibly "marked" with HTML tags. Links can point to this anchor and take the user to specific locations within one HTML document.

applet   Another name for a Java miniprogram. Applets are the Java elements that run through Java-enabled browsers. In JavaScript, these are called "scripts" instead of applets.

arithmetic operator   Any of the following symbols: * (multiply), +, –, / (divide), % (modulus), ++ (increment), – – (decrement), or – (negation). Arithmetic operators are used with variables or numeric values in an expression to yield a mathematical result.

array   An object with a list of properties. In an array, the properties are named in numerical sequence, as in arrayname[0], arrayname[1], and so on.

assign   To refer a value to a variable name.

assignment   The act of designating a value to a variable name; for example, purchases = 10.

assignment operator   One of the following symbols: =, +=, –=, *=, /=, or %=. All but = will perform the indicated arithmetic on the current variable value and its assigned value.

assignment statement   The whole syntactical construction of assignment: purchases += (mugs*orders);

attribute   An HTML structure that sets a particular parameter value for a given HTML tag.

binary   Numerical representation in base-2; for example, 10001100. This is the "alphabet" that the computer ultimately understands.

Boolean   An element of logic: true, false, and (&&), or (||).

browser   A program that enables you to navigate the *World Wide Web*. Browsers can be either text-based or graphical. Some examples of browsers are Netscape Navigator, HotJava, and Microsoft Internet Explorer.

bug   An error in a computer program. See *debugging*.

C   A common programming language, which JavaScript is partially based on.

C++   An object-oriented programming language; the closest relative to JavaScript.

call   To tell JavaScript to execute a function.

case-insensitive   In a case-insensitive language or operating system, the computer makes no distinction between lower-and uppercase letters; it considers them equal. Thus, "cat" is the same word as "Cat" and "CAT."

case-sensitive   In a case-sensitive language or operating system, the computer distinguishes between lower- and uppercase letters; it considers them different characters. Thus, "cat" is a different word from "Cat" and "CAT."

CGI (Common Gateway Interface)   The programming interface that enables Web servers to perform special functions. CGI programs are commonly written in *Perl* and can perform such tasks as complex database searches, custom Web page construction, or secure Web access control. CGI is regarded as complex; JavaScript is a simpler alternative for performing similar programming feats.

clause   A portion of a full JavaScript statement. For example, within the if...else statement, both the if portion and the else portion are clauses.

command   Any "word" that tells the computer to do something.

comment-out   To insert proper comment symbols into code, telling JavaScript not to attempt to execute the words that follow.

comments   Author-entered descriptions in program code that are meant for human programmers to read, not for JavaScript interpretation.

comparison operator   One of the following symbols: ==, <, >, <=, > =, or !=. Returns true if the comparison is valid; otherwise, it returns false.

compiler A program that converts a collection of programming language statements from "near-human-readable" form (which is what the programmer writes) to "computer-readable" form so that the computer can run them.

compressed files Computer files that have been reduced in size by a *compression program*. Compression programs are available for all computer systems. For instance, PKZIP is used on DOS machines, WinZip is used with Windows, *tar* and *compress* are used with UNIX, and StuffIt is used on Macintosh computers.

concatenate Combine any number of strings into one longer string. For example, "my" + "dog" + "loves" + "me" yields "my dog loves me".

conditional statement A JavaScript statement that directs program flow based on the validity or invalidity of a comparison. Examples include if...else and while.

constant A variable that is assigned a value that is never meant to change.

cyberspace The "area" or space in which computer users travel when "navigating" or *surfing* around on a network or the Internet.

debug The irritating act of attempting to track down errors or design flaws in a program.

debugger A program designed to help track down *bugs* in other programs. See *bug*.

decompress To convert compressed, unreadable data into uncompressed, readable data.

define In JavaScript, to describe the name, parameters, and statements of a function.

definition In JavaScript, the name, parameters, and statements that make up a function.

document object The JavaScript object that contains properties and methods relevant to the HTML document. These include colors, anchors, links, and form elements.

download To transfer information from one computer to another. You *download* a file from another computer to yours. The reverse process (transferring a file from your computer to another) is called *uploading*.

element A screen element is any widget on the computer screen. A form element is one portion of an HTML form, such as a text box, a check box, a radio button, a submit button, or a selection box.

e-mail Short for *electronic mail*, this is the system that enables people to send and receive messages with their computers.

embed To insert an item into a text file. JavaScript programs are "embedded" into HTML files.

empty string A string variable that contains no value. You can create an empty string with the assignment stringname="".

error   An illegal statement in the JavaScript program that JavaScript cannot understand.

error handler   A programming statement that changes program flow in case an error is encountered.

evaluate   To perform the specified calculation or comparison. JavaScript "evaluates" expressions such as arithmetic operators or comparisons.

event   When a user performs some action that JavaScript recognizes, such as a mouse click in a certain location.

event handler   A JavaScript structure that responds to (handles) a particular event or response by the user of the browser. Event handlers are identified by special HTML *attributes*.

event watching   When JavaScript keeps an "eye out" for an event to happen. Defining an event handler for an event tells JavaScript to event watch.

execute   To perform the actions specified in the program code.

explicit code   Instead of calling a function, to write out the code to execute the function directly. (Used in relation to defining an event handler.)

expression   Virtually any "phrase" of JavaScript code, such as an assignment, arithmetic, or comparison.

eZine   An electronic magazine.

false   The value returned from a comparison operation if the comparison is invalid.

FAQ   Short for *Frequently Asked Questions*, a *FAQ* is a document that contains a collection of the most commonly asked questions on a particular subject and their answers.

focus   When a user clicks on a form element and it becomes "active" for interaction, it is said to "have the focus."

form   Any number of user-interactive features in a Web page, including text entry boxes, check boxes, radio buttons, selection boxes, and any other buttons.

frame   A subwindow within the browser window.

FTP (File Transfer Protocol)   A *protocol* that defines how files are transferred from one computer to another. Also, the name of a program that uses this protocol to move files between computers. (Sometimes you'll find **ftp** used as a verb: "Ftp to ftp.netscape.com.")

function   A collection of JavaScript statements that perform a particular operation. Also called a *method*.

function call   When JavaScript is told to execute a named and defined function. Occurs in the form functionname(parameters).

Gamelan   The premier Web site of Java applets and Java/JavaScript-related information and links: **http://www.gamelan.com**.

Gopher   A hierarchical information-retrieval protocol that was popular on the Internet before the Web (which uses the http protocol).

hash mark   The symbol #. In an URL, the hash mark is used to specify an anchor to start the user at; for example, **http://www.machine.com/~*userid*/index.html#*anchorname***.

helper application   An independent program used to process files that the Web browser does not know how to process.

history list   The list of URLs that have been visited during the current Web browsing session.

hostname   The Internet address (or "name") of a machine that holds a particular HTML document; for example, **www.machine.com**.

HotJava   The browser developed by Sun Microsystems that runs Java applets. HotJava itself is written in Java. HotJava does not yet support JavaScript programs.

HTML (HyperText Markup Language)   The formatting language supported by the World Wide Web. Web documents are written using various HTML *tags*, which control how the information in the document is presented through the browser.

HTTP (HyperText Transfer Protocol)   The *protocol* used by the World Wide Web to transfer HTML documents.

hypertext   A system in which documents contain links that, when clicked, enable readers to move between areas of the document or between documents, following subjects of interest in a variety of different paths. The World Wide Web is a hypertext system.

image map   A Web page graphic that the user can click on and be directed to a certain place depending where in the image he clicked.

increment   To increase the value of a variable, usually by 1.

index number   The number referring to one of the properties in an object. Alternate terminology would refer to a list element of an array (both are the same in JavaScript).

initialize   To assign a starting value to a variable. Often this is 0, but it doesn't have to be.

input   When a user enters data requested by the program; also the name of an HTML tag (<INPUT>), which defines a form element.

instance   A particular object created from an object definition. An object definition defines the skeleton structure of an object, whereas an instance refers to an actual object based on that skeleton.

instantiate   To create an instance of an object. This is done by assigning an object definition (a function) to a new variable using the new keyword, such as instanceobject = new Objectdefn();

internet   Spelled with a lowercase *i,* the term refers to computer networks that are joined together (or *interconnected*).

Internet   Spelled with a capital *I,* the term refers to the collective of interconnected networks that are globally accessible.

Internet provider   A company that provides connections to the Internet. See also *service provider.*

interpreter   A program that translates computer language statements into computer-readable form and executes them at the same time (at "run time"). This is in contrast to a compiler, which interprets and converts the statements into computer-readable form and then saves the result into a separate file that can be executed later.

iterate   To repeatedly move through a program loop.

iteration   One sweep through a program loop.

Java   A programming language that extends the Web to handle the distribution of *interactive content*: video, audio, multimedia, and so on. Java programs are called *applets* and run from within a Java-enabled browser such as HotJava or Netscape Navigator 2.0.

JavaScript   An English-like *scripting language* that supports much of Java's capabilities but doesn't require extended programming knowledge.

JDK   The *Java Developer's Kit,* created by Sun Microsystems to assist Java programmers in creating Java applets.

.js extension   If you are including a file of JavaScript code via the SRC= attribute of the <SCRIPT> tag, the file's name must contain the extension .js.

keyword   Any one word that JavaScript recognizes as having meaning to it (such as if, then, var, new, and so on).

link   Text or an image in a Web page that, if clicked, takes the user to another Web page or to another location within the current Web page (an anchor).

literal   An actual numeric value or string value such as "5" or "cats". String literals must be enclosed in single- or double-quotation marks.

LiveScript   The scripting language developed by Netscape that was the predecessor to *JavaScript.*

load   To retrieve an HTML file and display it in the Web browser.

loading   Retrieving data into a Web browser either from the local hard drive or from across the Internet.

logging off   The opposite of *logging on*, where the computer service is informed that you want to terminate the connection. The process usually involves typing a command such as "exit," "logout," "logoff," or "bye."

logging on   Slang for the process of connecting to a central computer network or service from a local computer (sometimes referred to as *logging in*). The process usually involves entering a *username* and *password*, which ensures that only authorized individuals can use the computer service.

logical operator   Any of the following: && (AND), || (OR), ! (NOT). Used in conditional expressions; returns true or false.

login   The procedure of *logging on*.

loop   A section of program code that is executed over and over in repetition until some condition changes.

loop counter   A variable that changes through each iteration of the loop in correlation with how many times the loop has been executed. The loop counter is often used in the condition that continues or ceases the loop.

Lycos   A popular Web search engine that locates information anywhere on the World Wide Web; **http://www.lycos.com**.

megabyte   A measure of the quantity of data, disk space, or computer memory (*RAM*). One million bytes.

method   A function that is a property of a JavaScript object.

Microsoft Internet Explorer   A Web browser from Microsoft, intended to compete directly with Netscape Navigator. Internet Explorer 3.0 offers support for JavaScript 1.0.

MB   The abbreviation for *megabyte*, which is roughly one million bytes.

module   A miniprogram, essentially equivalent to a function.

modulo   The % operator.

modulus   The result of the modulo (%) operator, which returns the remainder of a division operation. Thus, 10%3 results in 1.

multimedia   Any computer program that uses one or more of the following: text, graphics, sound, and video.

nest(ed)   When a statement is used as part of another statement. For example, were the if clause of a statement another if...else statement, these would be nested. Also, when bookending symbols such as brackets { } or parentheses ( ) are used within one another.

Netscape   Short for Netscape Communications Corporation, the company that produces the highly popular Netscape Navigator Web browser.

Netscape Navigator   The Web browser product available from Netscape (**http://home.netscape.com**). Supports Java and JavaScript, and virtually every other Web capability.

newline character   The symbol that represents a linefeed to the computer. The JavaScript method document.writeln() sends a newline character at the end of the output, whereas document.write() does not.

null   Literally "nothing." No value—especially not 0, which *is* a value. Just *nothing*.

numeric variable   A variable that contains a numeric value, such as 5.

object   A very important feature of JavaScript. An object is a variable that is, in fact, a set of subvariables known as *properties*.

operand   A variable or value used in an operator expression. For example, in the expression orders*10, both orders and 10 are operands.

output   Any data that is sent to the screen (or, perhaps, to the printer).

parameter   Additional information that is passed to a Java applet or a JavaScript function. Parameters supply applets and functions with information they need to complete their task.

parameter passing   The act of sending values to a function or applet. Done either in a function call or <APPLET> tag.

parent object   If object A contains property B, where property B is also an object, A is the parent object to B.

parse   To pull desired data from a larger set of data. Often used in reference to a string, where one uses a method to pull specified parts of the string out of the whole one.

Pascal   Another programming language, somewhat similar to C.

pass   To send data or values into a function or applet.

Perl   A popular UNIX-based scripting language that's often used in partnership with CGI.

pixel   One dot of light on the computer screen. Common computer screens contain 640 horizontal × 480 vertical pixels. Depending on the video configuration and monitor size, other computers may have screen sizes of 800 × 600 pixels, 1024 × 768 pixels, or even 1200 × 1024 pixels (on a 21" monitor, lest the user go blind).

placeholder   A book convention wherein you insert some text that refers to actual variables or values you would put in its place if you were actually writing the code. For example, lunch(parameters) means to call the function lunch() with some parameters appropriate to the particular situation.

port   In the context of the Internet, a *port* is similar to a CB radio channel. Different Internet applications (*FTP*, the *World Wide Web*, *Telnet*, and so on) communicate on different ports throughout the Internet.

program flow   The order in which program commands and statements are executed. Normally, they are executed in sequence (from top to bottom), but conditional statements and function calls are frequently used to alter program flow.

programming language   Any set of keywords and syntax that you can combine to instruct the computer to perform some tasks.

property   A subvariable of an object. An object is a set of related variables known as properties, and each property is a variable or function in and of itself. In JavaScript, they are referred to in the form object.property. For example, status is a property of the object window, and it can be assigned a string to display in the browser status line.

protocol   A set of rules that defines how computers transmit information to each other, enabling different types of computer hardware and software to communicate with each other. Each type of Internet application (*FTP*, *Telnet*, and so on) has its own protocol.

public domain software   Software that is not owned by anyone and is freely available for use and redistribution.

relative address   A URL without the machine name specified; it's understood that such an address starts at the same directory as the current document. For example, extras/more.html is a relative address referring to the specified subdirectory and file name, assuming the same starting path as the current document.

reserved word   One of the words that JavaScript recognizes for its own uses, and which, therefore, cannot be used as a variable name. Reserved words include all keywords that are part of JavaScript statements.

return   A keyword that is used to return a value at the conclusion of a JavaScript function. This value is assigned to a variable if the function was called in an assignment; for example, result=functionname();

REXX   A somewhat popular scripting language that's similar to PERL. Commonly used in OS/2; a variation is used on the Amiga (AREXX).

run   To execute a computer program.

script   A series of program statements that instruct the computer on how to accomplish a task.

scripting language   The set of rules and keywords that comprise a functional script. Same as a programming language, except that scripting languages are traditionally less strict and simpler to learn.

self   A synonym for a window object; self.status is equivalent to window.status. Can be used to avoid conflicts with other labels in the JavaScript program.

self-extracting archive   A compressed file that can be run like a regular program, except that the "program" that runs is the decompressor, and the result is a reconstructed collection of programs or files.

server   A program or computer that "services" another program or computer (referred to as the *client*). For example, within the World Wide Web, your *browser* is the *client*, and the computer you connect to is the *server*.

service provider   A company that provides a connection to the Internet for a fee. Different providers charge different fees; shop around for the best deal before you subscribe to a particular provider.

source code   The actual text that comprises the program itself.

statement   A JavaScript construction that usually winds up affecting program flow. Loops and conditionals, such as for and if…else are statements.

status line   The small message window at the bottom of the browser window. The status line can be programmed to display specified messages using the window.status property.

string   A value that consists of a series of alphanumeric characters enclosed in quotation marks.

submit   To send the user-entered form data to a specified action, either another URL or some data processing function in JavaScript.

subvariable   A variable that is a property of an object.

Sun Microsystems   The company which, besides manufacturing very fast, very expensive UNIX computers, also created the Java language and the HotJava browser. Sun partnered with Netscape to create JavaScript.

supervariable   An object. This is a variable that consists of a set of variables.

support   In software lingo, refers to the capability of an application to handle some task. A browser that "supports" JavaScript is capable of running JavaScript programs.

surf   To view Web pages. Often implies moving from one page to another to another via links. Surfing is supposed to make you cool.

syntax   The grammatical rules of a programming language.

table   An HTML design element that formats and displays data in an on-screen table structure.

tag   An HTML "code" that defines how a portion of a Web document is to be formatted by the browser for display.

Telnet   An Internet facility by which you can connect ("log in") to another machine anywhere on the Internet.

template   A skeleton design. Serves to define an outline.

The Web   More Internet shorthand for the World Wide Web.

this   A JavaScript object that is used as shorthand to refer to the current object in question. Used in relation to forms and method definitions.

trigger   An onEvent definition, which tells JavaScript "what to do" when a specified event occurs.

true   A logical (Boolean) value, returned from a comparison.

unary   An operator that takes only a single operand; for example ++ (increment), -- (decrement), and – (negate).

UNIX   A computer operating system; one that the majority of *hosts* connected to the Internet run. There are several different versions of UNIX available today, fondly referred to as *flavors*.

upload   The process of transferring information from one computer to another, specifically from your computer to someone else's (either another user's computer or a server).

URL (Uniform Resource Locator)   An "address" that defines the exact location (and *protocol*) of a computer or document on the Internet.

UseNet   The world's largest public "bulletin board," where folks post messages and reply to messages from others. UseNet is divided into many thousands of subtopics of interest (known as "newsgroups").

user   Whoever is visiting your Web page and, therefore, "using" and interacting with your JavaScript program.

validation   The practice of evaluating data to see whether it meets some criteria.

value   Some form of data. A numeric value is a number. A string value is a string. Either can be assigned to a variable. A literal value is a specific number of string explicitly stated, not assigned to a variable.

variable   A "label" that refers to some value. Often, the value may change, which enables the programmer to use named labels to keep track of various quantities or other forms of changeable data.

W3   Internet shorthand for the World Wide Web.

WebCrawler   Another (somewhat old) Web search engine; **http://www.webcrawler.com**.

widget   A prewritten JavaScript program that creates a small user-interaction doohickey, such as a scroll bar.

window   The on-screen area in which the browser displays a Web page's contents related to the current browser window.

window object   The JavaScript object that contains properties related to the current browser window.

World Wide Web   A *hypertext* system that allows users to "travel through" (or *surf*) *linked* documents, following any chosen route. World Wide Web documents contain a variety of topics; selecting various *links* leads you from one document to the next. The nature of the system allows links to span computers, literally taking you from one part of the world to the next with the click of a mouse.

WWW   Yet more Internet shorthand for the World Wide Web.

Yahoo   The premier subject catalog for the World Wide Web, with search facilities; **http://www.yahoo.com./**.

Index